STUDIA PINDARICA

STUDIA PINDARICA

BY
ELROY L. BUNDY

UNIVERSITY OF CALIFORNIA PRESS
BERKELEY AND LOS ANGELES
1986

University of California Press

University of California Press, Ltd., London, England

First published in 1962 as Volume 18, nos. 1 and 2, of the
University of California Publications in Classical Philology

This combined edition published 1986

Library of Congress Cataloging-in-Publication Data

Bundy, Elroy L.
  Studia Pindarica.

  (California library reprint series)
  ''First published in 1962 as volume 18, nos. 1 and 2,
of the University of California publications in
classical philology''—T.p. verso.
  Bibliography: p.
  Includes indexes.
  Contents: The eleventh Olympian ode—The first
Isthmian ode.
  1. Pindar—Criticism and interpretation. 2. Pindar.
Olympian odes. 11. 3. Pindar. Isthmian odes. 1.
4. Odes—History and criticism. I. Title. II. Series.
PA4276.B93 1987   884'.01   86-6992
ISBN 0-520-05098-3
ISBN 0-520-05111-4

0 1 2 3 4 5 6 7 8 9

CONTENTS

	Publisher's Note	vii
I.	The Eleventh *Olympian Ode*	1
II.	The First *Isthmian Ode*	
	Introduction	35
	The Opening Foil, Lines 1–13: Prooimion	36
	The First Crescendo, Lines 14–32: Kastor and Iolaos	44
	The Second Crescendo, Lines 32–40: Asopodoros	47
	The Third Crescendo, Lines 41–63: Herodotos	53
	The Concluding Crescendo, Lines 64–68: Prayer for the Future	76
	Selected Works Cited	93
	Index Locorum	95
	Subject Index	125
	Index of Greek Words	137

PUBLISHER'S NOTE

In May 1959 the University of California Press accepted for publication Elroy Bundy's book-length manuscript entitled *Hesukhia: A Study of Form and Meaning in Pindar*. Two years later, after trying out his methodology on seminar students, Bundy became dissatisfied with the manuscript and withdrew it. He then distilled the essence of this methodology into two short monographs, *Studia Pindarica I* and *II*, which appeared in 1962 in the University of California Publications in Classical Philology. On these two slender books—wrote W. S. Anderson, L. A. MacKay, and A. Renoir after Bundy's sudden death in 1975—"an international reputation was slowly built."

The monographs have long been out of print and hard to find. Reprinting was first suggested by Robert Renehan of the University of California, Santa Barbara, at a meeting of the editorial board of the journal *Classical Antiquity*. Mark Griffith, a Berkeley member of the same board, spoke up in agreement. Both men helped in gathering opinions and making arrangements. An independent proposal came from John Dillon, once of Berkeley and now Regius Professor of Greek at Trinity College, Dublin. Several other scholars, when queried, declared the reprinting clearly desirable.

After discussion among all those concerned and consultation with Barbara Bundy, the author's widow, the decision was made—with some regret—not to include other published and unpublished writings of Bundy's. So the two monographs are here presented quite as they first appeared, with but a few typographical corrections and without critical introduction or commentary. The only additions are three indexes and a list of works cited; these were prepared by Thomas Walsh, with the assistance of Andrew Miller and Donald Mastronarde.

I
The Eleventh Olympian Ode

PINDAR's Tenth and Eleventh *Olympians* for Hagesidamos of Epizephyrian Lokris have suffered much at the hands of critics and scholars from being treated not as individual unities, but as subordinate parts of a unity achieved by the two odes together. This pernicious tradition goes back to the Alexandrians, who placed the Eleventh after the Tenth in their editions because the word τόκος in *O*. 10 seemed to designate *O*. 11 as interest in payment of a debt long overdue.[1] Although this view still has adherents today,[2] modern scholarship most often reverses the ancient judgment.[3] Attacking the odes in the same spirit as the Alexandrians, scholars take the future κελαδήσω in *O*. 11.14 as a reference to *O*. 10 and label the former as an improvisation performed at Olympia immediately after the victory. *O*. 10 is then the "regular" ode composed for a later celebration in the victor's home town.

With the truth or falsehood of these theories it is useless to concern oneself, for not a shred of evidence can be found in either ode to support either of them, or any other view of the relation between the two odes—so long, at least, as Pindaric studies continue on their present track. As for the evidence adduced in τόκος and κελαδήσω: this is nonexistent, for certain rhetorical conventions make the true meaning of these words inconsistent with reference to anything beyond the compass of the odes in which they appear.[4] It is, indeed, to this question of convention, in matters small and large, that scholarship must now address itself if it is to add in any significant way to our knowledge of Greek choral poetry.[5]

---
[1] See scholia *O*. 11 inscr. τῷ αὐτῷ τόκος. All references to Pindar and Bakkhulides in this essay are to the editions of Turyn (Krakow, 1948), and Snell (Leipzig, 1949).
[2] E.g., A. Puech, *Pindare, Olympiques* (Paris, 1949), p. 124.
[3] Turyn, in his edition, puts the view succinctly: "Hoc carmine . . . Pindarus promisit se victoriam Hagesidami uberiore poemate celebraturum. Et reapse postea poeta carmine Olymp. X promissum suum exsecutus est."
[4] τόκος refers to the extra pains taken in the elaboration of *O*. 10. Cf. the similar metaphor at Themistios 1.4b; and see p. 33. Promises of this type are no different from that made by κελαδήσω in *O*. 11.14, on which see below, pp. 21 f. The embarrassment displayed in *O*. 10.1–8 is used as foil to heighten the force of the opening crescendo introduced by the stereotyped ὅμως δέ in line 9.
[5] I intend, after preparing the way in this series of studies, to publish a detailed investigation of the conventions of choral poetry as they affect form and meaning, both in the lyrists (chiefly Pindar) and in the dramatists.

What we know of this poetry is woefully inadequate; nor can we ascribe this condition to the paucity of our texts; were a hundred odes to be unearthed tomorrow, we should proceed to assign their contents to the same complacent categories that are the badges of our present ignorance.[6] In dealing with Pindar, misconceptions are the rule: the odes do not have a linear unity; the transitions are abrupt; the poet devotes much time to his personal preoccupations, triumphs, and embarrassments, as well as to irrelevancies of other kinds.[7] These myths have arisen from a failure to understand the conventional aspects of choral communication.

Thus no commentator will inform his readers that εὐφροσύνα in *N.* 4.1 (personified abstract for concrete) is a poetic word for a victory revel. Yet the fact that it is contrasted with ἀοιδαί (line 3) makes this certain. We may compare the contrast of συμπόσιον with ἀοιδᾷ in *N.* 9.48 f.; θαλίαις with εὐφαμίαις in *P.* 10.34 f.; εἰλαπινάζοισιν εὐφρόνως with χοροί, λυρᾶν, and αὐλῶν in *P.* 10.38–40; συμποσίων with ὕμνοι in Bacch. frag. 4.39 f.; εὐφροσύνα with δόξα in *P.* 11.45; and κῶμοί τε καὶ εὐφροσύναι (hendiadys) with ὑμνεῦσι in Bacch. 11.12 f. This is a small matter, yet the sense and force of *N.* 4.1–8 depend upon their use of the importance of the victory revel as foil for the importance of song as a permanent record of achievement (see pp. 11, 22 f.). What is more serious, words like εὐφροσύνα, left vague in line after line, so attenuate the concrete sense intended that it is impossible for a reader to follow it or for a critic to know what he is criticizing.[9]

Again, no commentator informs his readers that the sentence ὠκεῖα δ' ἐπειγομένων ἤδη θεῶν / πρᾶξις ὁδοί τε βραχεῖαι in *P.* 9.69 f. would signal to the audience the end of the tale of Apollo and Kurana and promise a transition to the ἀρεταί of the victor. Yet the same topic concludes the

---

[6] This has already proved to be true of the Bakkhulides papyrus and the newly recovered remains of the *Paeans* of Pindar.

[7] For the history of Pindaric scholarship in modern times and for assessments of the current state of the problem, see A. B. Drachmann, *Moderne Pindarfortolkning* (Copenhagen, 1891); and G. Perrotta, *Safo e Pindaro* (Bari, 1935). Both of these writers despair of finding sense in the odes. G. Norwood's description of the state of the problem in his *Pindar* (Sather Classical Lectures, vol. 19; Berkeley and Los Angeles, Univ. Calif. Press, 1945) is marred by inaccurate reporting and a faulty historical perspective.

[8] "Festivity" (drinking and merriment to celebrate an event), not "feasting" (Sandys, *The Odes of Pindar* [London, 1946] 344), is the meaning of the word. Cf. *I.* 3.10.

[9] ἄριστος, *N.* 4.1, may indicate to some that there is no *contrast* between εὐφροσύνα and ἀοιδᾷ. What, then, shall we say of the identical contrast between εὖ παθεῖν and εὖ ἀκούειν in *P.* 1.99–100b, where εὖ ἀκούειν is δεύτερον to the πρῶτον of εὖ παθεῖν? ἄριστος in *N.* 4.1 means "most desirable in the immediate present." Cf. Phoc. 9 D³: δίζησθαι βιοτήν, ἀρετὴν δ' ὅταν ᾖ βίος ἤδη. In its longevity, song outweighs the revel. See pp. 11, 22 f.

tale of Perseus in *P*. 10 (lines 48 ff.) and introduces the transition back to Hippokleas and his victory, just as a variation of it is employed at *P*. 2.42–52 (key words θαυμαστός and θεός) before the transition (lines 52–56) back to Hieron. The topic appears also at *Bacch*. 3.57 f. to signal the end of a tale and the introduction of Hieron a few lines later. Comparing finally *P*. 1.26–28 and *O*. 13.80, we see that what all these passages have in common is that they intensify, and sometimes also signal, the *climax* of a story or long description by calling attention to the marvelous powers of the divinity or supernatural agency that directs or determines the events or phenomena described.[10] One can be certain that a transitional formula of one kind or another will shortly follow this type of foil.

Here then are two examples of convention operating to control form and meaning in choral poetry. For both I have given examples from the two poets of whose work complete specimens survive, in order to suggest that they are not mannerisms of a given poet but conventions protecting the artistic integrity of a community of poets working within well-recognized rules of form and order. I have observed and catalogued a host of these conventions and find that they point uniformly, as far as concerns the Epinikion, to one master principle: there is no passage in Pindar and Bakkhulides that is not in its primary intent enkomiastic— that is, designed to enhance the glory of a particular patron. This conclusion, if it can be substantiated, should provide solid comfort to those who have complained of willful irrelevance in the odes, although I fear that these have, in truth, been more comforted than surprised by the spectacle of a professional admirer of athletes who will not stick to his business. Yet it should be evident that the Epinikion must adhere to those principles that have governed enkomia from Homer to Lincoln's *Gettysburg Address*, so that when Pindar speaks pridefully in the first person this is less likely to be the personal Pindar of Thebes than the Pindar privileged to praise the worthiest of men.[11] If he protests that he

---

[10] In *P*. 9.69 f. the treatment of this motive is particularly dexterous, since in ὠκεῖα πρᾶξις and βραχεῖαι ὁδοί these lines incorporate the conventional language of abbreviation used in such contexts as that of *P*. 4.247 f., and achieve the desired end without self-consciously interrupting the tale: as the god brings events quickly to a close, so the tale of those events is shortened by the poet's statement to that effect. In *N*. 10.49–54 the θαῦμα motive is used to ease the transition from a victory catalogue to a mythical narrative. See p. 14.

[11] Cf. *O*. 1.115 ff., *I*. 5.51 ff., *O*. 2.91–97, and *N*. 4.41 ff. Only misinterpretation can make personal passages of these. In *N*. 4.41 ff., for example, the enkomiast, according to the rules of order mentioned in lines 33 ff., momentarily hesitates to continue the catalogue of Aiakid heroes (begun with Telamon in line 25 and concluded with Peleus in line 68). These rules and his own desire he thrusts aside in lines 36–43, where he contrasts himself with the stinter (φθονερὰ δ' ἄλλος ἀνὴρ βλέπων) whose mechanical obedience to rules ignores what every discerning person can see: for such

is truthful, he is not making an ethical statement about his own person, but quieting murmurs from his audience with the assurance, "He is every bit as good as I say he is," or "My words shall not fall short of his deeds."[12] If he seems embarrassed by irrelevance, or by the poverty of his expression, or by his failure to do justice, these inadequacies have been rigged as foil for the greatness of the laudandus.[13]

Unfortunately for those who would prefer a Pindar that makes sense even in praise of athletes to a Pindar that rises to gorgeous irrelevance in avoiding his unpromising subject, the enkomiast's rhetorical poses may take forms that speak to one unschooled in the conventions with something less than the precision intended. Thus $N.$ 7, a straightforward enkomion, has been canonized by those who follow one guess reported by the scholia as the poet's personal apology for offensive references to Neoptolemos in the ode we now possess fragmentarily as $Pa.$ 6;[14] and similar embarrassments have been discovered in $P.$ 2.[15]

As a counter to the continuing efforts to find unity in Pindar on assumptions that presume disunity from the start, and as a justification of my plea for attention to the conventional elements of Pindar's style, I should like to present my reading of $O.$ 11, an ode short enough for detailed analysis in brief compass. I shall treat it, as it deserves to be treated, in complete isolation from $O.$ 10, which nowhere presupposes $O.$ 11 and to which $O.$ 11 contains no references. I apologize to the reader at the outset for the terms I have been forced to invent to facilitate reference to certain devices in the odes. These terms are often awkward, but they are the best I have been able to devise.

The ode begins with a formal device first discussed as such in connection with Greek choral poetry in Dornseiff's monograph on Pindar's style.[16] In Germany, where it has been the object of considerable study,

---

heroes as the Aiakids you must abandon the rules. Here the way of φυά (natural enthusiasm) is preferred to the way of τέχνα (mechanical praise). (See pp. 29–32.) After this he begins a new crescendo in lines 43 ff. and completes his catalogue. Thus what Farnell (*The Works of Pindar* [London, 1930] I 179) calls "an expression of arrogant egoism" is in reality rhetorical foil to enhance the glory of the Aiakids. The school of interpreters that cons the odes for gossip should be further warned that the ἄλλος ἀνήρ of line 39 is a type, not an individual poet close to or far from the scene of the celebration.

[12] Cf. $O.$ 4.19 f., $N.$ 1.18, $O.$ 6.89 f. (ἀλαθέσιν λόγοις is the full praise with which the laudator escapes the charge of ἀπαιδευσία or ἀμαθία).

[13] Cf. $N.$ 7.64–69, 102–105, $P.$ 11.38–40 (foil for the introduction of the victor in lines 41–45), and $P.$ 10.4 (dismissing lines 1–3 as irrelevant to the praise of Hippokleas).

[14] The authors of the scholia had only the odes to aid them, as is suggested by the phrasing of the scholium on line 102, ὁ μὲν Καλλίστρατος . . . ὁ δὲ 'Αριστόδημος κτλ. My view of this ode will be given in a subsequent study in this series.

[15] I believe that this ode, on which I am preparing a monograph, contains nothing personal to Pindar.

[16] See F. Dornseiff, *Pindars Stil* (Berlin, 1921) 97–102.

it is known as the priamel (*praeambulum*).¹⁷ Elsewhere it is scarcely mentioned, even though it is a frequent manifestation of perhaps the most important structural principle known to choral poetry, in particular to those forms devoted to praise. The subject is extremely complex, and full discussion of it is beyond the scope of this essay, yet some idea of the possibilities of the device is necessary to an appreciation of *O.* 11.1–15.

The priamel is a focusing or selecting device in which one or more terms serve as foil for the point of particular interest. A straightforward example is Sappho A.16(L.-P.).1–4:

οἱ μὲν ἱππήων στρότον οἱ δὲ πέσδων
οἱ δὲ νάων φαῖσ' ἐπὶ γᾶν μέλαιναν
ἔμμεναι κάλλιστον, ἔγω δὲ κῆν' ὅτ-
τω τις ἔραται·

Here a host of cavalry, a host of foot, and a host of ships are foil for the writer's own choice, which she states in a general proposition. This proposition is then glossed by an exemplum (lines 5–14), which is in turn used as foil for the introduction in line 15 of the poetess' favorite Anaktoria. The concrete climax, Anaktoria, fulfills the gnomic climax of lines 3 f. introduced by ἔγω δέ. Such concrete climaxes, or caps, whether preceded or not by a gnomic climax, are often accompanied, as here in Sappho A.16(L.-P.).15, by the adverb νῦν.¹⁸ Typical also of climactic

---

¹⁷ See, above all, W. Kröhling, *Die Priamel (Beispielreihung) als Stilmittel in der griechisch-römischen Dichtung*, Greifswalder Beiträge für Literatur- und Stilforschung, Heft 10 (Greifswald, 1935). This is an excellent introduction to the form, but by no means an adequate discussion of its functions. A number of important types are not noticed.

¹⁸ νῦν (νυν) and the like very frequently follow exempla to mark them as foil for the topic of particular interest, or occur in the climactic term of a priamel in which the foil involves either other times and occasions or a gnome. Cf. *N.* 6.8 (after gnomic foil), *O.* 1.105 (after the tale of Pelops), *O.* 3.36b (after the tale of Herakles' planting of the olive at Olympia), *O.* 7.13 (see below, p. 7), *O.* 9.5 (contrast between a celebration at home and the celebration at the scene of the victory), *O.* 10.81, *P.* 1.36 (ταύταις ἐπὶ συντυχίαις, after the gnomic foil [see below, pp. 7 f.] of lines 33 ff. [note that the *superlative* πρῶτα in line 33 abbreviates a list]), *P.* 1.50 (note the list [see pp. 7–10] implied by οἵαις ἐν πολέμοισι μάχαις in the summary foil of lines 47–50), *P.* 6.44 (after the summary dismissal in line 43 of the story of Antilochos), and *P.* 9.73 (after the story of Apollo and Kurana). Bacch. 14.19 f. combines νῦν, name cap (Κλεοπτολέμῳ), and χρή (see pp. 10 f.) following a complex combination of summary and list foil. Other expressions, some metaphorical, are also used. Cf. τὸ παράμερον ἐσλόν (*O.* 1.99), τὸ πρὸ ποδός (*I.* 8.13), τὸ ἐν ποσὶ τράχον (*P.* 8.33), ἔπειτεν (*I.* 7.20). In this essay and in others to follow, I shall employ the word "cap" to designate the culminating term of a priamel—the term, that is, which "caps" one or more preliminary foil terms. A cap which prominently displays a pronoun to designate either the laudator or the object of the laudator's meditations—usually the laudandus or a category that embraces him—is called a "pronominal cap." If the name of the laudandus is prominently displayed, I refer to the cap as a "name cap." If both a pronoun and a name are used, I employ the term "pronominal name cap."

terms, whether gnomic or concrete, is Sappho's pronominal cap ἔγω δέ. The second and third personal pronouns are also used in capping terms.[19] So the gnomic climax of *O*. 11.4 ff. (amplified by lines 7–10) is followed by the concrete climax of lines 11–15 introduced by the words ἴσθι νῦν, Ἀρχεστράτου / παῖ, τεᾶς, Ἀγησίδαμε κτλ, where the adverb νῦν, the name Ἀγησίδαμε, and the pronominal adjective τεᾶς combine the conventional elements represented in Sappho A.16(L.-P.) by νῦν (line 15), Ἀνακτορίας (line 15), and ἔγω (line 3).

The priamel, because it selects some one object for special attention, is a good prooimial device; it will highlight one's chosen theme. In the well-known prooimion to *O*. 1, water, fire, gold, and the sun exist as foil for the introduction of the Olympian games, but the real climax, postponed for effect to the end of the strophe, comes with the mention of Hieron.[20] In *P*. 10.1–6 Lakedaimon and Thessaly are foil for Pytho (the place of victory), Pelinna (the victor's home town), and, mentioned last for effect, the victor himself. Here the poet goes so far as to reject explicitly as themes for his song (τί κομπέω παρὰ καιρόν, "Why this irrelevant vaunt?") the items used as foil.[21] *I*. 7 is more complicated. The foil, in imitation of a traditional hymnal priamel, takes the form of a question ("In which of your ancient splendors, O Theba, do you take particular delight?") and is followed by a list of tentative themes, each introduced by the disjunctive ἤ, which are eventually thrust aside (on the ground that they are ancient history) in favor of the victor Strepsiadas.[22] Here the foil includes so many terms that it must be recapitulated and rejected, in what forms (here in transition, often elsewhere in intro-

---

[19] In Pindar, pronominal caps, mostly in the first and second persons, abound. Almost any page will contain one or more of these or of the closely related name caps illustrated below *passim*.

[20] The main terms are water, gold, and the Olympian games. To gold is subordinated, in a simile, fire; to the games, also in a simile, the sun. After mention of the games and before the introduction of the name of Hieron are inserted references to the laudator himself (generalized in σοφῶν) and Zeus, the appropriate god. There are many similar contexts. In the opening priamel of *O*. 2 we have god, hero, and man, Zeus (Pisa), Herakles (Olympian games), and Theron (chariot race, Akragas, ancestors), while the laudator is introduced in line 2.

[21] Elsewhere when this happens the foil has usually achieved, through sheer length, a quasi-independent status, and the laudator can pretend, in order to highlight his next topic, that he has strayed from his theme. Since the long foil is most often legendary or mythical, the narrative matter, more often than other foils, triggers elaborate transitional priamels. See my remarks on *I*. 7, pp. 6 f. Cf. *O*. 13.45–52, 89–96, *O*. 1.97–105, *O*. 2.91–105, *O*. 9.107/8–120 (on which see below, p. 16), *P*. 1.81–86, *P*. 2.49–61, *P*. 10.51–63, *P*. 11.38–45, *I*. 5.51–61, *I*. 6.53–56. These all belong to types illustrated in this essay.

[22] On this passage, see W. Schadewaldt, "Der Aufbau des pindarischen Epinikion," *KGG*, 5. Jahr, Heft 3 (Halle, 1928) 267. Only a complete misunderstanding of the form of lines 1–22b can lie behind the determination on the part of all but a handful of scholars to find in lines 16 f. an irrelevant allusion to ungrateful Spartan neglect of Theban interests. For this and other grotesqueries, see Farnell, *op. cit.* I 277–281.

duction) a priamel of the *summary* type. Other examples of this priamel with transition to climactic term are N. 10.1–24 and P. 8.22–35.

In the summary priamel, of which there are a number of variations, the foil appears in summary or gnomic form. Most frequently this will involve the idioms ἄλλοι ἄλλα, ἕτεροι ἕτερα, and equivalents, or some form of the words πᾶς, πολύς, or the like.[23] At O. 8.12 we find ἄλλα δ' ἐπ' ἄλλον ἔβαν / ἀγαθῶν as foil for Timosthenes and his victory at Nemea, and at O. 7.11 we find as foil for Diagoras and his Olympian victory ἄλλοτε δ' ἄλλον ἐποπτεύει Χάρις. In the former example there is a vocative name cap (Τιμόσθενες, line 15) in combination with a pronominal cap (ὔμμε δ', line 15); in the latter the name of Diagoras is introduced by the frequent καί νυν. Often the summary foil is expanded by a list, as in I. 1.47–51 the sentence μισθὸς γὰρ ἄλλοις ἄλλος ἐπ' ἔργμασιν ἀνθρώποις γλυκύς is followed by a list of concretes:[24] the shepherd, the plowman, the fowler, and the fisherman are all foil for a generalization (gnomic climax) about athletes and warriors in lines 50 f., which in turn serves as foil for a catalogue of victories (concrete climax) introduced by the pronominal cap ἄμμι δ'. A second bit of summary foil containing the key word πᾶς is subjoined to the list of occupations.

Thus in this form of the summary priamel the vicissitudes of nature or the diversity of human life become the burden of the foil. The most characteristic use of vicissitude as foil is to highlight victorious achievement or merit in general, but it may also be used to emphasize the need to praise it. Summary priamels of the latter type are employed at P. 2.13–20 (note the name and pronominal caps in line 18) and N. 4.91–96 (note the name cap Μελησίαν in line 93) to set in the light the current need to praise Hieron and Melesias, respectively. The gnomic material representing vicissitude need not involve the ἄλλοι ἄλλα motive. At O. 8.52, for example, the gnomic sentence τερπνὸν δ' ἐν ἀνθρώποις ἴσον ἔσσεται οὐδέν (cf. ξ 228, ἄλλος γάρ τ' ἄλλοισιν ἀνὴρ ἐπιτέρπεται ἔργοις) is foil for the laudator's need to praise Melesias (see p. 16). Here, as in many priamels, a pronominal cap referring to the laudator is combined with a name cap referring to the laudandus.[25] Finally, any gnome (generalizing

---

[23] Other expressions of the former type are ὁ μὲν τά, τὰ δ' ἄλλοι (N. 7.55), τὰ (τε) καὶ τά (I. 5.58 and often), ἀλλασσόμεναι (N. 11.38), ἐν ἀμείβοντι (N. 11.42), ἀμειβόμεναι (N. 6.9), πεδάμειψαν (O. 12.12), and πόλλ' ἄνω, τὰ δ' αὖ κάτω (O. 12.6). Cf. also P. 8.96 f. Other expressions of the latter type are μακρός (N. 4.33), ἕκαστος (O. 13.45), ἀφνεὸς πενιχρός τε (N. 7.19), κοινός (N. 7.30, N. 1.32), εὐμαχανία (I. 4.2), μυρία παντᾷ κέλευθος (I. 4.1), οὐ γὰρ πάγος, οὐδὲ προσάντης ἁ κέλευθος (I. 2.33), ἄλλαι / ὁδῶν ὁδοὶ περαίτεραι (O. 9.113/4), ἑτοῖμος ὕμνων θησαυρός (P. 6.7 f.), and τίνα κεν φύγοι ὕμνον (O. 6.6). There are many others.

[24] For another example of a list following a gnome, see O. 9.31–50, which are discussed on p. 9.

[25] Cf. I. 1.14, P. 1.42, N. 6.59–63, N. 7.20 f., O. 13.47–52, O. 10.100–110, and O. 3.40 f.

as it does *many* human experiences illustrating by analogy or contrast the laudator's chosen theme) may serve as foil. At *P.* 5.1-11 the statement that under certain circumstances wealth has great power is foil for an address to Arkesilas in which the laudator ascribes to him wealth and power. At lines 12 ff. of this same ode the statement that the σοφοί carry God's gift of power more nobly than others is followed by praise of Arkesilas on this ground. In the former passage the pronominal and name caps are combined (σύ and 'Αρκεσίλα); in the latter the pronominal cap (σὲ δ') suffices. At lines 43 ff., still in this same ode, the statement that gratitude must attend good works is followed by the vocative 'Αλεξιβιάδα and the pronoun σέ, introducing praise of Arkesilas' charioteer in return for services rendered.

A second form of summary priamel is characterized by the use of πᾶς, πολύς, μακρά, or the like, to summarize a list of themes to be dismissed or abbreviated.[26] These are frequent in transitions or rhetorical pauses that create an ἀπορία as foil for the selection of a subject or a manner of treating it. Thus in *N.* 4.69-75 the laudator finds himself in an ἀπορία defined by his inability to exhaust (ἄπαντα ... διελθεῖν) the glories of the Aiakidai, which he accordingly dismisses in sum (ἄπαντα) in favor of the Theandridai. Here the Aiakidai and their glory are foil for the Theandridai and theirs. This passage may be labeled as purely transitional only because the catalogue of Aiakid heroes has grown so long (see n. 11). Actually, it is no different in function from the transition to the climactic term in the opening priamel of *I.* 7 (see pp. 6 f.). In such transitional priamels it is useful to think of the foil as diminuendo and the climax as crescendo.

These terms will apply as well to priamels in rhetorical hesitations such as those of *N.* 4.33-46 (see n. 11) and *O.* 1.28-51. In the latter passage, which (as we see from θαύματα in line 28) is akin to the topic discussed on pages 2 f. above, πολλά (line 28) abbreviates a list of marvels that are traditional subjects of poetry and were "suggested" to the laudator by his carefully contrived mention of the ivory shoulder of Pelops in the previous lines. From the convention in which the legendary or mythical foil of a given ode is often introduced by a relative pronoun (τοῦ, line 25) the audience know that the laudator is committed to praise Pelops.[27] The conventional θαύματα will then inform them that the poet

---
[26] For other expressions, see n. 23.
[27] The use of the relative pronoun in major transitions is descended from the use of the relative in cult hymns to introduce descriptions of the god's powers, and in the rhapsodic hymns to introduce the central narrative illustrating the god's greatness. In Pindar it most characteristically introduces mythical exempla (at times it is strictly hymnal, as in *P.* 1.3), but can as well introduce current themes in transition from legendary matter, particularly when the latter is in some way very closely

has entered upon a diminuendo that will produce a new approach to the story of Pelops. In this way convention assures them that the purpose of the rhetorical pause is to set up the summary list of marvels as a foil to focus attention on the laudator's enkomion of Pelops. From the contrast of ἀλαθῆ with ψεύδεσι in lines 28b f. they will infer certainly that his attitude toward the traditional story is unfavorable (he rejects it out of piety in line 36) and possibly that he will substitute another θαῦμα—as it turns out, the θαῦμα of Pelops' translation to Olympos—for that of the ivory shoulder. In any case the θαύματα πολλά of line 28 are focusing foil for the θαῦμα of lines 36–45. When the crescendo comes in line 36, it is introduced by the combination of a vocative name cap (υἱὲ Ταντάλου) and a pronominal cap (σὲ δ'). We note further that προτέρων (line 36) implies a νῦν. In O. 9.30–50 a similar θαῦμα, this time not labeled as such, signals a transition. To illustrate the principle—to which he appeals in his desire adequately to praise the Opountians—that all human ability comes from God (this by-passes art in favor of inspiration), the laudator cites Herakles' battles with Poseidon, Apollo, and Hades. The implication is that it would take the divine strength and daring of a Herakles to equal in praise the divine merits of the Opountians. But the exemplum, while illustrating very well the point for which it was introduced, verges (and the laudator has carefully so contrived it) on impiety in its comparison of mortals to gods. The laudator must accordingly dismiss the theme (his admiration of the Opountians has carried him away) and does so with a fervor appropriate to the Opountians' good taste in hearing their own praises (cf. E. I. A. 979 f., αἰνούμενοι γὰρ οἱ ἀγαθοὶ τρόπον τινὰ / μισοῦσι τοὺς αἰνοῦντας, ἢν αἰνῶσ' ἄγαν). He can now turn to a consideration of the merits of the city of Protogeneia on a less dangerous and presumptuous level. Here the priamel is introduced by gnomic foil (lines 30 f.) illustrated by an exemplum incorporating a list (Poseidon, Apollo, Hades) of Herakles' successful struggles against the immortals.[28] Although the passage omits the typical πᾶς or the like, it is nevertheless a summary priamel (πάντα might have been included before τὰ τέρπν' in line 30; cf. O. 1.30, P. 2.49, P. 1.41) and well illustrates the use of appeals to piety in transitional or hesitatory priamels. It will be seen that such passages are entirely too sophisticated and rhetorical to be taken in a straightforward religious sense. For transitional priamels of the πᾶς-πολύς type, see further I. 6.53–56, I. 5.51–65, O. 13.89–93, P. 1.81–86,

---

connected in an aetiological or exemplary way with the present. Other pronouns or pronominal adverbs occur; κεῖνον (P. 5.57), νιν (P. 9.73), ὅθεν (O. 2.50/1), ἐξ οὗ (O. 6.71), καὶ νυν (see n. 18), τόθι (O. 7.77), ἔνθεν (P. 4.259) are all transitional. For the relative pronoun in particular, see τάν (P. 9.5), τόν (O. 8.31), τάν (O. 3.13).

[28] For gnome followed by list, see p. 7.

N. 6.47–65, N. 7.50–53, etc., and for hesitatory priamels of one or another type, see N. 4.33–46, N. 5.14–21, N. 8.19–39, and N. 7.17–34. N. 8.19–39 is complicated by an exemplum (lines 23–34) subjoined to the summary priamel (lines 19–22). This exemplum (it is a θαῦμα preparing the transition to the climax) restores the laudator's confidence and is accordingly followed by a vigorous restatement in full priamel dress (lines 35–39) of the general gnomic climax (νεαρὰ ... / ... ἐρίζει, lines 20 ff.) of the summary priamel. The concrete climax is reached, after another priamel, in the name cap of lines 44–48. N. 7.17–34 is extremely complicated. ἀφνεὸς πενιχρός τε (line 19) provides the πᾶς motive; ἐγὼ δέ (line 20) gives the pronominal cap, which is only a paradigmatic form of the still postponed climactic term. This paradigm is further expanded by an explanatory parenthesis (lines 24–30), after which the πᾶς motive is resumed in κοινόν (line 30). This motive then serves as foil (lines 30 ff.) for the concrete climax (lines 33 f.) in favor of Neoptolemos.[29]

These are some of the forms and some of the uses of the priamel in Pindar. If I have treated the subject at too great length, my purpose has been to justify my plea for a careful assessment of the role of convention in the poetry of Pindar and to provide a background of examples rich enough to make appreciation of the high rhetoric of O. 11 possible.

Turning to O. 11 itself, we observe that the ode begins with a priamel capped by a gnomic climax. This suggests that a concrete climax will follow. The preliminary foil is of the occupational type illustrated above (p. 7) by I. 1.47–51. There the shepherd, the plowman, the fowler, and the fisherman were foil for athletic and military success in general; here sailors and farmers, who have need of wind and rain, respectively, are foil for achievement in general. In I. 1.47–51 μισθός and in O. 11.1–6 χρῆσις express the natural yearnings and fulfillments of the activities in question. In N. 3.6 f., δίψῃ and φιλεῖ serve the same function in a summary priamel. In the priamel of N. 9.48–55, φιλεῖ has the same sense. (Cf. ποθεινός in the simile—a two-term or abbreviated priamel—of O. 10.90–97b,[30] and μισθός in N. 7.63, where the summary priamel occupies lines 54–63.) This motive is often reversed: as merit seeks out song, so song seeks out merit. Thus δίψαν (P. 9.108) expresses in transition the laudator's still unsatisfied thirst for songs of Telesikrates.[31] The necessity

---

[29] At the end of line 32 place a full stop; in line 32 read βοαθόος or Farnell's βοαθοῶν; in line 34 read the imperative μόλε, and compare lines 30–34 with I. 7.16–21.

[30] For the two-term priamel, see N. 4.1–6, 82–90, P. 10.67–72, O. 2.108 ff., O. 13.42–44b, O. 6.1–4, O. 7.1–10.

[31] "As I seek a subject to slake my thirst for song, someone (Telesikrates) bids me duly bring to life the ancient glory of his ancestors." The notion, developed by Farnell, that "Pindar was just going to unyoke and refresh his tired horses when

or propriety that determines the relationship between song and merit is expressed in countless other ways. We may compare, among other words, χρή (cf. *I.* 3.7 f.), χρέος (*P.* 8.34), πρέπει (*O.* 2.50/1), τέθμιον (*I.* 6.18), τεθμός (*N.* 4.33), ὀφείλω (*O.* 10.3), πρόσφορος (*N.* 7.63), and above all καιρός in such passages as *P.* 10.4.[32]

Passing over a host of minor conventions that implement the force of this opening priamel,[33] we may note that the foil is employed to establish a relation between song and achievement in which song sets a permanent seal on high deeds. Yet the foil has not served its eventual purpose, for the song is still selecting its subject. At first, the focus is wide: man is dependent on nature in different ways at different times. Those familiar with the conventions will think of farmers and sailors,[34] but the language leaves them free to apply it as universally as possible. The focus now narrows upon achievement and its natural rewards. The audience know that the laudator is thinking of athletic success, but the language still permits them to apply it universally. Elsewhere, in need of a different kind of foil, Pindar can distinguish two natural longings of those who have achieved success: celebration amid the congratulations of one's fellows, and song to immortalize one's achievement. The one serves an immediate, the other an enduring need.[35] The superlative πλεῖστα (line 1) allows room for this thought. Even when men have most need of wind, they have other needs too; and if immortalization in song be the dearest longing of the successful, they have other longings too. A priamel of like force at *N.* 3.6 ff. is careful not to exclude this thought:

> διψῇ δὲ πρᾶγος ἄλλο μὲν ἄλλου·
> ἀεθλονικία δὲ μάλιστ' ἀοιδὰν φιλεῖ,
> στεφάνων ἀρετᾶν τε δεξιώτατον ὀπαδόν·

---

someone requires him to yoke them again for a second journey" attributes to the laudator a remarkable indifference to merits as great as those of Telesikrates. Who could grow tired of these? δίψα in Pindar is a thirst *for song* (whether of the laudator or the laudandus), not the thirst the songs feel when they have worn themselves out in ungrateful toil.

[32] On this motive, see Schadewaldt, *op. cit.* 278 n. 1.

[33] For the superlative in priamels, see *N.* 6.58 (μάλιστα), *P.* 6.45 (μάλιστα), *I.* 7.2 (μάλιστα), *O.* 1.1 (ἄριστον), *O.* 1.100 (ὕπατον), *O.* 3.44 (ἀριστεύει and αἰδοιέστατος), *O.* 13.46 (ἄριστος), *N.* 5.18 (σοφώτατον), and many others. The comparative also occurs frequently; e.g., *P.* 7.7 (ἐπιφανέστερον), *P.* 11.57 (καλλίονα), *I.* 1.5 (φίλτερον), *I.* 8.13b (ἄρειον), *N.* 5.16 (κερδίων). For εἰ δὲ ... τις κτλ., see *O.* 6.4 ff., *N.* 5.19, *O.* 1.3 f. For πιστὸν ὅρκιον (here generalizing the asseverative principle in enkomia), see *O.* 6.20, *N.* 11.24, and see pp. 17, 20, 24, and 27 below.

[34] For other priamels of this occupational (or preoccupational) type, see *O.* 14.5–17 (note in particular line 7), *O.* 12.1–21, *I.* 5.1–11, frag. 260, *I.* 1.47–51, Bacch. 10.35–56, Hor. *Carm.* 1.1, 4.3, Verg. *Georg.* 2.503–515, *Aen.* 6.847–853.

[35] Cf. *N.* 4.1–8, *N.* 9.48 ff., and see pp. 2, 22 f. and n. 9.

The superlative adverb μάλιστ' extends the same invitation to comparison as does πλεῖστα in O. 11.1. Thus the dependency of achievement on song stands out against a background that has both depth and breadth. The viewer may locate it on two spectra of desires: those of the achiever and those of other men. It is a yearning that has dimension also in time, having begun with dedication in the past (σὺν πόνῳ, line 4) and extending its hopes into time hereafter (ὑστέρων, line 5).

Yet, as we have seen, the focus must narrow further: a single favored man must be made to stand out against this background of desire and fulfillment. Accordingly the process of selection continues. The sentence ὕμνοι / . . . / τέλλεται is glossed by a second gnome of slightly greater precision that focuses upon Olympic victors in particular. More important, the gnome, as now restated, can serve as foil for the introduction of the victor, Hagesidamos, in the name cap of lines 11–15. Lines 7–10, which consist of summary foil (lines 7–9) capped by a gnomic crescendo (line 10), have never been properly explained, because they contain verbal elements that have, in combination, a conventional meaning not easily deduced from their individual meanings. The most important of these elements are ἀφθόνητος, informing the audience that the laudator is preparing a second priamel, and ἐκ θεοῦ (line 10), informing them that his praise will be brief, but heartfelt and to the point. To appreciate the precision with which the foil accomplishes its purpose, we must turn to a group of priamels, extremely common in Pindar and Bakkhulides, employing the contrasting elements ἀφθόνητος and ἐκ θεοῦ, that articulate the meaning of O. 11.7–10.

On pages 8 ff. we have already distinguished a type of summary priamel that exhibits some such word as πᾶς, πολύς, μακρός, or the like, in the foil, and in note 23 are listed some of the variations of which this motive is capable. If we examine the contexts from which these examples are taken we shall see that in some of them the foil sets forth categories applicable by contrast or analogy to the laudandus (objective type) and in others highlights the laudator's prospective treatment of a theme (subjective type).

In the subjective group the foil often states or implies that the merits of the laudandus provide material in such abundance as to make it impossible for the laudator to recount, or the audience to hear, the whole story. This simple rhetorical theme achieves such astonishing variety and boldly original expression in the hands of an artist of Pindar's stature that its presence in his work has scarcely been noted. In its less transparent forms it is regularly misunderstood and is likely to be labeled as a typical Pindaric outburst in a personal vein.[36] For this reason we must examine first an unambiguous example. In discussing it I shall consider all the transitions of the ode, in order to present the single example as one tactical move in a complex strategy of design.

N. 10 opens in true priamel fashion with a long catalogue of Argive glories which is preceded by the statement (lines 2 f.) ['Άργος] φλέγεται δ' άρεταῖς / μυρίαις ἔργων θρασέων ἕνεκεν. Now it is immediately evident from μυρίαις that the laudator can hardly intend to exhaust his theme. The hyperbole is at once a rhetorical enlargement of that theme and an excuse for abandoning it whenever the laudator sees fit. μυρίαις is now picked up by μακρὰ μέν (line 4) and πολλὰ δέ (line 5), both abbreviations of extensive topics. After these entries, rhetoric is abandoned for some twelve lines in which the impression created by μυρίαις, μακρά, and πολλά is confirmed by the cataloguing of five more formally distinct items. When the foil has done its work, the laudator proceeds, as in the opening priamel of I. 7, to recapitulate it as a means of effecting a transition to the athletic successes of Theaios and his clan, reserved to this position of emphasis as the climactic term of the priamel. Here are the poet's words:

βραχύ μοι στόμα πάντ' ἀναγήσασθ', ὅσων 'Αργεῖον ἔχει τέμενος
20 μοῖραν ἐσλῶν· ἔστι δὲ καὶ κόρος ἀνθρώπων βαρὺς ἀντιάσαι·
ἀλλ' ὅμως εὔχορδον ἔγειρε λύραν,
καὶ παλαισμάτων λάβε φροντίδ'·

We observe the critical πάντ', which resumes the μυρίαις, μακρά, and πολλά of lines 3–5. βραχύ μοι στόμα marks the incapacity of the laudator to relate, and κόρος ἀνθρώπων that of the audience to endure, the full tale of Argive glory. Nevertheless (ἀλλ' ὅμως is conventional in such climaxes)[37] he now burdens their ears with a catalogue of the successes of Theaios and his clan that continues without major rhetorical interruption to line 45, at which point the now-familiar motive injects itself once more:

45 ἀλλὰ χαλκὸν μυρίον οὐ δυνατόν
ἐξελέγχειν· μακροτέρας γὰρ ἀριθμῆσαι σχολᾶς·
ὅν τε Κλείτωρ καὶ Τεγέα κτλ.

"But I can't bring to witness the countless bronzes (I simply don't have the time) set as prizes at Kleitor, Tegea, etc." μυρίον, οὐ δυνατόν, and μακροτέρας are the key words and require no further explanation. This

---
[36] On O. 2.91–105, P. 2.46 ff. (the θαῦμα motive, on which see, in the present study, pp. 2 f., 8 f., 14, and n. 10), N. 4.33–43, I. 5.51–61, N. 4.93–96 (climactic term of a priamel), see Farnell, op. cit. I 16, 90, 178 f., 273 f., 182.
[37] Cf. P. 1.85, I. 5.57. Cf. also ὅμως (O. 10.9) and ἔμπα (N. 4.36, P. 5.55).

concludes the catalogue, but so impressive has it been that it can now be converted into foil for the concluding tale of Kastor and Poludeukes by the insertion (lines 49–54) of the θαῦμα motive in a form very much like that of *P*. 10.48–50 (see pp. 2 f. and 8 f.). Neither the laudator nor his audience can wonder at such spectacular success when they consider its source in the benign influences of the Dioskouroi. Thus the laudator is permitted to conclude his ode with a glowing narrative tribute to the heroic patrons of Theaios' clan.

All this is extremely adroit and hardly the production of a poet whose bursts of inspiration carry him beyond the bounds of sense and relevance. At every point he is in perfect control, and if this is typical of the Theban eagle, our estimate of his irrelevant outbursts and violent transitions (as of much else) must be revised.

But I digress. Let us turn to less transparent examples of the form, in contexts that will bring us near *O*. 11.7–10. We may use *I*. 4.1–19 to bridge the gap between the more- and the less-transparent forms. The ode begins:

> ἔστι μοι θεῶν ἕκατι μυρία παντᾷ κέλευθος
> ὦ Μέλισσ', εὐμαχανίαν γὰρ ἔφανας Ἰσθμίοις,
> ὑμετέρας ἀρετὰς ὕμνῳ διώκειν·

Without discussing the context, I shall only note that these lines introduce summary praise of the Kleonumidai, which occupies lines 4–15. (Note the summary ὅσσα in line 9 and μακροτέραν in line 13, an oblique summary akin to the use of ὠκεῖα and βραχεῖαι in *P*. 9.69 f.: see pp. 2 f. and n. 10.) The last item in the tale of Kleonumid glory, their prowess in war (line 15), provides the transition to the climactic term, introduced in line 18; for the death of four of the clan in battle serves as dark foil for the brightness of Melissos' recent (on νῦν δέ in line 18, see p. 5 and n. 18) victory, which heads a catalogue of Kleonumid successes and failures in the games.[38] The key words μυρία, παντᾷ, and εὐμαχανίαν, taken together, suggest a prose parallel that may lighten our task. In the prooimion to his *Epitaphios*, Lysias has the following sentence: τοσαύτην γὰρ ἀφθονίαν παρεσκεύασεν ἡ τούτων ἀρετή ... τοῖς ποιεῖν δυναμένοις ... ὥστε καλὰ μὲν πολλὰ τοῖς προτέροις περὶ αὐτῶν εἰρῆσθαι, πολλὰ δὲ καὶ ἐκείνοις παραλελεῖφθαι, ἱκανὰ δὲ καὶ τοῖς ἐπιγιγνομένοις ἐξεῖναι εἰπεῖν. All that precedes the ὥστε clause is as perfect a prose equivalent of *I*. 4.2 f. as we

---

[38] The victories are summarized in lines 25 ff., and the failures in lines 28 ff. The latter allow the laudator to set up vicissitude foil (in summary gnomic form) which he then illustrates with the story of Aias. The climactic term comes in line 43, but is itself prepared for by exemplary subjective foil (lines 37–42).

could hope to find.³⁹ The prose equivalent of εὐμαχανίαν ἔφανας is ἀφθονίαν παρεσκεύασας, and this suggests at once that ἀφθόνητος in O. 11.7 is not "beyond envy," as it is regularly taken, but "ungrudging," "abundant." This gives us control of one of the critical terms in O. 11.7–10; the other, ἐκ θεοῦ, could be elucidated from θεῶν ἕκατι in I. 4.1, but there are other parallels that bear more precisely on this point while illustrating further the force of ἀφθόνητος. Let us proceed to these, noting only that the metaphor in κέλευθος is frequent in such contexts. We may compare N. 6.47, I. 2.33, Bacch. 19.1, 9.47 (all subjective), and 10.36, I. 6.20/1 (both objective).

For μυρία κέλευθος we find elsewhere such phrases as μυρίαι τέχναι (Bacch. frag. 20C.19 f.), μυρίαι ἀρεταί (N. 3.40, Bacch. 14.8) μυρίαι ἐπίσταμαι (Bacch. 10.38), τέχναι δ' ἑτέρων ἕτεραι (N. 1.25), ἄλλαι / ὁδῶν ὁδοί περαίτεραι (O. 9.112 f.), and the like. Though all these passages bear on the use of ἀφθόνητος and ἐκ θεοῦ in O. 11.7–10, we may concentrate our attention on two of them. Bacch. frag. 20C.19–24 will reveal at once the point of ἐκ θεοῦ:

> 20 τέχν]αι γε μέν εἰσ[ι]ν ἄπα[σαι
> μυρία]ι· σὺν θεῶι δὲ θ[α]ρσή[σας πιφαύσκω
> οὔτι]ν' ἀνθρώπων ἕ[τερον καθορᾶι
> λε[ύκι]ππος Ἀώς
> τόσσ[ο]ν ἐφ' ἁλικία[ι
> φέγγος κατ' ἀνθρώπ[ους φέροντα

We observe at once the extreme compression to which the motive has been subjected. There is no gloss to tell us whether the summary foil is subjective or objective. Bakkhulides may intend either, "There are many ways of life; but I can say confidently that he . . . ," or, "Many are the arts of praise; but (by-passing these arts) I say confidently that he . . ." The same ambiguity exists in 5.16–35 (see especially lines 31 f.), O. 9.107/8–120, and perhaps in N. 1.25–30, N. 3.38–40, N. 5.40 f., O. 2.91–105; and interpretation is complicated by the fact that a foil term may be subjective (or objective) when first introduced, but become objective (or subjective) before the capping term is reached. The most obvious example of this shift of emphasis is P. 1.81–86, but there are other striking examples. From Bacch. 14.1–11 one infers that the success of Kleoptolemos will be set against the background of vicissitude in human life: "People succeed or fail in their various endeavors. But Kleoptole-

---

³⁹ Lysias follows this sentence with the explanation, οὔτε γὰρ γῆς ἄπειροι οὔτε θαλάττης οὐδεμιᾶς, πανταχῇ δὲ καὶ παρὰ πᾶσιν ἀνθρώποις οἱ τὰ αὐτῶν πενθοῦντες κακὰ τὰς τούτων ἀρετὰς ὑμνοῦσι. For this sequence in Pindar, see N. 6.47–55, I. 2.33–42 (lines 41 f. give a metaphorical version of the πανταχῇ motive), I. 6.20/1–26. Cf. also I. 4.41 f.

mos, by holding to the precepts of propriety, the mistress of all virtues, has succeeded. Let us therefore praise him." Yet the argument takes a different turn in line 12: "In battle, choral performances are out of place; celebratory occasions do not admit the sounds of war. Each activity (war, peace) has its own propriety (not its own "right time," since "war" and "peace" are themselves the "times" and ὀμφά and καναχά the "proprieties"). What is proper *now* (νῦν χρή in line 20 introduces the climax of this elaborate priamel) is to praise Kleoptolemos."

Although Bacch. frag. 20C.19 f. are similarly ambiguous, I believe that the summary foil which they contain is subjective (at least with reference to the capping term introduced by σὺν θεῷ δέ in line 20), just as in 14.8 ff. the summary foil μυρί]αι δ' ἀνδρῶν ἀρε[ταί] κτλ. is subjective with reference to νῦν χρή in line 20.[40] The laudator means to say, "Though the resources of art are boundless, I shall abandon all device and say simply and with confidence that the sun never looked on a better man." But the audience, familiar with the conventions, will perceive the precise implication, "Whatever approach I take, I can't please everybody, for each will have his own vision of Hieron's greatness, but I know all will agree when I say...." This implication is explicit in *O.* 8.53 ff.:

> τερπνὸν δ' ἐν ἀνθρώποις ἴσον ἔσσεται οὐδέν.
> εἰ δ' ἐγὼ Μελησίᾳ ἐξ ἀγενείων κῦδος ἀνέδραμον ὕμνῳ,
> 55 μὴ βαλέτω με λίθῳ τραχεῖ φθόνος·

The sense is, "I can't please everybody, I know, yet I hope that no one will criticize me for eulogizing Melesias."

What, then, is the point of σὺν θεῷ in Bacch. frag. 20C.20? Clearly, it contrasts inspirational with mechanical praise; the laudator will have recourse not to the devices of art, which are impoverished by his theme, but to a natural and spontaneous enthusiasm that is divinely inspired. There are times when the subject must speak for itself. *Ipsa se virtus satis ostendit.*

Elsewhere (as in *O.* 2.94/5, *N.* 1.25), the work of σὺν θεῷ is done by φυᾷ (= "natural" as opposed to "mechanical" praise). In *N.* 4.41 f. both concepts (σὺν θεῷ and φυᾷ) are appealed to. But perhaps the finest illustration of the topic is *O.* 9.107/8–116 (note the contrast of φυᾷ with ἄνευ θεοῦ), used to terminate a long catalogue of athletic successes and introduce a simple, unaffected concluding vaunt. This passage contains many delightful combinations and variations of conventional themes. Note, for example, αἰπειναί in line 116, which exactly reverses, owing to

---

[40] Whether the foil is subjective or objective does not, however, affect the point of σὺν θεῷ.

a slight difference in the rhetorical situation, οὐ πάγος, οὐδὲ προσάντης in *I*. 2.33; note also the amazingly adroit handling in lines 112 ff. of a motive that appears in its regular form at Bacch. 14.8 f. But we have perhaps dwelt overlong on this subject. We must note, before returning to *O*. 11.7–10, another aspect of Bacch. frag. 20C.19–24.

The crescendo, or climactic term, in such contexts is regularly attended by an oath or some other form of asseveration. In Bacch. frag. 20C.21 οὔτιν' and ἕτερον are conventional in this sense (cf. *O*. 2.102/3 f., *P*. 2.60, *N*. 6.26, Bacch. 8.22 ff.); so is 'Ἀώς as witness in line 22 (cf. Bacch. 5.40, ἀέλιος in Bacch. 11.22–30). The asseveration takes a variety of forms. We may compare Bacch. 5.42 f., 3.92 f., 63 ff., 1.159 f., 8.19 f., *O*. 13.94 f., *O*. 2.99 ff., *O*. 13.50, *P*. 2.58–61, *N*. 7.49 f., 102 ff., *N*. 11.24. In *O*. 11 the asseveration is taken care of in the name cap of lines 11–15 by ἴσθι and by ἐγγυάσομαι in line 16; and for the sequence ἀφθόνητος, ἴσθι after an opening priamel we may compare *O*. 6.1–9, where τίνα κεν φύγοι ὕμνον (= ἀφθόνητον ἂν ὕμνον ἔχοι) and ἀφθόνων ἀστῶν (= "unstinting townsmen") are followed by ἴστω introducing a name cap.[41]

We have only to identify the motives employed in τὰ μὲν ἁμετέρα / γλῶσσα ποιμαίνειν ἐθέλει (*O*. 11.8 f.) and in ὁμοίως (line 10) before venturing a paraphrase of our passage. We may take ὁμοίως first.

The word is used in exactly the same sense in *P*. 9.81. Here is the context:

ἀρεταὶ δ' αἰεὶ μεγάλαι πολύμυθοι·
βαιὰ δ' ἐν μακροῖσι ποικίλλειν
ἀκοὰ σοφοῖς· ὁ δὲ καιρὸς ὁμοίως
παντὸς ἔχει κορυφάν.

As we see from καὶ νῦν (see p. 5 and n. 18) in line 73, the laudator has completed his transition from the tale of Apollo and Kurana to the victor. After mentioning Telesikrates' Pythian victory (lines 75/6 ff.) as the first item in a catalogue, the laudator introduces a rhetorical pause; he hesitates before the complexity of his theme while seeking a method of presenting it. In lines 79–82 he decides to select a few of Telesikrates' successes for elaboration: what is important is the spirit, rather than the letter, of the truth. In lines 82 f. comes the second entry, a victory in the Iolaia at Thebes.[42] The transition (lines 83–89) to the

---

[41] Imperatives of οἶδα are conventional in oaths. Cf. τ 303. For these forms in capping terms, see *I*. 3.15, *I*. 7.27, *N*. 9.45, *N*. 5.48.

[42] This sentence is all but universally misunderstood. The subject of ἀτιμάσαντα is Ἰόλαον; its object is νιν (Telesikrates). Every element in the line is conventional. Cf. *O*. 7.83 in a victory catalogue (ὅ τ' ἐν Ἀργεῖ χαλκὸς ἔγνω μιν), where we have ἔγνω, ὁ ἐν Ἀργεῖ χαλκός and μιν to match ἔγνον, Θῆβαι, and νιν (witnessing word, place of victory and witness, victor). *P*. 9.81 f. has two witnesses (Θῆβαι, the place of victory, and Ἰόλαον), two witnessing words (ἔγνον and ἀτιμάσαντα), and the victor (νιν). For this

third item, a victory in the Herakleia (lines 90–92b)[43] he effects by exploiting the relation between Iolaos and Herakles; the transition (lines 92b f.) to the fourth and fifth (lines 93 ff.) by an appeal to the Kharites for continued inspiration (cf. the appeals to the Muses introducing catalogues in Homer); the transition (lines 96–99) to the sixth (lines 100–107), a summary list (see πλεῖστα, line 100; πᾶσιν, line 106) of local successes, by an appeal to the Kyrenaians (this is transparently foil) to praise Telesikrates. Here is a catalogue relieved of tedium by brevity (βαιά, line 80) and variety (ποικίλλειν, line 80).

Thus the meaning of the sentence ὁ δὲ καιρὸς ὁμοίως / παντὸς ἔχει κορυφάν is, "By judicious selection and treatment (καιρός) I can convey the spirit (κορυφάν) of the whole *just as well.*"[44] We may illustrate this meaning of ὁμοίως from two prose examples of the topic. The first is Dem. 61.27: ἅπαντας μὲν οὖν εἰ διεξιοίην τοὺς ἀγῶνας, ἴσως ἂν ἄκαιρον μῆκος ἡμῖν ἐπιγένοιτο τῷ λόγῳ· ἑνὸς δ', ἐν ᾧ πολὺ διήνεγκας, μνησθεὶς ταῦτά τε δηλώσω καὶ τῇ τῶν ἀκουόντων δυνάμει συμμετρώτερον φανήσομαι χρώμενος. The laudator will not describe all the successes of his favorite, but is confident that by recalling a single outstanding success he will accomplish all that the complete tale could hope to accomplish. ταῦτά is clearly equivalent to ὁμοίως in *P*. 9.81. The second passage is Isoc. 9.34: εἰ μὲν οὖν πρὸς ἕκαστον αὐτῶν τὰς πράξεις τὰς Εὐαγόρου παραβάλλοιμεν, οὔτ' ἂν ὁ λόγος ἴσως τοῖς καιροῖς ἁρμόσειεν οὔτ' ἂν ὁ χρόνος τοῖς λεγομένοις ἀρκέσειεν· ἢν δὲ προελόμενοι τοὺς εὐδοκιμωτάτους ἐπὶ τούτων σκοπῶμεν, οὐδὲν μὲν χεῖρον ἐξετῶμεν, πολὺ δὲ

---

manner of cataloguing victories, see also *O*. 9.105 f., σύνδικος δ' αὐτῷ Ἰολάου τύμβος, where σύνδικος = witnessing word, αὐτῷ = victor, and Ἰολάου τύμβος = the witness (both the patron of the games and the place); Bacch. 11.22, οὐκ εἶδέ νιν ἀέλιος κτλ.; Bacch. 13.193, τὰν (μελέταν Μενάνδρου) ἐπ' Ἀλφειοῦ τε ῥοαῖς θαμὰ δὴ / τίμασεν ἁ χρυσάρματος / ... Ἀθάνα, where Ἀθάνα is the witness, μελέταν Μενάνδρου, the dedication of the trainer, and τίμασεν, which well illustrates οὐκ ἀτιμάσαντα in *P*. 9.82, the witnessing word. For οὐκ ἀτιμάσαντα, cf. also οὐκ ἐμέμφθη (*I*. 2.20) and τίμασε (*N*. 6.22). See O. Schroeder, *Pindars Pythien* (Berlin, 1922) 85; H. Fraenkel, *Dichtung und Philosophie des frühen Griechentums*, Mon. Amer. Philol. Assn., 13 (New York, 1951) 567 ff.; H. J. Rose, "Iolaos and the Ninth Pythian Ode," *CQ* 25 (1931) 156–161.

[43] With the language, here quoted, of Telesikrates' prayer, cf. Thgn. 341 f. *P*. 9.92 f. may be (as I think it is) a thank offering for a victory already achieved or (παθών = "when I shall have experienced") a prayer for a future victory. For such hopes expressed in the middle of a victory catalogue, cf. *N*. 10.29–33, *O*. 13.99–102.

[44] So far as I am aware, only Norwood (*op. cit.* 169 and 265 n. 20) construes ὁμοίως correctly. Yet he mistranslates the sentence and misunderstands the entire context because he harbors the popular misconception about the word καιρός in Pindar and is totally unaware of his author's rhetorical sophistication. On καιρός in Pindar, see Fraenkel, *op. cit.* 568 n. 10, and M. Riemschneider-Hörner, "Die Raumanschauung bei Pindar," *Zeitschrift für Aesthetik und allgemeine Kunstwissenschaft*, 36 (1942) 104–109. In *P*. 9.81 f., ὁμοίως and παντός together make one think of the verbal formula that links ὁμοίως (ὁμῶς) with some form of πᾶς, and this makes it all but impossible to see the point of ὁμοίως (the fact that a line ends between ὁμοίως and παντός is perhaps significant) until one has grasped the rhetorical purpose of the passage. One marvels the more at Norwood's instinctive grasp of the grammar.

συντομώτερον διαλεχθησόμεθα περί αυτών. The phrase ούδέν χείρον in this passage is clearly equivalent to ταύτά in Dem. 61.27 and ομοίως in P. 9.81. For κορυφάν we may compare the phrase έπί κεφαλαίου, frequent in prose examples of the topic.[45] The sense of O. 11.10 is therefore clear: "Praise in song will achieve as fine a bloom in simple and unaffected congratulations as it will in a pedantic catalogue of individual merits." ομοίως is litotes for "better."

What then is the meaning of lines 8 f.? Now that we have identified and documented all the other elements of the passage, a single parallel should serve to illustrate their sense and function.

In N. 6.47 the laudator warms to his task of praising the Aiakidai in these words, πλατεΐαι πάντοθεν λογίοισιν έντί πρόσοδοι / νάσον εύκλέα τάνδε κοσμεΐν, which by this time require no explanation. The laudator goes on to indicate the extent of their fame in lines 48–55, then in a *praeteritio* (lines 55 f.) dismisses them in favor of Alkimidas, his clan, and his trainer in lines 57–69 (for τό δέ πάρ ποδί κτλ. introducing the climactic term, see n. 18). Here is the *praeteritio*:

55   καί ταύταν μέν παλαιότεροι
    οοον άμαξιτόν εύρον· έπομαι δέ καί αύτός έχων μελέταν·
    τό δέ πάρ ποδί ναός έλισσόμενον αίεί κυμάτων
    λέγεται παντί μάλιστα δονεΐν
    θυμόν.

"Such is the highway of song opened by the bards of old, and while my thoughts incline me to follow their lead, yet the concerns of the present have a greater claim on my affections." In this *praeteritio* the sentence έπομαι δέ καί αύτός έχων μελέταν is the exact rhetorical equivalent of O. 11.8 f., in which the laudator expresses solicitous concern for each item in the ledger of Hagesidamos' glory only to dismiss the full tale in favor of a brief but spirited vaunt. This gives point to ποιμαίνειν, of which Gildersleeve says only, "The figure is not to be pressed." But ποιμαίνειν is more than a faded metaphor for μελέτα. The shepherd is concerned for all his sheep and will count them into the fold. O. 11.7–10 may then be paraphrased: "Bounteous is the praise laid up for Olympian victors, but while my tongue would tend those flocks of song, God's prompting brings my thought to surer bloom."[46]

---

[45] Cf. Hypereides 6.4; Isoc. 2.9, άν γάρ έν κεφαλαίοις τήν δύναμιν όλον τού πράγματος καλώς περιλάβωμεν, ένταύθ' άποβλέποντες άμεινον καί περί τών μερών έρούμεν; and Dem. 60.6.

[46] See B. Gildersleeve, *Pindar, The Olympian and Pythian Odes* (New York, 1890), ad loc. For the figure we may compare Nikos Kazantzakis, *The Odyssey: A Modern Sequel*, translated into English by Kimon Friar (New York, 1958) 29 (Book I, lines 1126–1129): "Like a great master-shepherd, owner of many flocks, / who stands straight by his sheepfold and selects with care / his fattest ram to slay at his best friend's reception, / so did my mind rise up *to count its flocks of song*." (Italics mine.)

Let us review now what has been accomplished in the focusing process initiated in line 1. Against the general background of human desire and fulfillment there emerged in the strophe a foreground filled with achievers and singers, the former seeking fulfillment, the latter proffering it. In the antistrophe the focus narrowed to success in the Olympian games in the sphere of achievement, but opened a prospect without limit in the sphere of song. From this the singer turned away, finding the solution to his ἀπορία in the abandonment of all device. We know now that a simple comprehensive statement will complete the laudator's praise of Hagesidamos and the Lokrians. Thus, line 10, the gnomic cap to the summary foil of lines 7–9, is followed by the concrete name cap of lines 11–15. The introductory words ἴσθι νῦν are formulaic, νῦν being a word frequent in the introduction of climactic terms and ἴσθι being the regular asseveration after the type of priamel that is employed in lines 7–10. In the climactic term, in which a single man is finally selected to occupy the foreground of our attention, the father of the victor and the event are duly named. The laudator promises to enhance (κόσμον) the crown of olive worn by the victor, while—but here we must pause, for κελαδήσω (line 14), the commentators tell us, is Pindar's postponement of an ampler ode. Still, we may more easily refute their claim if we first attend to an important feature of these lines, the preparation for the summary vaunt promised in κελαδήσω.

The effect of the focusing foil of lines 1–10 has been to make Hagesidamos the cynosure of all eyes for no more than three lines, for in the fourth, formally belonging to the victor, the laudator is turning from him to praise the Western Lokrians. This shift of focus is frequent in this position (after the opening foil has given way to praise of the victor) and occurs in a variety of forms. In *O.* 7.13 we find the victor and his polis introduced by the climactic καί νυν, as follows: καί νυν ... σὺν Διαγόρᾳ κατέβαν ... ὑμνέων ... Ῥόδον. This is then glossed (ὄφρα) and expanded in lines 14–19: ὄφρα / ... ἄνδρα ... / αἰνέσω πυγμᾶς ἄποινα / ... πατέρα τε Δαμάγητον ... / ... τρίπολιν νᾶσον ... / ... ναίοντας. The passage has all the elements of *O.* 11.11–15: naming of victor, father, polis, and event (πυγμᾶς ἄποινα = πυγμαχίας ἕνεκεν); the participle ὑμνέων = ἀλέγων, and the virtual future ὄφρα αἰνέσω = the future κελαδήσω. And the whole introduces praise of the island of Rhodes (in narrative form), as its counterpart in *O.* 11 introduces praise of Western Lokris. *P.* 9.1–4 is simpler. The laudator, dispensing with focusing foil, opens with a spirited declaration of intent: ἐθέλω ... Πυθιονίκαν ... ἀγγέλλων / Τελεσικράτη ... γεγωνεῖν / στεφάνωμα Κυράνας. Though all translators treat στεφάνωμα as if it were in apposition to ἄνδρα, it is in truth the inner object of γεγωνεῖν: the song is a wreath to crown Kyrene.[47] This brings the passage, which introduces narrative praise of the victor's polis, very near O. 11.11-15, where the singer will add luster to the victor's crown while showing due concern for the city of the Western Lokrians. The fact that ἐθέλω . . . γεγωνεῖν in P. 9.1 f. = κελαδήσω in O. 11.14 indicates that this future expresses a present intention and contains no promise of an ampler ode. These examples may perhaps suffice to illustrate the frequent shift of emphasis from victor to polis after the opening vaunt, whether prepared for or not by focusing foil. In O. 11.15 the shift informs the audience that Hagesidamos will no longer be the direct concern of the laudator. The focus now widens to include an entire community of men dedicated to the pursuit of ἀρετά. The shift of emphasis will be completed by the pronominal adverb ἔνθα, as in P. 9.5 it is effected by the relative pronoun τάν (see n. 27). Thus the vaunt for Hagesidamos, promised by ἐκ θεοῦ and ἴσθι κελαδήσω, will formally praise the community of which he is part.

While O. 7.13-19 and P. 9.1-4 illustrate the transfer of attention from victor to polis after the opening vaunt, αἰνέσω in O. 7.16 and ἐθέλω γεγωνεῖν in P. 9.1-3 indicate that the future indicative in O. 11.14 expresses a present intention. The laudator's use of the future indicative in the first person (when the song, or another witness, is the subject, the third person is used) is, in fact, a conventional element of the enkomiastic style. It never points beyond the ode itself, and its promise is often fulfilled by the mere pronunciation of the word. Thus κωμάξομαι in the last line of I. 4 does not promise a second ode in praise of the victor and his trainer, but informs the audience of the importance of the trainer's role in securing the current victory: "In praising him I would add the name of Orseas." φθέγξομαι (O. 1.36), στάσομαι (N. 5.16), κελαδήσομεν (O. 2.2), αὐδάσομαι (O. 2.101), τέγξω (O. 4.19), μαρτυρήσω (O. 6.21), πίομαι (O. 6.86: πίομαι . . . πλέκων = πινόμενος πλέξω), πέμψω (O. 9.27: cf., under the same circumstances, πέμπω in N. 3.74), τείσομεν (O. 10.12), οὐ ψεύσομαι (O. 13.50), διασωπάσομαι (O. 13.87b), μαρτυρήσει (O. 13.104), ἀρέομαι (P. 1.75), ἀναβάσομαι (P. 2.62), δέξεται (P. 9.75/6, of Κυράνα, bearing witness to Telesikrates' victory),[48] and a whole host of other

---

[47] See O. Schroeder, *Pindari carmina* (Leipzig, 1900) 44 f., and B. Gildersleeve, op. cit., ad loc.

[48] For Farnell (op. cit. II 201), δέξεται proves that the ode was performed at Thebes. He is thus able to take πόλιν τάνδ' (line 94), the formulaic designation of the laudandus' home city (see n. 53), as a reference to Thebes. This in turn enables him to interpolate a long irrelevance concerning Theban relations with Athens. On the context, see the works mentioned in n. 42.

examples of such futures, refer without exception to the present, and only by treating a given ode in a philological vacuum can one refer them to a time beyond the occasion of the ode itself.[49]

It is in lines 16–21, then, that the promise of κελαδήσω is fulfilled by the vaunt for Hagesidamos carefully prepared for in lines 1–15. In this vaunt his glory will be linked in the conventional manner with that of his polis; he and his fellow Lokrians will eagerly await the expected praise of their city. This praise has three parts. The first is introduced by the conventional ἔνθα (see n. 27) and directs the impulse of the song. In the second (lines 16–19), the laudator confides to the Muses, his messengers, the special qualities which they will find in the Lokrians deserving of their praise. This is the formal vaunt, and its importance is emphasized by asseveration (ἐγγυάσομαι). The third (lines 19 ff.) consists of an explanatory gnome which has never been satisfactorily explained. We shall discuss the separate motives in their contextual order.

In the phrase ἔνθα συγκωμάξατ' two conventional motives are combined. One of these, the "arrival" motive, appears in ἔνθα and is carried forward into ἀφίξεσθαι in line 19; the other is the linking of the song to the κῶμος. It will be best to discuss the latter first.

Song and revelry are the two elements of the victory celebration. We have noted this above, and have seen that πλεῖστα in the first line of our ode leaves room for both elements in the opening priamel (pp. 2, 11 f.). Two examples will illustrate the motive. The first is *N.* 9.1–3:

κωμάσομεν παρ' Ἀπόλλωνος Σικυωνόθε, Μοῖσαι,
τὰν νεοκτίσταν ἐς Αἴτναν, ἔνθ' ἀναπεπταμέναι ξείνων νενίκανται θύραι,
ὄλβιον ἐς Χρομίου δῶμ'. ἀλλ' ἐπέων γλυκὺν ὕμνον πράσσετε.

The conventionally contrasted elements are expressed here in κωμάσομεν (line 1) and ὕμνον (line 3). From ἀλλ', dismissing the former, we see that the κῶμος is here foil for the song, as it is in *N.* 4.1–8 (see p. 2 above).[50] Starting from Sikuon, the scene of Khromios' victory, the Muses are to proceed in a κῶμος, bringing mirth and revelry to Aitna, where guests fill to overflowing the halls of Khromios. They will join the merrymakers in their congratulations to Khromios, but will add their own priceless boon of song in obedience to the law that achievement must be heralded. The motive appears again at lines 48–55 of this same ode:

---

[49] κωμάσομαι (*P.* 9.92) may be, though I strongly doubt it, an exception, but then it would have this status within the requirements of a set topic, for which see n. 43; φάσει in *N.* 7.102 is modified by οὔποτε ("not now or ever").

[50] Similarly, ἀλλά in line 8 marks the preceding gnomic material as foil; ἀλλά and ἀλλὰ γάρ frequently signal a climax.

ἡσυχία δὲ φιλεῖ μὲν συμπόσιον· νεοθαλὴς δ' αὔξεται
μαλθακᾷ νικαφορία σὺν ἀοιδᾷ. θαρσαλέα δὲ παρὰ κρατῆρα φωνὰ γίνεται·
50 ἐγκιρνάτω τίς μιν, γλυκὺν κώμου προφάταν,

ἀργυρέαισι δὲ νωμάτω φιάλαισι βιατὰν
ἀμπέλου παῖδ', ἅς ποθ' ἵπποι κτησάμεναι Χρομίῳ πέμψαν θεμιπλέκτοις ἅμα
Λατοΐδα στεφάνοις ἐκ τᾶς ἱερᾶς Σικυῶνος. Ζεῦ πάτερ,
εὔχομαι ταύταν ἀρετὰν κελαδῆσαι σὺν Χαρίτεσσιν, ὑπὲρ πολλῶν τε
    τιμαλφεῖν λόγοις
55 νίκαν, ἀκοντίζων σκοποῖ' ἄγχιστα Μοισᾶν.[51]

Here we have a priamel of the type in which a generalized foil and climax precede a concrete foil and climax.[52] φιλεῖ, as we have seen (p. 10), is one of the many versions of the motive marked by χρῆσις in O. 11.2. μέν and δέ (line 48) contrast the revels (συμπόσιον, line 48) with the song (line 49). The second term caps the first: when a man's victorious labors are over, he longs to celebrate with his friends; but song heightens the bloom of the celebration, causing the victory to live again. Lines 49–53 concretize the κῶμος (note κώμου in line 50) and present a vivid picture of merriment beside the wine bowl. Lines 53 ff. cap the joy of the present with the laudator's wish, expressed in a prayer, that he may outdo all rivals in conferring on the ἀρετά of Khromios a (lasting) glory.

These two passages, juxtaposing the complementary elements of the celebration, are like all others that employ this motive in assigning to song the capping position. Song, as the more lordly of the two, rules the celebration, and for this reason, when elaboration is not required, the κῶμος sometimes represents the chorus, not so much as a band of revelers, as in their role as laudator. In I. 4.72, for example, κωμάξομαι puts the chorus as laudator in the role of revelers. This is the force of συγκωμάξατε in O. 11.16, where the Muses, who are on the scene to convey the spirit of merrymaking and song to the city of the Lokrians, appear in the personae of celebrants, secure in their own identity as laudatores.

The second motive in ἔνθα συγκωμάξατε is the "arrival" motive, which brings the song, or a divine projection of the song, to the scene of the celebration.[53] The transitional ἔνθα sets the scene, and N. 9.1 f. suggest

---

[51] A full stop, rather than a colon, is needed after ἀοιδᾷ in line 49. The gnomic priamel ends with ἀοιδᾷ as the concrete priamel begins with θαρσαλέα.
[52] Cf. O. 2.1–8.
[53] The scene is designated or referred to by some form of pronominal reference. Most frequent is a demonstrative adjective. Cf. τάνδ' ἐπιστείχοντα νᾶσον (I. 6.19), δάπεδον ἂν τόδε (N. 7.83), πόλιν τάνδε (P. 9.94), ἔμολον . . . / τάνδ' ἐς εὔνομον πόλιν (I. 5.23 f.), τόνδε λαόν (O. 13.26). This type of expression refers always to the home of the laudandus.

that ἔνθα συγκωμάξατε means, "Go there and join the revels," not, as those who follow the scholia take it, "There join in the revels." This motive will be illustrated below in connection with ἀφίξεσθαι in line 19. For the present, the reader may consult O. 6.22–28 for a general parallel.

Moving to his actual praise of the Lokrians, the laudator reinforces ἴσθι κελαδήσω with an even stronger asseveration. ἐγγυάσομαι, like ἴσθι νῦν, rhetorically heightens the laudator's praise by setting itself firmly and confidently against imaginary objections.[54] From these words, and from ἐκ θεοῦ in line 10, the audience will know that categorical praise of the Lokrians will follow. The eulogy itself is cast in an entirely conventional form. The items that may appear in such catalogues are limited in number, but the possibilities for selection and arrangement are practically unlimited. In our passage two doublets contain the laudator's direct praise of the Lokrians. These are φυγόξεινον στρατὸν / μήτ' ἀπείρατον καλῶν and ἀκρόσοφόν τε καὶ αἰχματάν. Both are conventional motives. The latter, praising qualities of mind and body, appears frequently by itself in abbreviated or expanded form;[55] the first element of the former, praise of ξενία, appears frequently as an independent motive, either alone, or coupled with praise of ἀρετὰ φιλόπολις so as to achieve a universalizing force similar to that of ἀκρόσοφόν τε καὶ αἰχματάν.[56] As an illustration of this coupling we may take O. 13.2 f., οἶκον ἥμερον ἀστοῖς, / ξένοισι δὲ θεράποντα, in which the universality of the doublet is defined by the words ἀστοῖς and ξένοισι. The second element of φυγόξεινον στρατὸν / μήτ' ἀπείρατον καλῶν we can identify only from an examination of examples of such catalogues in both abbreviated and elaborated forms.

It will be evident that the individual items employed to make up the ensemble must vary according to the particular merits of the laudandus and according as the laudandus is a person, a clan, or a community. In P. 5, after a brief rhetorical preface (lines 107 f.), Arkesilas is praised for his qualities of mind and spirit (lines 109–112), his physical prowess (line 113), his sophistication in the ways of the Muses (line 114), his skill in chariot racing (line 115), and his participation in athletic contests (lines 116 f.). In O. 13, after a brief rhetorical preface (lines 11 ff.), the sons of Alatas (i.e., the Korinthians) are praised for their athletic victories (lines 14 f.), their discoveries in the arts and sciences (lines

---

[54] The use of imaginary objections as foil is well illustrated by ἄπιστον ἔειπ' in N. 9.33.

[55] See N. 8.8, P. 2.63–67, P. 4.281 f.

[56] Other typical universalizing doublets are: land and sea (P. 1.14, I. 4.41 f., O. 12.3 ff., O. 6.10, I. 5.5 f.), north and south (I. 2.41 f.), beginning and end (P. 10.10, P. 1.34 f., O. 7.26, frag. 117.1–4), youth and age (P. 4.281 f., P. 2.63–67), good fortune and good repute (I. 5.15, I. 6.9–11b, O. 5.23 ff., P. 1.99–100b), rich and poor (N. 7.19, Bacch. 1.172 ff.), friend and foe (P. 9.96).

16–21b), their sophistication in the ways of the Muse (line 21b), and their prowess in war (lines 22 f.).[57] In *O*. 10, after the focusing foil of lines 1–12 has done its work, the Lokrians are praised for their sense of justice in human intercourse (lines 13 f.),[58] their concern for the Muse (line 14), and their prowess in war (line 15). In *I*. 4, after the focusing foil of lines 1–6, the Kleonumidai are praised for their sense of justice in human intercourse (lines 7 ff.),[59] their manly exploits (generalized in lines 9–13), their equestrian skill (line 14), and their prowess in war (line 15).

These examples are sufficient to establish a pattern. What are praised, generally or specifically or both, are nonmilitary exploits, skills of mind and body, a sense of justice in human intercourse, an appreciation of poetry, and prowess in war. Beside these, service to the gods is a frequent category, and wealth another.[60] These motives may appear singly or in any combination and are subject to great compression or elaboration as the laudator chooses. Confronting our passage with these categories, we find the Lokrian sense of justice embodied in the phrase φυγόξεινον στρατόν, their skills of mind and body and their prowess in war in ἀκρόσοφόν τε καὶ αἰχματάν, and either their athletic successes or their sophistication in the ways of the Muses in μήτ' ἀπείρατον καλῶν. Yet as to καλῶν, athletic success cannot here be intended. The close connection of the phrase with φυγόξεινον στρατόν tells against this, as do certain specific parallels.

In Bacch. 3.63–71 Hieron is praised for his services to Apollo (lines 63–66), his equestrian skill (line 69), his skill in warfare (line 69), his hospitality,[61] and his sophistication in the ways of the Muses. The last two items give the same coupling as we are supposing in *O*. 11.17 f., and the same modesty of assertion (litotes) appears in μέρος ἔχοντα Μουσᾶν as in μήτ' ἀπείρατον καλῶν. The same order of listing (omitting the element represented by ἀκρόσοφον) appears in *O*. 10.13–15 as in *O*. 11.17 ff. (see n. 58). In *P*. 6.48 f. praise of Thrasuboulos' sophistication in the ways of the Muses is preceded by praise of his sense of justice. In *N*. 11.7 ff. the same coupling occurs, but the order is reversed. The evidence

---

[57] These items are immediately used as foil for the introduction (prefaced by a prayer to Zeus recapitulating the foil) of the victor in line 27.

[58] That this is the general sense of Ἀτρέκεια appears from topical considerations alone. Cf. *O*. 8.21–30, *N*. 11.8 f., frag. 1.5, *P*. 8.6 f., *N*. 4.11 ff., *O*. 9.16 f.

[59] The meaning of the second element in the doublet is clear from the meaning of the first. ξενία and ἀρετὰ φιλόπολις universalize this aspect of Kleonumid ἀρετά.

[60] For service to the gods see *I*. 2.39 and Bacch. 3.63–66; for wealth see *P*. 2.59.

[61] See the passages cited in n. 58, which make ξεινίου the most likely supplement in line 70, though any word of related meaning is possible.

thus indicates that ἀπείρατον καλῶν = ἀπειρόκαλον, ἄμουσον. The Lokrians have taste.[62]

Thus the laudator assures the Muses in O. 11.16 f. that among the Lokrians they will be well received and understood; φυγόξεινον points to the hospitality they will enjoy, and μήτ' ἀπείρατον καλῶν to the frequent experience their audience can be presumed to have had *of enkomia;* for to Pindar and his audience aesthetic sensibility is more than appreciation of poetry as such. It is a passionate love of the qualities praised in poetry and an appreciation of the good taste and discernment required of anyone who would praise them. In N. 7.7–10 Sogenes finds himself glorified in song because πόλιν . . . φιλόμολπον οἰκεῖ δορικτύπων / Αἰακιδᾶν· μάλα δ' ἐθέλοντι σύμπειρον ἀγωνίᾳ θυμὸν ἀμφέπειν. Similarly, when Bakkhulides says (5.1–6) that Hieron has no living superior as a judge of poetry, he implies that he has no living superior in ἀρετά; and Pindar makes the same statement at O. 1.104 f., where he adds praise of Hieron's ξενία. In the latter passage καλῶν . . . ἴδριν is a close parallel to μήτ' ἀπείρατον καλῶν. As a final parallel we may cite I. 2.30 ff., οὐκ ἀγνῶτες . . . δόμοι / οὔτε κώμων . . . / οὔτε . . . ἀοιδᾶν, where we note, besides, the explicit inclusion of the two complementary elements of the celebration, revelry and song, that are found in our passage in the words συγκωμάξατε . . . / . . . ὦ Μοῖσαι.

To return now to the doublet of O. 11.19, O. 13.16–21b will illustrate the general character of the σοφίσματα summarized in ἀκρόσοφον. Attributed to the Korinthians there are the development of the dithyramb, the bridle, and temple pediments. ἀκρόσοφον might, then, refer to the creations of native poets, as some assert,[63] or to any native proclivities toward the arts and sciences. Elsewhere this element of the doublet often refers to ability in the council chamber. For this we may compare frag. 238.1 f. and P. 8.3 f.; in the latter of these, praise of Hesukhia's prowess in deliberation and in war follows praise of her sense of justice. We must include this general deliberative ability among the objects of the laudator's praise in O. 11.19.

---

[62] One must beware of determining the meaning of the phrase μήτ' ἀπείρατον καλῶν with reference to specific parallels for either ἀπείρατον or καλῶν; the evidence is too various. See οὐκ ἄπειρον . . . καλῶν (I. 8.70), μοῖραν ἐσλῶν (N. 10.20), τύχαν τερπνῶν (O. 13.110b), μοῖραν . . . καλῶν (Bacch. 5.51), μοῖραν ὕμνων (I. 6.58), ἀέθλων . . . / μοῖρα (I. 3.9 f.), τούτων μοῖρ' . . . καλῶν (I. 5.17), καλῶν μοίρᾳ (O. 8.86), μοῖρ' εὐδαιμονίας (P. 3.84), διάπειρα (O. 4.20), πεῖρα (N. 3.67), οὐκ ἀγνῶτες . . . / . . . κώμων (I. 2.30 f.), καλῶν . . . ἴδριν (O. 1.104), ἀπειράτων (I. 4.30), πειρώμενον ἀγωνίας (O. 2.57), etc. The position of the phrase in its more or less conventional sequence is a better guide.

[63] See C. A. M. Fennell, *Pindar, The Olympian and Pythian Odes.* (Cambridge, 1879), *ad loc.*, and B. Gildersleeve, *op. cit., ad loc.* Against these commentators I read with Turyn μήτ' (Bergk) for μηδ' in line 18 and τε for δέ (E, F) in line 19. Line 19 is thus not a positive version of line 18 (i.e., μήτ' . . . δέ is not equivalent to μήτ' . . . ἀλλά). τε, as Schroeder points out, connects ἀκρόσοφον to line 18: τε, καί rather than τε καί.

We see, then, that O. 11.16–19 present in conventional categories, and in more or less conventional sequence, items that appear regularly in catalogues of the virtues of individuals, clans, communities, or, as once (P. 8.1–4), of divine projections of these human entities. Even the position of the catalogue in the ode is conventional,[64] and it is the audience's knowledge of these conventions that gives precise form and value to what might otherwise appear to be a vague and random list of epithets. That the catalogue is presented confidently on oath (ἴσθι κελαδήσω and ἐγγυάσομαι particularize for the Lokrians the πιστὸν ὅρκιον of line 6) gives its verity added force. That the arrival motive appearing in ἔνθα συγκωμάξατε (line 16) and ἀφίξεσθαι (line 19) points formally to the future gives no more indication than κελαδήσω (line 14) that in O. 11 the poet promises an ampler ode. The arrival motive refers always to the arrival of the *current* song at its contractual destination or in imagination at some scene invoked by the song itself in pursuance of its χρέος (see pp. 10 f., n. 32). Most often the laudator himself "arrives" or "has arrived" at the scene.[65] At times he himself is dispatched or personally dispatches the song.[66] At times it is he who takes his stand beside the laudandus[67] or is present at a place with no mention made of his arrival.[68] At other times the Muse or the song or a special messenger performs this duty for him.[69] When the Muse goes in his stead, she is by convention summoned or directed to her destination, as in a kletic hymn. At N. 3.1–5 the Muse is dispatched to Aigina:

Ὦ πότνια Μοῖσα, μᾶτερ ἁμετέρα, λίσσομαι,
τὰν πολυξέναν ἐν ἱερομηνίᾳ Νεμεάδι
ἵκεο Δωρίδα νᾶσον Αἴγιναν· ὕδατι γὰρ
μένοντ' ἐπ' Ἀσωπίῳ μελιγαρύων τέκτονες
5   κώμων νεανίαι, σέθεν ὄπα μαιόμενοι.

Though the epithet πολυξέναν does not belong to the γάρ clause, it partially justifies the summons, as does φυγόξεινον in O. 11.17; and within the γάρ clause the laudator attributes to the Aiginetan chorus the same appreciation of song as he attributes to the Lokrians in the words μήτ' ἀπείρατον καλῶν in O. 11.18. Note also that the Muse will join a κῶμος (τέκτονες / κώμων νεανίαι, lines 4 f.). The same conditions obtain at

---
[64] See further pp. 30 ff. In long odes, praise of the polis will ordinarily prove to be foil for the reintroduction of the victor. So with paradigmatic material. See P. 8.22–35, N. 4.20–79.
[65] See O. 1.10, O. 6.22–28, O. 7.13, O. 13.93, P. 2.4, P. 3.76, N. 4.74, I. 5.23, etc.
[66] See O. 4.2b, O. 9.27, N. 3.74, P. 2.68, etc.
[67] See N. 1.19.
[68] See N. 7.82 ff.
[69] See P. 4.1 f., O. 6.87–91, P. 4.277 ff., N. 5.2 f.

N. 9.1 ff. (see p. 22), where the words ἔνθα . . . ξείνων κτλ. fulfill the function served by φυγόξεινον in O. 11.17. Neither in these nor in any other of its forms does the arrival motive refer to a future not embraced in the song itself. For this reason it will require very pressing special considerations to justify taking any element of O. 11 as a reference to O. 10.

We come now to the concluding item in the laudator's praise of the Lokrians. The ode ends with a gnome that, so far as I am aware, has never been properly explained. To appreciate its force requires an acquaintance with certain conventions in the use of foil that we have not yet considered. Roughly speaking, there are two broad types of foil in Pindar and Bakkhulides: the subjective and the objective. The objective concerns itself with categories of experience the relevance of which is directly determined by the qualities of the laudandus; the subjective concerns itself with the laudator's relation to his theme (see p. 12). Although this distinction applies to all types of foil, we shall here be concerned only with the gnomic.

A gnome followed by a particular can, of course, be employed in conclusions, but it is perhaps more natural in prooimia and transitions, where it serves to highlight a prospective theme. When these elements are inverted, the gnome will broaden the perspective instead of narrowing it. In the normal order, the particular substantiates the gnome and derives luster from it; in the inverted order the gnome bears witness in some sense to the worth of the particular. In general, the inverted form will have greater relevance in conclusions than in prooimia and transitions, but it has other conventional uses; in narrative, for example, it often serves to relax tension between two peaks of interest (see N. 1.53 f., N. 10.72, P. 2.34 ff., P. 3.20–23). Gnomic foil to conclude an ode is frequent in Pindar. Examples are O. 3.46/7 f., O. 4.28 f., O. 7.94 ff., P. 1.99–100b, P. 7.19b–22, P. 10.71 f., P. 3.114 f., N. 7.104 f., P. 12.28–32, I. 3.18, I. 1.67 f., N. 11.37–48. An examination of these passages will show that although the order of the elements is inverted, the elements themselves have the formal characteristics which we have identified in priamels of the regular type. In O. 7.87–95, for example, vicissitude foil (lines 94 f.) follows a long catalogue of Diagoras' victories climaxed by a dedication to Zeus of his recent Olympian success. Among others, P. 7 and I. 3 end with vicissitude foil. In P. 10.69–72 a gnome about statesmen in general follows praise of the Thessalian princes; in O. 4.24–29/30 a concluding gnome supports the concrete vaunt that precedes it. The foil in these instances is objective; to the subjective type belongs the concluding foil of N. 7, which, by its declaration of impatience with further elaboration, adds force to the laudator's confident assertion that N. 7, his "hymn to Neoptolemos," has done justice to this hero and to the other laudandi of the ode.[70] O. 2.105–110 also belong to this class of gnomes.[71]

Returning to O. 11, we note that lines 16–21 employ the order in which a particular is capped by a gnome. We must, then, ask whether the gnome is subjective or objective, whether it reveals the laudator's attitude toward his subject or an aspect of the merit of the laudandus. According to the accepted view (and I am not aware that it has been challenged), the animal figures in lines 20 f., ἀλώπηξ and λέοντες, are symbolic representations of the qualities praised in ἀκρόσοφον and αἰχματάν. Commentators are content to cite I. 4.45–48 for the animal images and O. 13.13 for the sense of the gnome.[72] How inconsistent is this mechanical matching of motives without regard to context we shall presently see, for although both passages are relevant to our problem, in context the former praises the laudandus, while the latter expresses the laudator's attitude toward his subject.

Let us consider first the evidence of I. 4.45–48:

45   τόλμᾳ γὰρ εἰκὼς
θυμὸν ἐριβρεμετᾶν θηρῶν λεόντων
ἐν πόνῳ, μῆτιν δ' ἀλώπηξ, αἰετοῦ ἅ τ' ἀναπιτναμένα ῥόμβον ἴσχει·
χρὴ δὲ πᾶν ἔρδοντ' ἀμαυρῶσαι τὸν ἐχθρόν.

What are important to observe are the qualities praised. The lion is an emblem of τόλμα (θυμός); the fox, of μῆτις (elsewhere σοφία, τέχνη, etc.). That they are here the qualities of a successful wrestler is of little moment in establishing the sense of O. 11.19 ff., for these, as we shall see, are qualities that distinguish the successful singer too. Furthermore, there is more than a hint that under ordinary circumstances something less than approval would attach to the ways of the fox: χρὴ δὲ πᾶν ἔρδοντ' ἀμαυρῶσαι τὸν ἐχθρόν. It is only against bitter foes that the deviousness of the fox is an acceptable recourse. Elsewhere, too, straightforwardness (δύναμις) is preferred to device (τέχνη), unless an enemy is involved. Then the devious way is the straight way: the way of God, the way of nature, the way of truth. Thus in P. 2.77, the fox is a symbol of base deviousness; but in lines 83 ff. the laudator approves the way of

---

[70] The notion that these lines contain a reference to Pa. 6 is false. See p. 4 and n. 14.
[71] This passage makes no sense on the assumption that κόρος = "envy." What kind of Greek is that? κόρος = ἄκαιρον μῆκος. The μαργῶν ἀνδρῶν of line 106 are those who don't know when to quit once they get a taste of eulogizing fair deeds. Doing justice to a theme is to them a mere matter of enumeration, but they bury under an avalanche of words the very thing they would reveal. The μαργοί, like the κόρακες of line 96, are a type, not historical personages.
[72] See B. Gildersleeve, op. cit., ad loc.

the wolf, who loves (praises) his friends, but hates (censures) his enemies as he moves in ὁδοὶ σκολιαί, and in frag. 283, as we see from the fanciful interpretation of Ailios Aristeides, it is the laudator who declares, ὄπισθεν δὲ κεῖμαι θρασειᾶν / ἀλωπέκων ξανθὸς λέων.[73] A reasonable conjecture is that the foxes here are mere technicians (no definite allusion intended), with whom the straightforward lion confidently vies in praise of a given laudandus, having recourse only to the "plain blunt" force of natural enthusiasm. This would indicate that if ἀλώπηξ in O. 11.20 refers to the Lokrians, it must, with λέοντες, imply that when straightforward methods fail, they will try anything.[74] This is, of course, grotesque, and gives us reason to look for another interpretation. And since the animal images in frag. 283 may well define separate and opposing attitudes toward a laudandus, we may at least suspect that ἀλώπηξ in O. 11.20 is mere foil, and that λέοντες, the real point of the gnome, is a symbol of the singer's strong and confident approach to so promising a theme as Lokrian ἀρετά. Is τόλμα, then, of which the lion is a symbol, a quality appropriate to the laudator?

We have already touched on this theme in our discussion of ἐκ θεοῦ in O. 11.10, where we noted that Bakkhulides has the phrase σὺν θεῷ δὲ θαρσήσας at frag. 20C.20, and that Pindar, in O. 9.107/8–120, sets up a confident θαρσέων with a contrast between τὸ φυᾷ (line 107/8) and ἄνευ θεοῦ (line 111). In lines 86–89 of this same ode the laudator pauses to summon inventiveness, courage, and power to help him prepare a catalogue of athletic successes (recall Homer's appeals to the Muses at the outset of catalogues). Here are his words:

εἴην εὑρησιεπὴς ἀναγεῖσθαι
πρόσφορος (= καίριος) ἐν Μοισᾶν δίφρῳ·
τόλμα δὲ καὶ ἀμφιλαφὴς δύναμις
ἕσποιτο.

Clearly the singer must have τόλμα; else his subject would intimidate him: to praise a merit that one can never equal is a thankless task, but one can achieve a greater measure of success φυᾷ than τέχνᾳ. In O. 3.40b the laudator's θυμός forces him to say that the Emmenidai have the favor of the Tundaridai. Indeed, the theme of confidence, along with the com-

---

[73] See Ailios Aristeides, περὶ τοῦ παραφθέγματος 56 (II, p. 159, 19 Keil), πάλιν τοίνυν πρός τινα τῶν ἀκροατῶν, ἐπειδὴ νυστάζοντα ἑώρα, καὶ οὐκ εἰδότα ὅτῳ σύνεστιν, οὑτωσὶ πεποίηκεν.

[74] For the symbolism, cf. Zenobios I.93 (*Paroemiographi Graeci*, ed. Leutsch-Schneidewin, I 30, line 9): ἂν ἡ λεοντῆ μὴ ἐξίκηται, τὴν ἀλωπεκῆν πρόσαψον· ἂν μὴ φανερῶς δύνῃ βλάψαι, πανουργίᾳ χρῆσαι. ἂν μὴ κατὰ ῥώμην τὸ προκείμενον ἐξανύοιτο, μηχανῇ καὶ τέχνῃ περαινέσθω τὸ λειπόμενον. τάττεται ἡ παροιμία ἐφ' ὧν σοφίᾳ μᾶλλον ἢ τῇ δυνάμει προσήκει χρῆσθαι, ὡς ὁ ποιητής φησι, ἢ δόλῳ, ἠὲ βίηφι· ἢ ἀμφαδόν, ἠὲ κρυφηδόν.

plementary theme of hesitance, plays an important role in Pindar, as it does in the rhetoric of pleading generally. Both attitudes are natural foil for the worth of the laudandus, whose merits both intimidate and inspire.[75]

By this route we are brought to consider the second of the two passages generally cited as parallels to O. 11.19 ff. There an extended name cap is prefaced by these lines (O. 13.11 ff.):

ἔχω καλά τε φράσαι, τόλμα τέ μοι
εὐθεῖα γλῶσσαν ὀρνύει λέγειν,
ἄμαχον δὲ κρύψαι τὸ συγγενὲς ἦθος.

This passage, so far from being a mere parallel to O. 11.19 ff., is a capsule of the entire ode. It differs rhetorically from our passage only in that the actual praise of the Korinthians follows rather than precedes the gnomic comment on the stability of "inborn nature." In O. 13 the order of foil and concrete is regular; in O. 11, for the reason that the praise is being terminated rather than introduced, it is inverted. We have already seen (pp. 24 f.) that O. 13.1–22b are topically identical with O. 11.17 ff., and we may make the following additional identifications: opening foil (O. 11.1–6) = opening foil (O. 13.1–10), ἀφθόνητος δ' αἶνος Ὀλυμπιονίκαις / οὗτος ἄγκειται (O. 11.7 f.) = ἔχω καλά τε φράσαι (O. 13.11), τὰ μὲν ἀμετέρα ... ἐγγυάσομαι κτλ. (O. 11.8–19) = τόλμα τέ μοι / εὐθεῖα γλῶσσαν ὀρνύει λέγειν (O. 13.11 f.), τὸ γὰρ ἐμφυὲς κτλ. (O. 11.19 ff.) = ἄμαχον δὲ κρύψαι τὸ συγγενὲς ἦθος (O. 13.13). The first two of these equivalences require little comment. In O. 13.11 the laudator declares that he has a glorious theme; in O. 11.7 f., that he has a copious one. Clearly the laudator is making no firm distinction between quantity and quality (indeed, he follows καλά with πολλὰ μέν and πολλὰ δέ in O. 13.11–16). The next topic, involving the τόλμα motive, takes a simple form in O. 13.11 f., a complex form in O. 11.8–19. The two passages are alike in that they define the laudator's confident approach to his subject; they are different in that the former introduces a long list of particulars, whereas the latter introduces a categorical vaunt. This categorical vaunt in O. 11.17 ff. demands the special preparation of a *praeteritio* (see p. 19) to avoid the listing which is welcomed in O. 13.14–22b. The vaunt itself is controlled by ἐκ θεοῦ (line 10), ἴσθι νῦν (line 11), συγκωμάξατε (line 16), and ἐγγυάσομαι (line

[75] For the most transparent example of the ὄκνος motive in Pindar, see N. 8.19–34 (elaborated by exemplum and thrust aside in lines 35–39). Here the hesitation is prompted by fear of detraction aimed against the victor (see p. 10); in N. 7.17–30 use of the motive (elaborated by exemplum and thrust aside in lines 30–34) is prompted by fear of not doing justice to Neoptolemos and the Euxenidai (see p. 10); in P. 9.79–82 the laudator is overawed by the dimensions of his theme.

16)—all pointing to the laudator's τόλμα, which plunges him, as it does in O. 13.11 f., into the thick of his praises, here into an abbreviated vaunt, there into an expansive listing of individual merits. In both passages the laudator apologizes for his abruptness.[76] In O. 13.13 he explains, "I can't help myself. That is my way." Is it reasonable to suppose that this is not his meaning in O. 11? Does not the entire ensemble force us to take the gnome in O. 11.19 ff. as explanatory of ἐγγυάσομαι in line 16, which carries forward the sense of ἐκ θεοῦ in line 10? ἐγγυάσομαι is a powerful word. The laudator will put up bail on his assertions; he is no hedger; his praise is unqualified, categorical. That is his way.

If the fox and the lion are seen as laudatores, the epithet ἐρίβρομοι takes on specific meaning. It is emblematic of τόλμα and the laudator's ringing praise.[77] ἀλώπηξ becomes vivid foil for λέοντες, for the fox is the man of device who cannot come to the point, who fails to mark the occasions on which merit deserves vehement acclaim rather than the devious services of art.[78] The fox and the lion are symbols respectively of τέχνη and δύναμις (τὸ φυᾷ, τὸ σὺν θεῷ)—ideas contrasted again and again by Pindar in rhetorical elaboration of his themes. O. 2.91–105, 105–110 (see n. 71), O. 9.107/8–120, N. 3.77–80, N. 4.33–44, and N. 8.19–39, passages which we cannot here discuss in detail, exemplify Pindar's use of this rhetorical motive, in which the laudator, disdaining all device, makes his straightforward confidence and enthusiasm the measure of the laudandus' worth. In all such contexts, Pindar himself is hidden behind the conventional mask of the laudator; yet they are regarded by critical opinion as personal to the poet, often in embarrassing senses. What is required to set right our knowledge of these and other problem passages is a thorough study of conventional themes, motives, and sequences in choral poetry—in short, a grammar of choral style that will tell us what systems of shared symbols enabled the poet and his audience to view the odes as unified artistic wholes.

◇ ◇ ◇

---

[76] See B. Gildersleeve, op. cit., ad O. 13.12.
[77] Cf. βρομίαν in N. 9.8, βρέμεται in N. 11.7.
[78] On the paratactical inclusion here of (apparently) irrelevant categories (often opposites) as foil, cf. I. 1.50 (where ἀέθλοις is relevant and πολεμίζων is foil), P. 2.83 f. (where only φίλον εἴη φιλεῖν is relevant to the laudator), N. 6.1 (only ἀνδρῶν is relevant), P. 10.1 f. (only Θεσσαλία is relevant), I. 1.1–4 (Θήβαις is relevant, and Δᾶλος is foil), N. 11.29–32 (καταμεμφθέντ' is relevant, κενεόφρονες αὖχαι is foil), N. 8.42 ff. (τέρψις is relevant, τὰ μὲν ἀμφὶ πόνοις is foil), O. 3.46/7 f. (only σοφοῖς is absolutely required, and ἀσόφοις, exhausting the possibilities, is foil). The lion and the fox are like the eagle and the daws (O. 2.94/5 ff., N. 3.77 f., Bacch. 5.16–30), and Pindar intends, "I am the lion, and no one, fox or lion, can change his nature." οὔτ' αἴθων ἀλώπηξ / οὔτ' ἐρίβρομοι λέοντες = οὔτις, with the added point: "whether straightforward (as I am) or devious."

The Eleventh Olympian Ode

I have tried to indicate what such study might mean for our appreciation of Pindar by analyzing the thematic and motivational grammar of a single brief ode. Having completed my analysis, I seem to hear the question, "But what *is* the relation between O. 11 and O. 10?" My answer is that we do not know; that we have no evidence on which to base an answer save the odes themselves; that each is an independent work of art; that it is in no way probable, whatever their relation, that one of them refers to the other; and that certainly neither τόκος in O. 10.9b nor κελαδήσω in O. 11.14 has reference to anything beyond its own context. κελαδήσω is a conventional future, as we have seen, set in a context that will not allow it an unconventional meaning. As for τόκος, indicating the finer quality of a product delivered late, I invite attention to Themistios' prooimial use of this apologetic topic at 7.84b f.:

οἶμαι σὲ θαυμάζειν, ὦ βασιλεῦ, τί δή ποτε οὐ παραχρῆμα ἐπὶ τῇ νίκῃ καὶ ἐφεξῆς τοῖς πεπραγμένοις τὸ παρὰ τῶν λόγων τοῖς ἔργοις χαριστήριον προσενήνοχα· ἀλλὰ τοσοῦτον χρόνον διαλιπὼν δόξαιμ' ἂν ἴσως ἀπαντᾶν ὑπερήμερος τοῖς τοὺς μῆνας ὥσπερ δανείσματα λογιζομένοις, μηκέτι δὲ ἐνθυμουμένοις ὅτι τὰ φιλοσοφίας ὀφλήματα τοὺς βραδύτερον ἐκτίννυντας οὐδὲν θαυμαστὸν τοῦ καιροῦ μᾶλλον τυγχάνειν τῶν λίαν ἐσπουδακότων. καὶ δὴ τοῦτο αὐτὸ πρῶτον δεῖ σοφώτερον καταστῆσαι, ὅτι βέλτιον διαλύει τὸ χρέος ὁ λόγος εἰς τὸν παρόντα χρόνον ἀναβαλλόμενος ἢ εἰ τῶν πραγμάτων εὐθὺς κατηπείχθη.

Note the important word βέλτιον, which indicates that τόκος in O. 10.9b has a rhetorical function similar to that of ὁμοίως in O. 11.10. That the laudator may have to abbreviate his enkomion or deliver it late will not affect the quality of his praise, which will be all the better for the difficulties he must overcome. This is purely and simply a rhetorical use of foil.

Did Themistios have O. 10 in mind when he composed this prooimion? He may have, even though the topic is conventional. If he did (and he quotes O. 6.3 f. at the beginning of the next paragraph), he read his Pindar with an innate appreciation of the requirements of discourse not displayed by the authors of our scholia and the moderns who approve their methods.

II

The First Isthmian Ode

INTRODUCTION

IN THE FIRST PAPER OF THIS SERIES[1] I argued for the necessity of a new approach to the study of Pindar, and by presenting my reading of O. 11, tried to indicate what results we might hope to achieve if we discard what we "know" from Alexandrian sources and from modern researches based on the methods of those ancient witnesses, and let the odes speak for themselves, not separately, each in a philological vacuum, but together as the products of poetic and rhetorical conventions whose meaning, though at present dark to us, is recoverable from comparative study.

I suggested that the successful prosecution of such a program would remove from the odes those "blemishes" that in their sum constitute the "Pindaric Problem"; that the Pindar we know is a myth created by our acceptance of postulates at variance with the very nature of the odes themselves. We forget that this is an oral, public, epideictic literature dedicated to the single purpose of eulogizing men and communities; that these eulogies are concentrated upon athletic achievement; that the environment thus created is hostile to an allusiveness that would strain the powers of a listening audience, hostile to personal, religious, political, philosophical and historical references that might interest the poet but do nothing to enhance the glory of a given patron, hostile to abruptness in transitions, to gross irrelevance, to lengthy sermonizing, to literary scandals and embarrassments, hostile in short to all the characteristics of style and temper that we ascribe to Pindar. That we persist in ascribing them to him against the plain requirements of genre and, as I believe, of context in all the senses of that word, is perhaps owing to our distaste for the genre itself—a distaste that leads us to prefer the irrelevancies we invent to the perfect tact of what is really there. I cannot otherwise imagine how the multitude of conventional masks and gestures that appear in the odes could have been transformed into so many personal grotesqueries, or how so many passages, perfectly lucid if one but insist

---

[1] The first and second parts of the present work were originally published independently (see p. iv). The first part, "Studia Pindarica I: The Eleventh *Olympian Ode*," is referred to hereafter as Stud. Pind. I.

that they are enkomiastic, could have become, on other assumptions, celebrated obscurities.

Here, then, in examining a second ode, *I*. 1, on the assumption that it is an enkomion and adheres to the rules that govern other pieces of the kind, I shall seek to discover its design, and the place of each several topic in the linear development of the whole. I shall assume that my readers are acquainted with the first essay of the series.

THE OPENING FOIL, LINES 1–13: PROOIMION

Line 14 contains a pronominal name cap bringing together the laudator (ἐγώ) and laudandus ('Ηροδότῳ).[2] The cap is introduced by the conventional ἀλλά[3] marking lines 1–13 as focusing foil. The foil well illustrates a class of priamels that are also hymnal invocations. *I*. 7.1–22b, addressed like *I*. 1.1–3 to Theba, belong to this class,[4] but rather nearer *I*. 1.1–13 in certain formal characteristics are invocational priamels of the type of *O*. 12.1–21, *N*. 7.1–8, *N*. 8.1–5, and *I*. 5.1–11. Without discussing these priamels at length, we may note that they are all invocations that hypostatize the principle common to a group of terms serving to illustrate by contrast or analogy a category or object of climactic interest. We may take *N*. 7.1–8 as typical: "Although (summary foil) all men are born into this world of days and nights,[5] our fortunes differ. Now (name cap) young Sogenes is acclaimed victor at Nemea." The invocation to the goddess of birth, Eleithuia, which controls this priamel, hypostatizes the principle that unifies its foil and climax. Similarly, in *I*. 7.1–22b the unifying principle, Theban glory, is hypostatized in the person of Theba. Tukha in *O*. 12, Hora in *N*. 8, and Theia in *I*. 5 have a similar unifying function.[6]

Although in *I*. 1.1–13 the nymph Theba has something of this function in that she represents the victor's polis, we cannot say that she generalizes all the terms of the foil, whether listed or summarized, as she

---

[2] For the terms employed in this essay, see Stud. Pind. I (esp. 5 n. 18). One may find a pronominal cap, a name cap, or a combination of the two. Both the pronoun and the name may designate the laudandus (e.g., *P*. 5.45), or the pronoun may designate the laudator and the name the laudandus (e.g., *N*. 1.33, on which see p. 85).

[3] ἀλλά dismisses the foil. Cf. *O*. 1.84, *P*. 10.4 (on which see Stud. Pind. I 6), *I*. 7.37, *N*. 9.3 (on which see Stud. Pind. I 22), *O*. 8.74, *N*. 9.8, *O*. 9.5, *O*. 4.7.

[4] See Stud. Pind. I 6.

[5] For the motive, cf. *N*. 6.6 f., *P*. 4.256. For other universalizing doublets, see Stud. Pind. I 24, 24 n. 26.

[6] All are hypostatizations of aspects of success. Observe in each of these prooimia the priamel motive. *O*. 12: ναες (A), ἐν χέρσῳ (B), πόλεμοι (1), κάγοραί (2); summary foil (πόλλ' κτλ., lines 5–12); pronominal name cap (line 13); *N*. 8: τὸν μὲν ... ἕτερον δέ (summary foil); lines 4 f. (generic cap); lines 6–12 (exemplum); lines 13–16 (name cap); *I*. 5: ναες (A), ἵπποι (B), ἀέθλοισι (C); summing gnome for lines 1–11; priamel foil (δύο, πάντ'); pronominal name cap (lines 19 ff.).

The First Isthmian Ode

does in *I*. 7 or as Eleithuia in *N*. 7 generalizes both the climax and the summarized terms of the foil. Theba is rather one of the terms of the foil, and we must turn to another group of prooimial priamels for precise analogies. Two examples, neither invocational, will suffice to illustrate the formulaic skeleton on which *I*. 1.1–13 are erected. *N*. 6.1–7 read as follows:

Ἑν ἀνδρῶν, ἓν θεῶν γένος· ἐκ μιᾶς δὲ πνέομεν
ματρὸς ἀμφότεροι· διείργει δὲ πᾶσα κεκριμένα
δύναμις, ὡς τὸ μὲν οὐδέν, ὁ δὲ χάλκεος ἀσφαλὲς
αἰεὶ ἕδος
μένει οὐρανός. ἀλλά τι προσφέρομεν ἔμπαν ἢ μέγαν
5 νόον ἤτοι φύσιν ἀθανάτοις,
καίπερ ἐφαμερίαν οὐκ εἰδότες οὐδὲ μετὰ νύκτας
6b ἄμμε Πότμος
ἄντιν' ἔγραψε δραμεῖν ποτὶ στάθμαν.

The first line and a half give the substance of this priamel, as follows: ἓν ἀνδρῶν, ἓν θεῶν γένος = list foil; ἐκ μιᾶς δὲ πνέομεν / ματρὸς ἀμφότεροι = gnomic climax. Gods and men are the terms included in the foil, and are presented as separate and distinct categories.[7] The climactic term discovers a principle that will allow them to be grouped in a *single* category. This device, in which the climactic term may be either positive or negative, is common. A simpler form selects for special attention *one* of many categories proposed by the foil. We may consider two examples of this simpler form in foil overtly devoted to the selection of an appropriate theme or treatment of a theme. In Bacch. 14.1–18 Bakkhulides is working through summary foil to his statement in the climax (νῦν, line 20) that what is *now* appropriate is ringing praise of the son of Purrhikhos. But he must first reach the gnomic climax, "Propriety is best in all things." Accordingly he writes (lines 8 f.), μυρί]αι δ' ἀνδρῶν ἀρε[ταί,] (summary foil) μία δ' ἐ[κ / πασᾶ]ν πρόκειται κτλ. (gnomic climax): while there are countless excellences that bring distinction, the *single* greatest of these is the sense of propriety. Similarly, in *O*. 9.107/8–16 Pindar is working through summary foil to a categorical vaunt in behalf of the laudandus and therefore wishes to reject the devices of art as inappropriate. He does so in this language: ἐντὶ γὰρ ἄλλαι // ὁδῶν ὁδοὶ περαίτεραι, μία δ' οὐχ ἅπαντας ἄμμε θρέψει / μελέτα. Here, because of the need for rejection of material in the interest of abbreviation, the gnomic climax is

---
[7] The proof that ἓν ... ἓν (= ἕτερον ... ἕτερον) emphasizes the distinction between men and gods rather than their common origin is in the priamel form. For the generalization governing such proofs, see p. 92, last sentence of paragraph 1. For κεκριμένα as a priamel motive, cf. frag. 105.6, where τιμαὶ δὲ βροτοῖσι κεκριμέναι is the equivalent of such summary foil terms as τέχναι δ' ἑτέρων ἕτεραι (*N*. 1.25), μυρίαι δ' ἀνδρῶν ἀρεταί (Bacch. 14.8), and τιμὰν δ' ἄλλος ἀλλοίαν (Bacch. 14.6 f.).

negated. There are many ways in which to praise by the rules of art, and no *one* of them will please everyone equally. Pindar accordingly lets the subject speak for itself, as it were, in the concluding lines.[8] The formal characteristics of this device are a representation of diversity in the foil and the words εἷς or ἀμφότερος or both in the climax. Thus in *N.* 6.1 f. gods and men in the foil give an impression of diversity in the cosmos, while in the climax we find the key words μιᾶς and ἀμφότεροι, creating an emphatic image of unity against the background of the foil. After this first statement the movement repeats itself. Lines 2 ff. amplify the impression of diversity as lines 4–7 amplify the image of unity.[9] We note that this second priamel has a climax introduced by the conventional ἀλλά. Both priamels then serve as foil for Alkimidas in the name cap of the antistrophe. A final point of importance in the formula as here employed is the word ματρός in line 2: the unifying principle is one of parentage.

The second of the two parallels I have selected with which to illustrate *I.* 1.1–13 exhibits a similar use of this parental motive. *P.* 10 begins as follows:

Ὀλβία Λακεδαίμων,
μάκαιρα Θεσσαλία· πατρὸς δ' ἀμφοτέραις ἐξ ἑνός
ἀριστομάχου γένος Ἡρακλέος βασιλεύει.
τί κομπέω παρὰ καιρόν; ἀλλά με Πυθώ τε καὶ τὸ
Πελινναῖον ἀπύει
5 Ἀλεύα τε παῖδες, Ἱπποκλέᾳ θέλοντες
ἀγαγεῖν ἐπικωμίαν ἀνδρῶν κλυτὰν ὄπα.

Here two distinct place names are offered as foil, as the categories "gods" and "men" are offered as foil in *N.* 6.1. They are then united by common parentage in a third term including forms of both εἷς and ἀμφότερος. The priamel achieves a general relevance in its mention of Thessalia, the victor's homeland,[10] which must, however, give way to the victor as subject of the song. Accordingly, the entire priamel is recapitulated as foil and rejected by the hesitatory[11] τί κομπέω παρὰ καιρόν; in line 4. Perfect relevance demands the vaunt for Hippokleas which is now introduced by the conventional ἀλλά.

We observe that *N.* 6.1–7 and *P.* 10.1–3 both serve as foil for the laudandus, introduced in *P.* 10.4 ff. by ἀλλά and in *N.* 6.8 by καὶ νυν,

---

[8] See Stud. Pind. I 14–17.
[9] For the double priamel, the second glossing the first, cf. *P.* 5.1–11, 12–23, and see Stud. Pind. I 23, 23 n. 52.
[10] Note that μάκαιρα is an intensification of ὀλβία and rather contrasts than compares Thessalia with Lakedaimon.
[11] ὄκνος as foil for τόλμα (ἀλλά με κτλ.)—a frequent rhetorical device. τί κομπέω κτλ. = "Why this irrelevant vaunt?" For the recapitulation, cf. *I.* 7.16–19, on which see Stud. Pind. I 6 f., 6 n. 21.

both formulaic in such climaxes. Similarly, *I*. 1.1-13 serve as foil for Herodotos, introduced in line 14 by ἀλλά. We observe further that in *P*. 10 and *N*. 6 the foil terms (*P*. 10.1-3, *N*. 6.1-7) are themselves divisible into foil and climax, and that this minor foil and climax are in both odes articulated by a contrast between diversity and a unity that depends on common parentage. With these facts in mind we may return to consider *I*. 1.1-13.

Like *P*. 10, *I*. 1 begins with a name priamel, in which Theba and Dalos serve as foil for a third term that unites (ζεύξω, line 6, like μιᾶς in *N*. 6.1 and ἑνός in *P*. 10.2) the glories of both (ἀμφοτερᾶν, line 6). The whole then serves as foil for the name cap of line 14. As in *P*. 10.1-6, one of the names —here Theba, there Thessalia—achieves a general relevance in singling out a category applicable to the laudandus. So too in *N*. 6.1, the category ἀνδρῶν is applicable to Alkimidas. The parental motive is very much in evidence in line 1 (μᾶτερ) and in line 5 (τοκέων), but is used here to give precedence to one term of the foil (Theba) rather than, as in *N*. 6.1-8 and *P*. 10.1-6, to give unity to the composite term. This minor difference shows us how a poet's repertoire of formulae and themes, and hence the tradition in which he employs them, suffers modification and change. Structurally, then, *I*. 1.1-13 are formulaic. They bear a close resemblance to *P*. 10.1-6 and *N*. 6.1-8, priamels on the surface very different from that of *I*. 1.1-13 in force and meaning. Yet all three are variations of a single focusing device. They permit the poet to select his theme and highlight it against a background rich enough and layered enough to give it dimension and likeness to life. With this in mind, we may turn to certain other conventional aspects of the opening priamel of *I*. 1. Lines 7-13 of this priamel, though important for the focusing process, are in form explanatory of ἀμφοτερᾶν in line 6, and for this reason I have preferred to discuss them separately below.

Of many conventional motives embedded in these lines, three are common focusing devices. The first of these appears in ὑπέρτερον and φίλτερον, the second in μὴ νεμεσάσαι and εἶξον, and the third in πρᾶγμα and ἀσχολίας. We may consider them in that order.

I have discussed the role of comparatives and superlatives in priamels in the first paper of this series, and shall not repeat that discussion here.[12] We need only observe that ὑπέρτερον begins the process of selection by relegating Dalos to a deeper background than that which Theba will occupy when the spotlight finally focuses on Herodotos in line 14, while φίλτερον justifies the choice in terms of the compelling relationship appealed to in μᾶτερ (line 1) and τοκέων (line 5).

---

[12] See Stud. Pind. I 11 f., 11 n. 33.

μὴ νεμεσάσαι and εἶξον are negative and positive versions of a common motive: the use of real or imaginary objections as foil.[13] It is fully as common in choral as in prose rhetoric and is a frequent means of amplification in enkomia of all kinds.[14] It appears in as wide a variety of forms as there are kinds and degrees of objection: the laudator is too brief or too prolix, he is listless or overenthusiastic, he cannot stick to his subject or has no flair for the charmingly irrelevant, he is trying to please too many or too few of the interests represented in his audience, he is guilty of a breach of contract, and so on. So in *N.* 7.64, the laudator, fearing that he may be thought slack in his praises of the Euxenidai, or fearing that someone may resent his turning from Neoptolemos to the Euxenidai, counters this criticism by putting on witness a countryman of Neoptolemos (whom he has already praised at length), in these words: ἐὼν δ' ἐγγὺς Ἀχαιὸς οὐ μέμψεταί μ' ἀνήρ / Ἰονίας ὑπὲρ ἁλὸς οἰκέων.[15] In *N.* 8.19–22, thought of the criticism (φθόνος) which his praise may evoke among the enemies of Deinis induces him to pause (lines 19–22), even to illustrate the dangers of praising a man among his peers (lines 23–34), before he can confidently return to his task.[16] In *N.* 9.33 the words ἄπιστον ἔειπα reflect his fear that his confident praise of the Aitnaians will be disbelieved. In *N.* 10.20 the words κόρος ἀνθρώπων point to the strain he would put upon his listeners by further dilating on the glories of Argos.[17] Frequently he must put himself on oath to silence objections, as in *O.* 13.94 ff.,[18] or overcome resistance by elaborate apologies, as in *O.* 10.1–12.[19] In *I.* 1.1–13 he is overcoming the resistance of Dalos (in

---

[13] See Stud. Pind. I 24, 24 n. 54.

[14] For prose examples, cf. Dem. 60.6, 13 f., 61.33, Thuc. 2.35.2, Xen. *Ag.* 2.12 (ἀναμφιλόγως), 25 (πῶς οὐκ ἂν φαίη τις κτλ.), 5.6 (ἀλλὰ ταῦτα μὲν ὀλίγων εἰδότων πολλοῖς ἔξεστιν ἀπιστεῖν), 8.7 (εἰ δέ τις ταῦτα ἀπιστεῖ κτλ.).

[15] *N.* 7.64 f. is like the citations from Xen. *Ag.* in n. 14 above. Cf. also *O.* 8.54 f., on which see Stud. Pind. I 16. The notion that passages of this type reflect personal embarassments of the poet is misguided. At Himerios 38.9 (ed. Colonna), a close imitator in prose of choral style, occurs an interesting version of this motive: σὲ μὲν καὶ ὀρθόπολιν (cf. *O.* 2.8) ὀνομάζειν οὐδ' ἂν αὐτὸς ἡμῖν νεμεσήσειε (cf. *I.* 1.3) Πίνδαρος, οὐδ' ἂν ὁ Σικελιώτης ἐκεῖνος, ᾧ τοῦτο τὸ ὄνομα ἐχαρίσατο ὁ λυρῳδὸς ὁ Βοιώτιος.

[16] The concrete climax promised by the summary foil of *N.* 8.20 is not reached until the pronominal cap of line 44. After the exemplum of lines 23–34 (an illustration of the evils of φθόνος), the laudator again introduces himself and his προαίρεσις in a generic climax (lines 35–37) for which the gnomic priamel of lines 20 ff. (νεαρά ... ἐρίζει), together with its illustrative exemplum, is foil ("some people prefer φθόνος; I prefer praise"). Another priamel (lines 37–40) then reinforces this προαίρεσις and works into summary foil (lines 40–44, especially the sentence χρεῖαι δὲ παντοῖαι φίλων ἀνδρῶν· τὰ μὲν ... / ... μαστεύει δέ κτλ.), which introduces the concrete name cap (ὦ Μέγα, line 44) for which the whole of this complicated machinery of foil exists.

[17] On this passage, see Stud. Pind. I 13. See also below, pp. 74 ff.

[18] Cf. also *O.* 2.101 ff., *O.* 6.20 f., *O.* 11.16 ff., Bacch. 5.42, and often. Other forms of asseveration abound.

[19] On this passage, see Stud. Pind. I 1 n. 4, 33. I shall discuss the problem of this ode in a later essay.

whose interest he is composing a paian to be performed at Keos) to his juggling the order of his contracts.

It is a mistake to take any of these passages, or others like them, as reflecting serious embarrassment. The objections, whether real or imaginary, are all foil, and are all so handled as to enhance the glory of the laudandus. If no real objection is at hand, one is contrived and assigned to τις or τινες or, in some such phrase as κόρος ἀνθρώπων, to the audience itself. So in *I*. 1.1–13 the laudator's purpose is not at all to apologize to Dalos, or to Apollo, or to any Keans who may be within earshot (for these concerns are irrelevant in an ode for a Theban victor), but to turn the great reputations of Dalos, Apollo, and Keos to occasional advantage by asking them to yield to the demands of a more inspiring theme—the victory of Herodotos at the Isthmos. Yet since to put Herodotos above Apollo would have appeared tactless even to Herodotos, the apology to Apollo, once begun, must be put with consummate tact, and it is here that the parental motive, ready to hand in the formula we have analyzed, provides an aesthetic and ethical escape. Even so, Dalos, Apollo, and the Keans get interest on their debt,[20] for the laudator links them with Theba in his preliminary crescendo (lines 6–10). χορεύων (line 7) creates a virtual epiphany of Apollo as the laudator in imagination joins the seafaring men of Keos in their celebration of the god.[21] A further mark of the laudator's tact is κέχυμαι, which indicates the pains he has been taking over the composition of the paian. That the first person is thus the personal Pindar of Thebes is as irrelevant qua fact as is the embarrassment expressed by the apology qua embarrassment. The words will have a pleasing verisimilitude on the lips of the Theban chorus (χορεύων in line 7 is properly applicable only to them), and what every Theban will find infectious is the holiday mood which puts pleasure ahead of business and ranks the interests of his homeland ahead of such worthy themes as Apollo and Dalos.

This brings us to the motive expressed here in the words πρᾶγμα and ἀσχολίας. The laudator is frequently ἄσχολος before an aspect of his theme, as he is here before its entirety. According to his mood, he may find the difficulty insuperable, or face it with quiet confidence or reckless abandon. In *P*. 8.30–35, finding himself ἄσχολος to recount the entire tale of Aigina's heroic and historical greatness, he selects for treatment only her latest glory, the recent victory of Aristomenes. In *N*. 10.45–48 he abandons his catalogue of the victories of Theaios' clan with the explanation,

---

[20] For the τόκος motive, cf. *O*. 10.9b, on which see Stud. Pind. I 1 n. 4, 33.
[21] See K. Keyssner, *Gottesvorstellung und Lebensauffassung im griechischen Hymnus*, Würzburger Studien zur Altertumswissenschaft, Heft 2 (Stuttgart, 1932) 33, 157 n. 2.

μακροτέρας γὰρ ἀριθμῆσαι σχολᾶς. In *P.* 4.247 f. the pressure of time (ὥρα γὰρ συνάπτει) forces him to abbreviate what remains of his tale of the Argonauts. In *N.* 4.33–44 he has no further time to deal with the Aiakidai, but will nevertheless (ἔμπα, line 36) resist the considerations that conspire against him (ἐπιβουλίᾳ, line 37) and with quiet self-confidence will continue his catalogue of Aiakid glories.[22] Examples could be multiplied indefinitely, but these will perhaps suffice. For the analogy with *I.* 1.1–13 is clear: despite his lack of leisure, Pindar will let the holiday spirit prevail, asking Dalos to yield to Theba.

πρᾶγμα and ἀσχολίας in *I.* 1.2, ἄσχολος in *P.* 8.30, μακροτέρας σχολᾶς in *N.* 10.46, and ὥραι in *N.* 4.34 belong to a large group of words and phrases with which the poet refers to his obligations as laudator. In the first of these Pindaric studies I discussed the motive briefly in connection with χρῆσις in *O.* 11.2.[23] We may call it the χρέος–τεθμός motive, taking our cue from such passages as *N.* 4.33 f. and *P.* 8.34. In the former the laudator pleads, as reasons for abandoning his catalogue of Aiakid glories, lack of time (ὥραι), the exigencies of his τεθμός, his "assignment," and his own desire (ἴυγγι, line 35) to praise the Theandridai. In *P.* 8.34 it is the χρέος owed to Aristomenes that creates his lack of leisure for other matters. In *N.* 3.6 it is the thirst (δίψῃ) of success for song that calls the Muse to the banks of the Asopos. Elsewhere μισθός, χρή, πρόσφορος, πρέπει, and the like point to the laudator's obligation. In *I.* 1.2 πρᾶγμα and ἀσχολίας represent conflicting obligations. One proves stronger than the other.

Thus in *I.* 1.1–6, despite the originality of the composite, all the elements are conventional and formulaic. I have singled out only the most important motives and have commented on the way in which they serve the focusing function of the ensemble. It is the principle of foil that controls the deployment of the individual motives. The whole is tending toward the isolation of Herodotos' Isthmian victory as the central theme of the song. The completion of this process takes place in lines 7–13, which we must now examine.

As we have already noted, these lines are an amplification of the phrase ἀμφοτερᾶν . . . χαρίτων . . . τέλος, in line 6. ἀμφοτερᾶν is distributed into καί (line 7) . . . καί (line 9). The laudator will celebrate both Phoibos and the Isthmos. Here Phoibos and the Isthmos replace the Dalos and Theba of the first strophe respectively; as Dalos was foil for Theba, so now Phoibos at Dalos is foil for the Isthmos. With this substitution, attention converges on the games in which Herodotos is victorious, but the logic of the

---
[22] See Stud. Pind. I 3 n. 11.
[23] See Stud. Pind. I 10 f.

identity of interest between Theba and the Isthmos is left unexplained. Accordingly, this omission is now repaired in the ἐπεί clause of lines 10 ff., from which we learn that the Isthmos has bestowed on the laudator's fatherland the glory of six athletic successes.[24] This brings us close to the most important of these, Herodotos' own, but before seeing how the final transition is effected, we may observe that the linking of participles (here χορεύων, line 7) to voluntative enkomiastic futures (here ζεύξω, line 6) is conventional, as is the appending of ἐπεί or γάρ clauses (ὅτε once), containing the ground for praise (often itemized lists or summaries of ἀρεταί), to the singer's announcement of his readiness to praise.[25]

Lines 12 f., containing a reference to Herakles and the hounds of Geruon, form the bridge to the first full crescendo in lines 14 ff. This is an instance of the use of (comparative) irrelevance as foil—a device more common in transitions than elsewhere. Here, the laudator has every intention of introducing Herodotos, for whom lines 1–13 are foil, and no intention of wandering off into the legendary glories of Thebes. Yet he cannot introduce Herodotos at this point without ruining the effect of the implied series: not Dalos, not Thebes; not Apollo, not the Isthmos; but Herodotos. The name he is "seeking" to climax his meditations cannot follow immediately upon the climax reached in the mention of six Isthmian crowns. Attention must be directed away from these, allowed to relax, and then reawakened with a forceful name cap. The transitional matter must be sufficiently different from what precedes it to redirect the attention of the audience, but cannot be of such length or pointed interest that the force of the opening foil and its name cap will be dissipated. Nor can it be entirely irrelevant. This is a nice tactical problem, and to solve it, the poet resorts to an extremely abbreviated version of a topic that is conventional in certain forms of unreserved eulogy.

The topic frequently involves as foil Herakles' western adventures, and as this hero satisfies the requirement of nominal relevance to a Theban ode, it can be used here in a muted form.[26] Herakles' trip to Gades, where he subdued the hounds of Geruon, symbolizes the limit of human achievement beyond which neither the laudandus nor the lauda-

---

[24] Bury (*ad loc.*) believed that the six victories mentioned here are those enumerated in lines 53–59 (he believed also that Apollo is the subject of ὤπασεν in line 11), but πάντα (line 60) makes something else of this catalogue than a "punctual enumeration of *six* victories."

[25] Cf. *O*. 3.6, *I*. 6.57, frag. 106.23, *O*. 9.90, *N*. 6.48, *I*. 4.2, *I*. 7.21.

[26] Brief exempla of nominal relevance (usually introduced by a relative pronoun) are sometimes inserted between two peaks of interest to relax tension and avoid monotony. For the principle governing these insertions, see Aristotle *Rhet*. 1414b, ἅμα δὲ καὶ ἐὰν ἐκτοπίσῃ, ἁρμόττει, καὶ μὴ ὅλον τὸν λόγον ὁμοειδῆ εἶναι. Cf. *N*. 8.18 f., *N*. 3.21–24. Herakles καλλίνικος, εὐεργέτης, who won for himself a life of ease in heaven (a paradigm of fame after death), is at least nominally relevant to any epinikion.

tor who praises him can go. In *I*. 4.9–13 the topic is introduced in order to make possible the abbreviation, in a categorical vaunt, of all the witnesses to the glory of the Kleonumidai. At its end the sentence καὶ μηκέτι μακροτέραν σπεύδειν ἀρετάν serves to inform the audience that the Kleonumidai have achieved the heights and the laudator can say no more. Similar are *N*. 9.46 f., the end of *O*. 3, and *N*. 3.18–25. In the last of these the topic (lines 19 f. οὐκέτι ... εὐμαρές), introduced to enhance the glory of Aristokleidas, is made to assume digressive proportions (lines 21–25) in order that it may again serve as foil for the introduction of the Aiakidai.[27] But the topic occurs twice, without the symbolism of Herakles' western adventures, in a position between the opening foil and the subsequent pronominal name cap.[28] This full treatment is impossible, for reasons which we have seen, in *I*. 1.12 f. Instead, the motive is hinted at and dropped. The positioning of καί before τὸν ἀδείμαντον ... // παῖδα suggests, without fanfare, comparison of the six Isthmian crowns with Herakles' subduing of the hounds of Geruon. "Thebes" has suggested "Thebans"—first Herakles, then his modern compatriot, Herodotos, who emulates the standards he set. Thus ἀλλ' (line 14) rejects not Thebes, but *one* of her citizens in favor of *another* whose achievement satisfies, as that of Herakles does not, the category previously selected in the words Ἰσθμοῦ (line 9) and ἀέθλων (line 12). The comparative irrelevance of Herakles is emphasized by the mention of Geruon, which takes the audience to the conventional western limit of human exploration.[29] Beyond this the laudator cannot and will not take them. He therefore rejects the topic and turns with renewed force and vigor to Herodotos himself. The first full crescendo begins.

THE FIRST CRESCENDO, LINES 14–32: KASTOR AND IOLAOS

The opening foil has done its work of selection, and Herodotos is now the theme of the song. In the immediate background stand the Isthmos and Thebes, his mother city; in deeper background stand Dalos, Apollo, and the mariners of Keos. Five other victors offering crowns to Theba further complicate the scene, which gains temporal dimension from Herakles' legendary exploits. Against this background of varied interests ordered into two distinct groups, the Delian and the Theban, emerges the figure of a single favored man.

---

[27] With lines 25 f., proclaiming the passage as a digression, cf. *P*. 11.38–40.

[28] In *I*. 5.13–18 (forming the foil term for the pronominal name cap of lines 19 ff.) and in *I*. 6.9–11b (forming the foil term for the name cap of lines 12 ff.).

[29] Conventional, merely; since Greeks had long since sailed into the Atlantic. But that Pindar believed Gades to be the end of the world is the rash conclusion of Norwood from Pindar's use of this topic. See G. Norwood, *Pindar*, Sather Classical Lectures, vol. 19 (Berkeley and Los Angeles, Univ. Calif. Press, 1945) 45.

As the crescendo begins, the words ἀλλ' ἐγὼ Ἡροδότῳ show a piling up of key motives in an emphatic position. ἀλλά, as regularly, dismisses the foil, while ἐγώ and Ἡροδότῳ forcefully juxtapose the singer and his theme. Structurally, the rest of the sentence is typical of crescendos, which frequently display a verb in the first person (usually the future indicative, or ἐθέλω with an infinitive) supplemented by a participle. Here we have ἐθέλω / . . . ἐναρμόξαι and τεύχων.[30] Although the laudator praises Herodotos in these lines for his victory and for driving his own chariot,[31] he does so in the participle τεύχων, devoting the main verb ἐθέλω ἐναρμόξαι to selecting the *manner* of his praise. The selection motive appears in line 16 in the disjunctives ἢ . . . ἤ, which imply the preliminary question, "How shall I praise him?" Typical of this rhapsodic priamel motive is *h. Hom.* 3.19, 207, πῶς τ' ἄρ σ' ὑμνήσω πάντως εὔυμνον ἐόντα. Questions of this type may be followed as in the former (3.19) of these passages by an immediate selection, or as in the latter (3.207) by a list of tentative themes, each prefaced by a disjunctive, which culminates in the chosen one. This device is frequent in both prose and verse.[32] In Pindar, *I.* 7.1–22b and frag. 19.1–6 are the most conspicuous examples. A variation may be seen in the famous opening of *O.* 2: τίνα θεόν, τίν' ἥρωα, τίνα δ' ἄνδρα κελαδήσομεν; In *I.* 1.14–16 only two alternatives are presented: the laudator will link his praises of Herodotos to a hymn in honor either of Kastor or of Iolaos. The promised hymn does indeed follow in lines 17–32, but is introduced by the explanatory γάρ (line 17), so that the promise of ἐθέλω / . . . ἐναρμόξαι is never *formally* completed, since γάρ makes the hymn itself part of the prefatory promise. The use of the future indicative and of ἐθέλω with the infinitive, in which a promise is regarded as fulfilled the moment it is uttered, is a conventional mannerism of hymnal poetry.[33] Its presence here means that an overt choice is never made between Kastor and Iolaos, for the γάρ clause which explains the relevance of one *or* the other to the present celebration is itself the formal hymn. Yet this omission is purposeful, for of the alternatives posed by

---

[30] Cf. περιστέλλων . . . γαρύσομαι (lines 33 f.) and ἀμειβομένοις . . . κελαδῆσαι (lines 53 f.), ὀμόσσαις . . . μαρτυρήσω (*O.* 6.20 f.), πέμπων . . . ἱλάσκομαι (*O.* 7.8 f.), ἐθελήσω . . . ἀγγέλλων διορθῶσαι (*O.* 7.20 f.), ἐπιφλέγων . . . πέμψω (*O.* 9.23/4–27), ἐθέλω . . . ἀγγέλλων . . . γεγωνεῖν (*P.* 9.1 ff.), and often.

[31] Most wealthy competitors (as in modern horse racing) did not do their own riding or driving. When they did, this remarkable fact was regularly mentioned. Cf., e.g., in an agonistic inscription (*IG* 5.1, 213 ca. 440–435), τάδε ἐνίκαhε Δαμόνο[ν] τôι αὐτὸ τεθρίπποι αὐτὸς ἀνιοχίον.

[32] For prose examples, cf. Dem. *Ep.* 2.13–16, Isoc. 9.69 f. Cf. also *Pa.* 9.1–21, frag. *lyr. adesp.* 84 Bgk.⁴, Antagoras 1 (*Collectanea Alexandrina*, ed. Powell), Pind. frag. 254, frag. *lyr. adesp.* 34.8–11 (*Collectanea Alexandrina*, ed. Powell), Ariphron 1.D². 3–14 (an indirect way of listing the god's powers, implying, "Shall I hymn you for this . . . , or this [etc.]?"), *I.* 3.1 ff.

[33] See Stud. Pind. I 21 f.

the disjunctives in line 16 the first is foil; the audience, familiar with the motive, will know that this listing implies a choice. Kastor must be present throughout, but it is Iolaos in whom the laudator is chiefly interested, while the presence of Kastor adds luster to his name. The superior interest of Iolaos is indeed borne out in the next line, where the focus widens from the individual heroes to the city states to which they are a credit—Lakedaimon and *Thebes*. As Lakedaimon is foil for Thebes, so Kastor is foil for Iolaos. Thus the name patterns that distinguish the opening foil continue to play a role in the process of selection.

The evidence for the rhapsodic hymnal structure of lines 14–32 is unambiguous. What we require is a formal invocation, "I shall sing," or the like, and a formal close of any of the types found in the rhapsodic hymns. The relation of ἐθέλω / ἢ Καστορείῳ ἢ 'Ιολάοι' ἐναρμόξαι μιν ὕμνῳ to the introductory formulae of the rhapsodic hymns is clear, as is that of χαίρετε in line 32 to the concluding formulae. Consider *h. Hom.* 6.1 f., 'Αφροδίτην / ᾄσομαι, and 19, χαῖρε; 7.1 f., ἀμφὶ Διώνυσον ... / μνήσομαι, and 58, χαῖρε; 10.1, Κυθέρειαν ἀείσομαι, and 4, χαῖρε.[34] The only complication in *I*. 1 is the one announced by the laudator himself: he will harmonize praise of Herodotos with praise of Kastor or Iolaos. Even the γάρ of line 17 is compatible with the hymnal form in which the invocation is followed by the explanatory particle or an explanatory relative clause; for γάρ in hymnal openings is a characteristic not only of prayer hymns (cf. *P*. 8.6, *O*. 12.3) but also of hymns of praise (cf. *O*. 13.6, Bacch. 3.5, 4.4). With ἐθέλω / ... ἐναρμόξαι ... / ... γάρ, cf. further ζεύξω and ἐπεί in lines 6 and 10 (see p. 43 and n. 25).

The opening crescendo is thus a formal hymn to Kastor and Iolaos, who stand high among heroic patrons of the athletic arts. The body of the hymn is in form a summary victory catalogue which falls into two parts. Part one (lines 17–22) treats of prowess in chariotry, part two (lines 22–29) of excellence in other events. It is natural, in view of Herodotos' skills, that chariotry should receive greater emphasis than do the other accomplishments. The same plan is followed in each part. In line 17 the heroes are acclaimed as charioteers; in lines 18–22 we learn of their numerous (πλείστων, line 18) chariot successes. In lines 22–27 they are acclaimed as runners (stade and armed races), javelinists, and discus throwers; in lines 28 f. we learn of their frequent (θαμάκις, line 28) successes in these events.[35]

At the end of the second part we get again the play of foil in an array

---

[34] So too ἐγὼ δὲ ... γαρύσομαι in *I*. 1.32 is the rhapsodic αὐτὰρ ἐγὼ ... μνήσομ' ἀοιδῆς.

[35] For πλείστων (line 18) and ἀθρόοις (line 28) as summary catalogue motives, cf. πλεῖστα (*P*. 9.100), ἀθρόα (*O*. 13.94). For οἷα and ὁπότε in victory catalogues (or in the itemization of single wins), cf. οἷον (*O*. 9.95) and ὅταν (*P*. 2.10). Forms of ὅσος are more frequent in catalogues than forms of οἷος (*O*. 13.103, 42, *N*. 10.41). In line 18,

of names. The pair of place names introduced in line 17 is repeated twice, and the names of the heroes introduced in line 16, once. We note that the resulting total of five pairs produces not a single verbal repetition. Sparta is Λακεδαίμονι, παρ' Εὐρώτᾳ, and ὑψίπεδον Θεράπνας ... ἕδος ; Thebes is Θήβαις, ῥεέθροισι ... Δίρκας, and Σπαρτῶν γένει ; Kastor is Καστορείῳ and Τυνδαρίδας and Iolaos is Ἰολάοιο and Ἰφικλέος ... παῖς. *Variatio* (ποικιλία) is a typical feature of Pindar's style.[36] The cities had been introduced in the order Sparta, Thebes; at the close they appear in the order Thebes, Sparta, and the order of mention of the heroes is similarly inverted. It is clear that the one set of names (Sparta, Kastor) is again foil for the other (Thebes, Iolaos). Kastor and Sparta are this time mentioned last in order to make them the nearer object of the dismissal implied in the concluding hymnal χαίρετε (line 32).

The names that thus "ring" the exemplary agonistic material give it the proper weight and point, determining its emotional color and its bearing on the whole. So the first crescendo ends on a ringing muster of names. The glory of Herodotos is enhanced by his inclusion in the hymn to Kastor and Iolaos. The background becomes richer, deeper, more layered, but remains firmly structured. The laudator is in perfect control of the scene. The figures emerge and recede to take their place in the perspective, leaving always in the foreground that single figure to whom our eyes must return, Herodotos, victorious charioteer at the Isthmos. So now it is to him (τοῦδ' ἀνδρός, line 34) that we return in the second crescendo.

THE SECOND CRESCENDO, LINES 32–40: ASOPODOROS

χαίρετε in line 32, which concludes the hymn to Kastor and Iolaos, solves the laudator's problem of finding a foil for the pronominal name cap of line 32 with which a new crescendo begins. The moment of quiet achieved in χαίρετε provides the impetus for a new ἀναβολή to honor the victor's father. The mood of rejoicing is here tempered by a mood of sadness; else, the crescendo might have been set off by a more elaborate foil.[37]

τε is exegetical rather than additive and ἀγώνων (the genitive depends on ἀέθλοισι, not on θίγον [see Bury, *ad loc.*]) is "games" rather than "(various) contests." A comma should replace the colon at the end of line 17.

[36] Note the further patterns: (1) in the place names: regular place names, periphrasis using river names, other periphrases with a word to indicate the indwelling of the heroes (ὁμόδαμος, line 30, and οἰκέων, line 31), and (2) in the names of the heroes: given names, patronymics. The poet took considerable care in composing this series.

[37] Cf., for example, lines 41–51 introducing the catalogue (lines 52–63) of Herodotos' victories. Where a conspicuous personal success is not the burden of the climax, the foil is likely to be less highly wrought. The climax (lines 39 f.) of Asopodoros' crescendo is his son's victory. Thus, ἐγὼ δέ in line 32 would detract from Herodotos' own crescendo (lines 41–63), if it were preceded by too bright an amplifying foil.

We recognize in the crescendo the same mechanisms that were called into play in the crescendo of lines 14 ff. The adversative δέ is a muted ἀλλά; ἐγώ repeats ἐγώ; the names of Poseidon, the Isthmos, Onkhestos, Asopodoros, and Erkhomenos linked to τοῦδ' ἀνδρός (= Herodotos) do the work of Καστορείῳ and 'Ιολάοιο linked to 'Ηροδότῳ in lines 14 ff.; the future indicative γαρύσομαι does the work of ἐθέλω / . . . ἐναρμόξαι . . . ὕμνῳ in lines 15 f.; and the participial phrase περιστέλλων ἀοιδάν matches τεύχων . . . γέρας in line 14. The most important name is that of Asopodoros. Just as in the first crescendo the laudator linked his praise of Herodotos to that of Kastor and Iolaos, so here he links his praise of the son to commemoration of the father. But the conventions in which his eulogy of Asopodoros is cast are so allusive that it is hard to know exactly what it comes to. The crux of the problem is the point of ναυαγίαις in line 36 and εὐαμερίας in line 40. The scholia report two views, and each has its adherents among modern scholars. Bury and Farnell adopt the literal interpretation (real shipwreck),[38] but most scholars are agreed that ναυαγίαις is a metaphor for political disaster. Although the latter view is very probably right, it is rash to identify this Asopodoros with the Medizer of that name who commanded a squadron of Theban cavalry at Plataia (Herod. 9.69).[39] That the entire passage is metaphorical is put beyond doubt both by parallel passages and by the requirements of the context. In order to assess this evidence properly, we must observe certain formal peculiarities of our passage.

From νῦν δ' αὖτις in line 39 we see that lines 39 f. form a climax for which lines 36 ff. are foil. The brightness of the present is set against the darkness of the past. Further, assuming that lines 36 ff. are metaphorical, we note that the grief of the past is represented by storm (shipwreck), and the joy of the present by fair weather (εὐαμερίας, line 40). Two parallels then come to mind. The first is *I*. 7.23–38:

> φλέγεται δὲ ἰοπλόκοισι Μοίσαις,
> μάτρωΐ θ' ὁμωνύμῳ δέδωκε κοινὸν θάλος,
> 25   χάλκασπις ᾧ πότμον μὲν "Αρης ἔμειξεν,
> τιμὰ δ' ἀγαθοῖσιν ἀντίκειται.
> ἴστω γὰρ σαφὲς ὅστις ἐν ταύτᾳ νεφέλᾳ
> χάλαζαν αἵματος πρὸ φίλας
> 27b πάτρας ἀμύνεται,

---

[38] See below, pp. 50 f. The disagreement, as in most matters, goes back to the scholia. See Bury, *ad loc.*, and Farnell, *The Works of Pindar* (London, 1930), I 242, II 339.
[39] See Sandys, *The Odes of Pindar* (Cambridge and London, 1946), pp. 436 f., and Gaspar, *Essai de chronologie pindarique* (Brussels, 1900) 150–155. The identification, even as a guess, is unsound, since it poses several problems and solves none.

The First Isthmian Ode

λοιγὸν ἀμφιβαλὼν ἐναντίῳ στρατῷ,
ἀστῶν γενεᾷ μέγιστον κλέος αὔξων
30 ζώων τ' ἀπὸ καὶ θανών.
τὺ δέ, Διοδότοιο παῖ, μαχατάν
αἰνέων Μελέαγρον, αἰνέων δὲ καὶ Ἕκτορα
Ἀμφιάρηόν τε,
εὐανθέ' ἀπέπνευσας ἁλικίαν
35 προμάχων ἀν' ὅμιλον, ἔνθ' ἄριστοι
ἔσχον πολέμοιο νεῖκος ἐσχάταις ἐλπίσιν.
ἔτλαν δὲ πένθος οὐ φατόν· ἀλλὰ νῦν μοι
Γαιάοχος εὐδίαν ὄπασσεν
ἐκ χειμῶνος.

The important facts about this passage are these: (1) It occurs after the opening crescendo (lines 20-22b) and links praise of Strepsiades with commemoration of his maternal uncle of the same name. (2) The uncle has died in battle. (3) The death of the uncle is dark foil for the brightness of the current victory. (4) The joy of the present is represented by fair weather, the grief of the past by foul. (5) The climax is introduced by ἀλλὰ νῦν (line 37), as in *I*. 1.39 it is introduced by νῦν δ' αὖτις. Thus the position, form, function, and in part the specific content of *I*. 7.23-38 suggest comparison with *I*. 1.34-40 and give us every reason to suspect that the literal interpretation of these lines cannot be right. We seem to be dealing with a conventional topic, and this seeming becomes certainty when we turn to the second passage. This is *I*. 4.16-19:

ἀλλ' ἁμέρᾳ γὰρ ἐν μιᾷ
τραχεῖα νιφὰς πολέμοιο τεσσάρων
17b ἀνδρῶν ἐρήμωσεν μάκαιραν ἑστίαν·
νῦν δ' αὖ μετὰ χειμέριον ποικίλων μηνῶν ζόφον
χθὼν ὥτε φοινικέοισιν ἄνθησεν ῥόδοις

δαιμόνων βουλαῖς.

The important facts about this passage are: (1) It follows a crescendo in favor of the Kleonumidai. (2) It records the loss in battle of four men of the clan. (3) This disaster serves as dark foil for the brightness of the current victory. (4) The joy of the present is represented by spring (fair weather), the grief of the past by winter (foul weather). (5) The climax is introduced by νῦν δ' αὖ, as in *I*. 1.39 it is introduced by νῦν δ' αὖτις. This parallel is as close as the first and, with the first, strongly suggests that the literal view of *I*. 1.34-40 must be rejected. There can be no doubt that all three passages are versions of a set convention. In two of them it is used to honor men who have died in battle and to point up with dark foil the joy of the present.[40] How, then, is it used in *I*. 1?

We must understand first of all that everything from the original mention of Asopodoros in line 34 to the end of line 40 is reserved exclusively to the victor's father and that this entire interlude is being prepared as foil for a ringing return to Herodotus in line 41. Secondly, what these lines are celebrating is the ἀγακλέα ... αἶσαν (line 34) of Asopodoros—the glory of his lot.[41] This means that the climax of lines 39 f. must carry the burden of the praise, while the preceding lines serve as dark foil for this crescendo, which is introduced by˙ νῦν δ' αὖτις, where the words αὖτις ... Πότμος / ... εὐαμερίας take us back to ἀγακλέα αἶσαν in line 34: Asopodoros' once established glory, tarnished by some dark mischance (συντυχίᾳ, line 38), has now been restored to its former brightness.

Now according to Farnell this passage tells us "that ... Asopodoros had at some time in the past suffered severe losses from shipwreck and that he had retired to his family estate near Orchomenos, where he had regained his prosperity." We must note that if this interpretation is correct, then according to the literal language of the lines, Asopodoros was at the helm of his own ship when it went down, and on escaping from the icy waters of the sea, he found himself financially ruined and retired to live off his family near Erkhomenos, where he recouped his fortunes. Bury, perceiving in this some difficulty, thinks to escape it thus: "In another sense, however, the words may be metaphorical, but if so, it is a metaphor felicitous and transparent. *The wreck of the man's fortune is spoken of as if he had been wrecked himself* [italics mine]." Yet it is less than felicitous to make a shipwreck both a shipwreck and a metaphor for losses by shipwreck, and Bury himself does not see that his translation of ἀρχαίας ἐπέβασε Πότμος, "set him on board the ship of his old prosperity," marks the entire passage as metaphorical. To Bury's objection that there is nothing in the passage to mark it as metaphorical, εὐαμερίας is sufficient answer, since there is no possibility of taking this second member of the conventional pair "storm" and "calm" as literal. That

---

[40] Perikles apparently employed a version of this topic in his *Epitaphios*. See Aristotle *Rhet.* 1365a: οἷον Περικλῆς τὸν ἐπιτάφιον λέγων, τὴν νεότητα ἐκ τῆς πόλεως ἀνῃρῆσθαι ὥσπερ τὸ ἔαρ ἐκ τοῦ ἐνιαυτοῦ εἰ ἐξαιρεθείη. The use of dark foils is much more characteristic of Pindar than of Bakkhulides, with whom they rarely have more than their conventional rhetorical force. *P*. 8.50–57 (in narrative) is characteristically Pindaric: προτέρᾳ πάθᾳ (dark foil), νῦν ἀρείονος ... ὄρνιχος ἀγγελίᾳ (bright climax), ὀστέα λέξαις υἱοῦ (dark foil), λαῷ σὺν ἀβλαβεῖ (bright climax). Cf. the succession of dark and bright in *O*. 2.17–52.

[41] With ἀγακλέα αἶσαν, anticipating Πότμος συγγενής in lines 39 f., cf. *O*. 2.39 f., πατρῷον / ... τὸν εὔφρονα πότμον (anticipating the introduction of Theron's present happiness in lines 50/1–57).

the pair is conventional is assured. In *I*. 4.18 spring and winter represent εὐδία and χειμών; in *I*. 7.38 f. εὐδία . . . / ἐκ χειμῶνος displays the same metaphor; in our passage ναυαγίαις (a not infrequent metaphor for disaster) is χειμῶνι, and εὐαμερίας is εὐδίας; in *P*. 5.10 εὐδίαν . . . μετὰ χειμέριον ὄμβρον give the same metaphor in an abbreviated version of the topic (note μάκαιραν ἑστίαν both here and in *I*. 4.17b). Elsewhere, too, the ideas of storm (shipwreck) and calm represent disaster and success.

Since, then, the evidence of the context and of parallel passages suggests that the shipwreck is metaphorical, it becomes our business to inquire for what real disaster it stands. According to ancient conjecture (and it is no more than that), ναυαγίαις is a metaphor for political exile.[42] This is a responsible conjecture and there is a good deal of evidence to support it. Seemingly the disaster is not death in battle, as it is in *I*. 4 and *I*. 7. So glorious an end might well have been more than hinted at, and, although κρυόεσσα and the phrase ἄρουραν, / ἅ νιν . . . / . . . / δέξατο might suggest death and burial, lines 39 f. do not seem to accommodate the notion that Asopodoros is dead. I have tried other hypotheses, such as a near brush with death in a chariot crash (cf. S. *El*. 730, 1444), but these have only helped to solidify the conclusion that ναυαγίαις points to political exile. The case is a strong one and rests on the evidence of parallel passages.

Although the nearest formal parallels are *I*. 7.23–38 and *I*. 4.16–19, these will help us to identify others perhaps nearer *I*. 1.36–40 in point of the disaster hinted at. We may consider first the abbreviated version of *P*. 5.5–11, in which Arkesilas is said to add glory to his wealth because of the kindly influences of Kastor, patron of chariot racers, εὐδίαν δς μετὰ χειμέριον ὄμβρον τεάν / καταιθύσσει μάκαιραν ἑστίαν. From *P*. 4 we can be fairly certain (see the commentators) that χειμέριον ὄμβρον is here political trouble at Kyrene, while εὐδία, the calm after the storm, is Arkesilas' recent chariot victory at Pytho. This provides a parallel for ναυαγίαις in *I*. 1.36 = "political trouble" and εὐαμερίας = "Herodotos' chariot victory at the Isthmos." In like manner, in *P*. 4.291 ff., Damophilos' hope of repatriation after the civil storms that resulted in his banishment is expressed in a sailing metaphor: ἐν δὲ χρόνῳ / μεταβολαὶ λήξαντος οὔρου // ἱστίων. But the nearest parallel (save that the disaster is not expressed in a metaphor) is *O*. 12, a long priamel which turns political exile after a bloody revolt into dark foil for an Olympian success. The plan of the ode is simple. A priamel with a gnomic cap, in the form of an invocation to Tukha, fills the strophe (see p. 36), while the antistrophe glosses the

---

[42] The scholia report two views for which their authors had no evidence save the ode itself: φυγαδευθεὶς γὰρ ὁ 'Ασωπόδωρος Θήβηθεν ἐν 'Ορχομενῷ ἐπολιτογραφήθη and ναυαγήσας ὁ 'Ασωπόδωρος ἐν 'Ορχομενῷ ἐξερρίφη.

gnomic cap with vicissitude foil that then introduces the name cap, reinforced by asseveration,[43] of the epode. From the name cap we see that the vicissitude foil of the strophe and antistrophe is intended to provide a background for the changing fortunes of Ergoteles, who had been exiled from Knosia but, finding political sanctuary at Himera, has prospered and now (νῦν δέ, line 19) wears an Olympic crown. A bitter experience has proved to be a boon of fortune. We must note that in all examples of this topos (*I*. 1.34–40, *I*. 7.23–38, *I*. 4.16–19, *P*. 5.10 f., *O*. 12) the climactic term is a current athletic success.

P. 5.5–11 and *O*. 12 suggest that *I*. 1.36 ff. may have a political meaning. *I*. 7.23–38 and *I*. 4.16–19 suggest that they refer to death in battle. Since these passages are all the evidence we have (and the evidence of form is potent), we must decide in favor of one or the other interpretation. For reasons which I have already stated, I believe that *P*. 5 and *O*. 12 provide the proper analogies for *I*. 1. Asopodoros, after the wreck of his political fortunes, had returned to his birthplace at Erkhomenos, where fortune had smiled on him; and now the glory of his son's success at the Isthmos has restored him to his former place of honor. The passage is concluded by a gnome commenting on the value of bitter experience.[44]

Though many conventions on the levels of word, phrase, and sentence are deserving of comment in these lines, it is time to sum up and pass on to the next topic. The subjective crescendo of lines 32 ff., expressing the laudator's intent, has issued in the objective crescendo of lines 39 f. praising Asopodoros' good fame and fortune. The brightest part of that fame is the recent success of his son: family ability (Πότμος συγγενής) has at length asserted itself in this Panhellenic triumph. Thus, although a number of personages and places emerge into the foreground in lines 32–40, they are set in careful relation to Herodotos at the beginning (τοῦδ' ἀνδρὸς ἐν τιμαῖσιν),[45] and they recede into the background before the close. Only Asopodoros is left in the foreground, and even he now shares this place with his son in lines 39 f., since the words Πότμος συγγενής turn our attention to the fruition of this family's promise in Herodotos' Isthmian success. By convention, moreover, the gnome of line 40 will be heard as a signal that the promise of γαρύσομαι (line 34) has been fulfilled.

---

[43] On asseveration, overcoming real or imaginary objections, see n. 18 above and Stud. Pind. I 17, 17 n. 41, 24, 24 n. 54, 27.

[44] νόῳ is to be construed with φέρει (so scholia: ὁ παθὼν καὶ τῷ νῷ προμηθὴς γίγνεται) rather than with πονήσαις (so Lattimore, *Odes of Pindar* [Univ. Chicago Press, 1947]). Cf. *N*. 7.60, σύνεσιν οὐκ ἀποβλάπτει φρενῶν, and Thgn. 1237, νόῳ συνιεῖν. In such sentences φέρει apparently = τίκτει. Cf. E. frag. 237 N².3, οἱ πόνοι τίκτουσι τὴν εὐδοξίαν, and frag. 745 N².2 f., ὃ . . . / μόχθος πολλὴν εὐδαιμονίαν / τίκτει.

[45] Cf. *N*. 1.34, ἐν κορυφαῖς ἀρετᾶν μεγάλαις (i.e., those of Khromios), *O*. 13.49, ἐν ἡρωΐαις ἀρεταῖσιν (i.e., those of the Oligaithidai). In each of the three phrases the sense is, "while on the subject of this family's (or this man's) exploits."

We began with Herodotos and to him we shall now return. A dimension of suffering has been added to the scene, and in consequence our principal figure appears more solidly human beside his father than he had in the company of Kastor and Iolaos, whereas his crown gleams brighter for the reminder of vicissitude now included in the panorama. We may infer that Herodotos, like his father, is a man of experience who knows the measure of human life.

THE THIRD CRESCENDO, LINES 41-63: HERODOTOS

The transitional function of the gnome of line 40 is difficult to illustrate apart from a full discussion of gnomic foil in both straightforward and inverted forms. I have given some space to this subject in the first essay of this series and must refer my readers to that discussion.[46] It will suffice to state here one or two principles governing the disposition of such foil. A gnome providing a general category for a particular point of climactic interest may either precede (straightforward form) or follow (inverted form) its focal point; foil and climax may present a narrowing or widening of focus according as the foil is used to concentrate attention or to relieve it. The inverted forms are most common in the conclusions of odes or individual topics, but may be used simply to separate two peaks of interest (in narrative for example) by commenting on an obvious general truth illustrated by the first of two particulars to be emphasized. We shall discover that *I*. 1 ends with gnomic foil (lines 67 f.), as does the catalogue (lines 52–63) that precedes the final crescendo (lines 64–68). *N*. 1.53 f. well illustrate the use of inverted foil to separate two peaks of interest in a narrative. Other examples of gnomic foil in transition are *I*. 5.12 (the following gnome is foil for the name cap of lines 19 f.), *I*. 4.48, *P*. 2.34, and *N*. 10.72.

It is not difficult to see that in our passage the concentration on the good fortune that is once again the portion of Asopodoros is relaxed by the gnome of line 40, which generalizes his experience. Indeed it brings back in πονήσαις the memory of the bitter past, although in προμάθειαν it offers a measure of consolation. The laudator intends to begin a new crescendo in lines 41–46, but cannot juxtapose it to that introduced by νῦν δέ without diminishing the force of both. Accordingly, he brings back the dark past with πονήσαις that it may serve again as foil for the new crescendo. The sentiment attaches itself to the preceding lines and is therefore an example of inverted foil separating two peaks of interest. It provides a category for the first by analogy, and for the second by

---
[46] See Stud. Pind. I 28 f., 31.

contrast. In lines 41–63 the laudator will conduct his formal celebration of the son's victory, for this is the heart of the obligation by which he is bound. I use the word "obligation" advisedly, for the principal theme of the lines that follow is the χρὴ αἰνεῖν that defines the laudator's χρέος.[47] The motive appears in χρή (line 43), δόσις (line 45), μισθός (line 47), and κέρδος (line 51). All of these, organizing the laudator's generalized description of his duty, serve as foil for the particular and present ἔοικε (line 52) which introduces the victory catalogue of lines 52–63.

As we come to the third crescendo in line 41, it is equally impossible to supply ὁ πονήσαις (a gnomic reference to Asopodoros) or Asopodoros himself as subject of κατάκειται,[48] and to take the understood indefinite subject of that verb as a tacit reference to Asopodoros. The principal objections are topical: (1) The gnome of line 40 marks a division between topics. (2) The topic which occupies lines 41–51 never has a definite subject that is not *emphatically* expressed (see p. 59). We may observe further that if ὁ πονήσαις ("the sufferer") is subject of κατάκειται, then πόνοις ("dedicated toil") provides an ugly jingle and makes it hard to pass from one sense of πόνος to the other, and that the logic of χρή (line 43), δόσις (line 45), μισθός (line 47), and κέρδος (line 51) leads us straight through the generalized ἀέθλοις (line 50) to ἔοικε and the victory catalogue of lines 52–63 (a particularization of ἀέθλοις). Thus χρή enjoins praise of athletic success, and this belongs to Herodotos rather than to Asopodoros, who has already been congratulated (lines 32–40) for whatever may be his share in his son's success. To concede the most that is possible to Asopodoros, we may say that lines 41–51 put the general case, as lines 52–63 put the particular case, for praising the συγγενὴς Πότμος of his house; but the focus is on the current Isthmian success, and this is a definite breaking away from the previous concentration on Asopodoros.

Further, εἰ δέ in line 41 sharply separates the foil term (lines 41–51) of the new crescendo from the preceding gnome, which serves to conclude the praise of Asopodoros. εἰ δέ (sometimes εἰ in adversative asyndeton), introducing not a definite laudandus (in this form the laudandus is always named) but categories praiseworthy in a hypothetical laudandus or laudator, and followed in an apodosis by a command to praise, or a statement of the necessity or inevitability of praise on the assumptions stated in the protasis, grammatically separates all that follows εἰ δέ from everything that precedes it. If under these circumstances the subject of the protasis is not expressed, it is to be supplied grammatically not from the preceding context but from the apodosis that follows. The protasis

---

[47] See Stud. Pind. I 10 f.
[48] Yet this seems to be the accepted view. See Bury, *ad loc.*, Fennell, *ad loc.*

is a type of foil capped in the apodosis by a ringing injunction to praise; and this generic or gnomic cap is inevitably followed by a concrete cap, often accompanied by asseveration, praising the particular laudandus or laudandi generalized in the conditional sentence. εἰ δέ, then, takes a firm posture vis-à-vis the laudandus (thereby dismissing all previous concerns) and introduces an air of suspense by withholding the name of the laudandus but promising to surrender all reserve in calling attention to his marvelous qualities.

Let us examine a few typical uses of this convention, beginning with O. 6.1–7:

Χρυσέας ὑποστάσαντες εὐτειχεῖ προθύρῳ θαλάμου
κίονας ὡς ὅτε θαητὸν μέγαρον
πάξομεν· ἀρχομένου δ' ἔργου πρόσωπον
χρὴ θέμεν τηλαυγές. εἰ δ' εἴη μὲν 'Ολυμπιονίκας,
5 βωμῷ τε μαντείῳ ταμίας Διὸς ἐν Πίσᾳ,
συνοικιστήρ τε τᾶν κλεινᾶν Συρακοσσᾶν, τίνα κεν
    φύγοι ὕμνον
κεῖνος ἀνήρ, ἐπικύρσαις ἀφθόνων ἀστῶν ἐν ἱμερταῖς
    ἀοιδαῖς;

Here the focus widens from a concrete simile defining the laudator's attitude toward his subject to a gnomic generalization of that attitude: ἀρχομένου δ' ἔργου πρόσωπον / χρὴ θέμεν τηλαυγές. In χρή we observe the χρέος motive: the laudator owes something to his subject. The sense of the implied imperative is that he must begin with unqualified praise, with a categorical vaunt. The laudator will waste no time in getting to his subject and making its merit understood in simple, straightforward terms.[49] The categorical vaunt is introduced by εἰ δέ and builds up suspense through three separate factual suppositions that state the theme, before releasing the tension thus created in the statement (τίνα = οὐδένα) that achievements such as those listed call for unreserved praise. Not until line 8 is the general principle applied to Hagesias. It is important to observe that the unexpressed subject of εἴη (line 4) is to be supplied from κεῖνος ἀνήρ (= τοιοῦτος ἀνήρ) in line 7 in the apodosis of the condition. Comparing I. 1.41–63 with O. 6.4–21, we see that O. 6.4–7 = I. 1.41–51 as ἴστω γὰρ κτλ. (O. 6.8–21) = ἄμμι δ' ἔοικε κτλ. (I. 1.52–63).

I. 3 begins in the same fashion (lines 1 ff.):

Εἴ τις ἀνδρῶν εὐτυχήσαις ἢ σὺν εὐδόξοις ἀέθλοις
ἢ σθένει πλούτου κατέχει φρασὶν αἰανῆ κόρον,
ἄξιος εὐλογίαις ἀστῶν μεμεῖχθαι.

---

[49] The rhetorical point is easily understood from Diog. Apoll. 1 D-K⁶: λόγου παντὸς ἀρχόμενον δοκεῖ μοι χρεὼν εἶναι τὴν ἀρχὴν <u>ἀναμφισβήτητον</u> παρέχεσθαι, τὴν δὲ ἑρμηνείαν <u>ἀπλῆν καὶ σεμνήν</u>.

The self-sufficiency of the form is here assured, for it stands without introduction at the very beginning of the ode. The conditional particle (δέ is superfluous in this position) introduces a series of disjunctive propositions that reflect the hymnal device discussed on pp. 45 f.⁵⁰ These create a suspense that is released in the gnomic or generic crescendo of line 3: certain qualities and conditions demand (ἄξιος is here the χρέος word) unqualified response: one must praise them. The gnomic thought is subsequently brought closer to Melissos in the anaphoric χρή of lines 7 f., and in line 9 he is introduced by name. It is important to observe that the subject of κατέχει in line 2 is indefinite.

A somewhat different version of the topic appears in *I*. 5.13–18, *O*. 5.23 ff., *I*. 6.9–11b, *N*. 9.45 ff., *P*. 10.22–30, and *N*. 11.13–18. The relation of these passages to our own will be immediately evident on perusal. All involve conditional sentences that set up injunctions to praise or declarative catagorical vaunts. Perhaps the closest parallel to *I*. 1.41–51 occurs at *I*. 5.24–32. Only lines 24–27 need concern us here:

               εἰ δὲ τέτραπται
25   θεοδότων ἔργων κέλευθον ἂν καθαράν,
      μὴ φθόνει κόμπον τὸν ἐοικότ᾽ ἀοιδᾷ
      κιρνάμεν ἀντὶ πόνων.

We note the introductory εἰ δέ followed in the capping vaunt by ἐοικότα (cf. ἔοικε in *I*. 1.52) and the imperative μὴ φθόνει, which express the propriety and obligation involved in the χρέος motive. Here again εἰ δέ attracts attention to the laudator's posture vis-à-vis the laudandus. Since, as Mezger saw, the subject of τέτραπται is indefinite (the subject of the conditional clause in this topic is always indefinite when not emphatically expressed) and εἰ . . . τέτραπται = "if one has entered," we see that εἰ δέ breaks away from the previous avowals and begins the actual crescendo,⁵¹

---

⁵⁰ Cf. Ariphron 1.D², observing μετὰ σεῖο (line 7) and σέθεν δὲ χωρὶς οὐ κτλ. (line 9) = ἐκ σέθεν (*I*. 3.5). Pindar has adapted the hymnal motive to the praise of mortals. The effect of the disjunctives is to *list* the god's powers, of which a poet may or may not select one for special attention. Cf. also *O*. 14.7. The interrogative form (πῶς or the like) is equally a device for listing the divine attributes.

⁵¹ See F. Mezger, *ad loc*. The pronominal name cap of lines 21 f. (ἐμόν, Αἰακιδᾶν) turns from Phulakidas and Putheas to the Aiakidai. Lines 23 f. employ the motive displayed in *O*. 13.47, *N*. 6.59 (on these two passages see pp. 82 f.), *I*. 1.15 f., 33 f., and *N*. 1.33 ff., which links praise of one laudandus to that of another. Here the sons of Lampon *yield place* to their city (identified with the Aiakidai; for this identification, cf. *N*. 6.47 ff., *P*. 8.22 ff.), and the dative υἱοῖς gracefully suggests that they charged the poet with this duty. We shall now hear praise of the Aiakidai, but such a formidable subject cannot be approached before the laudator has gathered his powers and purified his heart from the envy naturally aroused by deeds so great as theirs. His meditations in lines 24–32 (foil for the catalogues of lines 33–50) thus represent a fresh start. Any grammatical link with the previous lines would be a blemish, ruining the effect of the rhetorical pause. What we require is *generic* foil

first in gnomic (μὴ φθόνει; cf. χρὴ φέρειν in I. 1.43 f.), then in particular form (ἀλλ' ἐν Οἰνώνᾳ at the climax of the priamel beginning in line 33; cf. ἄμμι δ' ἔοικε κτλ. in I. 1.52). φθόνει (cf. φθονεραῖσι in I. 1.44) and κόμπον (cf. κόμπον in I. 1.43) are further marks of the close kinship between the two passages, and all the words and phrases included in I. 1.41–46 have parallels in one or more of the passages cited above to illustrate the formal structure of this passage.[52]

It is clear, then, that in form and substance I. 1.41–46 is conventional, that the conditional clause would be heard as the introduction to a crescendo and that the force of εἰ δέ, juxtaposed with the concluding gnome of the previous topic, is strongly dismissive. Using Asopodoros' dark past as a springboard, it leaps to the son's Isthmian victory as a measure of the family's present good fortune. The crescendo itself (lines 43–51) has four movements. These are arranged in pairs, and each is marked by a version of the χρέος motive. The first pair appears in lines 43–46, and the second, in lines 47–51. The first pair is marked by the key words χρή (line 43) and δόσις (line 45), the latter explanatory of the former, whereas the second pair is controlled by μισθός (line 47) and κέρδος (line 51) governing the foil and the climax respectively of a full priamel explanatory of χρή.

The entire structure depends on χρή (line 43), which issues a very much stronger imperative than do the other forms in which the χρέος motive is cast. The conditional clause of lines 39 f. sets up the imperative χρὴ φέρειν, and the explanatory clause that follows justifies it in terms that repeat both the condition and the imperative. This order prevails also in I. 5.24–32, where εἰ δὲ τέτραπται κτλ. (lines 24 f.) does the work of εἰ δ' . . . κατάκειται κτλ., μὴ φθόνει (line 26) does the work of χρὴ . . . / μὴ φθονεραῖσι κτλ., γάρ (line 28) does the work of ἐπεί, and μελέταν δὲ σοφισταῖς does the work of κούφα δόσις ἀνδρὶ σοφῷ. Both passages depend on the notion that ἀρετά creates a debt that must be paid in the true

---

assigning the exploits which the laudator will praise to a *class*. We know, of course, the subjects intended, but their names must come in a climactic position and without previous distraction of πόλις as subject of τέτραπται. Finally, foil involving φθόνος is invariably gnomic. εἰ δὲ τέτραπται κτλ. = "Where entry has been made into the highroads of deeds, etc."

[52] εἰ δ' has been fully illustrated; ἀρετᾷ = ἀρετάς (I. 6.10) and ἀρετᾷ (P. 10.23); κατάκειται = τέτραπται (I. 5.24); πᾶσαν ὀργάν = ὀργαῖς (I. 6.12), glossing χαρείς (line 9); ἀμφότερον δαπάνᾳ τε καὶ πόνοις = δαπάνᾳ . . . / καὶ πόνῳ (I. 6.9 f.); χρή = the imperative mood of μὴ φθόνει (I. 5.26) and ἄξιος (I. 3.3); νιν εὑρόντεσσιν = πράσσει . . . ἀρετάς (I. 6.10), ἄρηται κῦδος (N. 9.46 f.) and τὰ μέγιστ' ἀέθλων ἕλῃ (P. 10.24); ἀγάνορα κόμπον = κόμπον τὸν ἐοικότα (I. 5.26); μὴ φθονεραῖσι φέρειν γνώμαις = μὴ φθόνει (I. 5.26) and ἀφθόνως (O. 6.7); ἐπεί = γάρ (I. 5.28); κούφα δόσις = ἄξιος (I. 3.3) and τίνα κεν φύγοι ὕμνον (O. 6.6); ἀνδρὶ σοφῷ = σοφισταῖς (I. 5.31); ἀντὶ μόχθων παντοδαπῶν = ἀντὶ πόνων (I. 5.27); ἔπος εἰπόντ' ἀγαθὸν κτλ. = εὐλογίαις . . . μεμεῖχθαι (I. 3.3) and αἰνεῖσθαι (N. 11.17). Still other passages contain closer parallels for some of these expressions.

coin of praise. The metaphor, implied by ἀντί in *I.* 5.27, is explicit in our passage in δόσις (= δαπάνα), μισθός ("wage"), and κέρδος ("lucre"), as it is in the word χρέος itself whenever it appears. The metaphor is frequent in still other forms and is one of the set conventions of the genre. Such, then, is the skeletal structure of the passage, and we may use its fourfold division to control our selection of the details to be commented on.

The sentence introduced by χρή contains the whole of the thought; the rest is amplification. The understood indefinite subject of κατάκειται (τις = men in general) and the category (ἀρετᾷ) selected by the conditional clause are resumed in the phrase νιν εὑρόντεσσιν, in which νιν = ἀρετάν and εὑρόντεσσιν are the achievers (τις), who are also the subject of κατάκειται. Here I would remind the reader that the shift from the singular in the protasis to the plural in the apodosis of conditional sentences is frequent in Greek (e.g., ὅστις or εἴ τις ... τούτοις κτλ.). Others take φέρειν = "bear aloft," κόμπον as the object of εὑρόντεσσιν, and εὑρόντεσσιν as the subject of φέρειν, but it must be understood that εὑρόντεσσιν resumes and amplifies the conditional clause.[53] Its function will be clear if we note that in this topic the conditional clause requires a verb expressing the achievement or possession of ἀρετά and not merely the disposition, however passionate, toward it: δαπάνα and πόνος do not assure achievement, and only achievers are crowned. πράσσει performs this function in *I.* 6.10. Compare also ἄρηται in *N.* 9.46, ἄρδει, ἐξαρκέων, and προστιθείς in *O.* 5.23 ff., εἴη in *O.* 6.4, ἔλῃ in *P.* 10.24, ἔχων, παραμεύσεται, and ἀριστεύων in *N.* 11.13 f., πάσχων and ἀκούῃ in *I.* 5.15, and εὐτυχήσαις in *I.* 3.1. Nor is *I.* 5.24 f. an exception, for ἔργων turns the dedication of τέτραπται into achievement, and τέτραπται with κέλευθον ἂν καθαράν = "entered." For the expression νιν (ἀρετάν) εὑρόντεσσιν we find the parallels ἀρετάν ... λαβεῖν in *O.* 8.6, and πράσσει ... ἀρετάς in *I.* 6.10; and an exact parallel in ἀρετὰν εὑρόντα in *O.* 7.89. The phrase ἀγάνορα κόμπον, the high point of the crescendo, anticipates in the epithet the point of μὴ φθονεραῖσι, which, by litotes, is equivalent to παντὶ θυμῷ, "unreservedly"; but ἀγάνορα κόμπον is more than a "vigorous vaunt," for ἀγάνορα is suggested by the qualities of the achiever. ἀγάνορα κόμπον is a "lordly" vaunt to match "lordly" deeds. The epithet obeys that common enkomiastic imperative "to match the deed in words."[54] "Praise to match" is the overt point of κόμπον τὸν ἐοικότα

---

[53] εὑρίσκω and ἐξευρίσκω are used equally of laudator and laudandus. For the sense demanded here, cf. *O.* 7.89 ἄνδρα τε πὺξ ἀρετὰν εὑρόντα.

[54] There are two main attitudes: the laudator exhorts himself (or claims) to do justice to the deed (he may neither exaggerate it nor fall short of it) or confesses that his powers are not equal to it. For the latter, cf. *O.* 2.108 ff., *O.* 13.43–44b, *N.* 4.69–75, *N.* 10.19 f., *I.* 1.60–64; for the former, cf. *I.* 2.35 ff., *O.* 4.19 f., *O.* 6.27 f., 87–91 (ἀλαθέσιν λόγοις = τῷ σὺν δίκᾳ ἐπαίνῳ), *O.* 13.89–93, *P.* 1.41–45; *P.* 9.96–99 (αἰνεῖν ... παντὶ θυμῷ σὺν τε δίκᾳ), *N.* 1.18, *N.* 5.50 f., *N.* 6.27 ff., *N.* 7.49, 63, 65 ff., 102 ff., Bacch. 3.94–98, 5.187–190, 8.19 ff. The theme is tacitly present in every exhortation to praise. For prose examples, cf. Lys. 2.1 f., Dem. 60.1, 61.7.

("the vaunt they deserve," i.e., a lordly one) in *I*. 5.26 (cf. also ποτίφορος ... μισθός in *N*. 7.63, and πρόσφορον / ... κόμπον in *N*. 8.48 f.

We move on next to the phrase μὴ φθονεραῖσι φέρειν γνώμαις. To follow this motive through its myriad transformations, to place all its other settings beside *I*. 1.41–51 and move first to one, then another and another, each displaying a new inflection, until one arrives, through a deftly graded series, at contexts like *N*. 6.47–55 and *I*. 2.33–46, or like *O*. 11.7–21, *O*. 9.107/8–120, and *N*. 1.25–30, is a fascinating study in literary technique. In Pindar, and even in Bakkhulides, close study of the motive discloses a marvelous mastery of the craft of versemaking, and in Pindar especially an equally marvelous creative energy shaping and reshaping the nuances and colors of traditional form. Here we can do no more than indicate in stringent selection a few of the possibilities.

The conditional clause that attends categorical vaunts of the type illustrated above may, as may all other foil terms, follow rather than precede the vaunt.[55] The condition may be expressed in a relative clause, a participle, an adjective or an adverbial phrase.[56] Or the condition may vanish and be replaced by any comparable generic expression, such as "Olympian victors";[57] or the condition may be retained and its generic force may vanish, leaving a particular, such as "this man" or "this city."[58] In this last form (see p. 54) the particular must be emphatically expressed (I add this as a warning against taking πόλις to be the subject of τέτραπται in *I*. 5.24 and Asopodoros to be the subject of κατάκειται in *I*. 1.41). The categorical vaunt may be subjective ("one must praise such men") or objective ("such men have reached the height of human achievement"), or both, as in *N*. 11.13–18.[59] Either the condition (with all its modifications) or the vaunt (with all its modifications) may be attended by strong asseveration.[60] Either may be expressed metaphorically;[61] either may take, or be incorporated into, any of the multiforms

---

[55] Cf. Bacch. 5.187–190, *O*. 1.17 f., *P*. 10.22–26. Anyone who doubts the propriety of terming the protases of such conditions "foils" and such conditional sentences "priamels" may compare *O*. 3.44–48 first with *O*. 1.1–11 and then with *N*. 3.18–25 and its congeners. Note ἀβάταν in *N*. 3.20 and ἄβατον in *O*. 3.46/7. μηκέτ' in *O*. 1.5, just as does μηκέτ' in *N*. 5.50 (cf. μηκέτι in *I*. 4.31, *O*. 1.114, and οὐκέτι in *N*. 3.19, *N*. 9.47), abbreviates the "pillars of Herakles" topic and its equivalents (e.g., *N*. 9.47): "One must seek *no further* for surpassing greatness." The reader may expand for himself the list of resemblances.
[56] Cf. *N*. 1.29 f., *N*. 4.93–96, Bacch. 3.67–71.
[57] Cf. *O*. 11.7 f., *P*. 5.12 f., 44 f.
[58] Cf. *N*. 5.50 f., *N*. 4.93–96, *N*. 3.18–25.
[59] Subjective: *I*. 3.1 ff., Bacch. 5.187–190; objective: *O*. 5.23 ff., *I*. 6.9–11b.
[60] Cf. *I*. 7.27–30 (ἴστω), *O*. 2.58/9 (μάν), *O*. 6.77–81 (ἐτύμως), *N*. 9.45 ff. (ἴστω). Sometimes the asseveration is independent of both condition and vaunt. Cf. Bacch. 3.63–71 (with οὖτις the asseverative word, on which cf. 5.43, 8.22, frag. 20 C.21, *P*. 2.60, *N*. 6.26), *O*. 6.1–8 (ἴστω).
[61] Cf. *N*. 3.18–25, *N*. 9.45 ff., *O*. 5.23 ff. (ἄρδει, μὴ ματεύσῃ κτλ.).

(I adopt this objectionable term to facilitate reference to variants of a theme or form) of the priamel;[62] either part may be suppressed for rhetorical effect,[63] or the two parts may be so combined as to be formally inseparable.[64] Each change of form may bring with it additional possibilities for embellishment,[65] but throughout them all the ruling idea is that of praise without stint. These are some of the possibilities, a few of which may be illustrated here.

In Bacch. 5.187–197 we encounter this variation:

χρὴ] δ' ἀλαθείας χάριν
αἰνεῖν, φθόνον ἀμφ[οτέραισιν
χερσὶν ἀπωσάμενον,
190   εἴ τις εὖ πράσσοι βροτῶν.

Βοιωτὸς ἀνὴρ τάδε φών[ησεν, γλυκειᾶν
Ἡσίοδος πρόπολος
Μουσᾶν, ὃν ⟨ἂν⟩ ἀθάνατοι τι[μῶσι, τούτωι
καὶ βροτῶν φήμαν ἔπ[εσθαι.
195   πείθομαι εὐμαρέως
εὐκλέα κελεύθου γλῶσσαν οὐ[κ ἐκτὸς δίκας
πέμπειν Ἱέρωνι·

We note that the leading idea is that of praise without stint, that the order of condition and vaunt has been reversed, that the explanatory gnomic material (lines 191–194) is put in the mouth of an ancient authoritative witness (the use of μαρτυρίαι, πίστεις, βάσανοι, and the like is another topic of great importance in enkomia),[66] that the notion of

---

[62] Cf. O. 3.44–48. Cf. also O. 11.1–6, where the conditional clause in line 4 of the capping term provides a second runway for the ultimately climactic ὕμνοι.

[63] In O. 2.62 the conditional sentence εἰ δέ μιν ἔχων τις οἶδεν τὸ μέλλον requires completion by a categorical vaunt, but the theme of life (paradigmatically = fame) after death (see pp. 84–90) is so extended (lines 63–91) that there must occur a transition (lines 91–99) to the climactic vaunt (lines 99–105), which now assumes a form incompatible with the conditional sentence. For the suppression of the conditional sentence, cf. O. 11.16–21, N. 1.13–18.

[64] Cf. I. 4.1 ff., where ὑμετέρας ἀρετὰς ὕμνῳ διώκειν = εἰ . . . διώκειν ἔλδομαι. Cf. I. 6.20/1 ff., where the condition is understood from the preceding ῥαινέμεν εὐλογίαις.

[65] As, for example, in I. 6.20/1 ff., the metaphor μυρίαι κέλευθοι brings in the geographical topic of lines 22–26, which is used (metaphorically) also in I. 2.33–42 (cf. N. 6.47–55, Lys. 2.2).

[66] The laudator must convince his audience (and sometimes his patron) that he is doing justice to his theme. A wide variety of devices serve this purpose, among them the presentation of witnesses, assurances, and "touchstones" or tests. Cf. P. 10.64–68 (πέποιθα, on which see N. 7.65, O. 1.103, Bacch. 5.195, and βασάνῳ, on which see N. 8.20 ff., N. 4.82–85, frag. 130.13, Bacch. frag. 14), N. 8.42 ff. (πιστόν, on which see N. 10.39 ff., O. 11.6, O. 1.31), O. 13.94 f., O. 2.101 ff. (oaths and other forms of asseveration are frequent in assurances), O. 6.82–91 (on ἀκόνα = "touchstone," cf. Scol. Anon. 33 D²), where the genealogy of lines 84 ff. is a test (cf. Soph. frag. 101 N², γένος γὰρ εἰς ἔλεγχον ἐξιὸν καλὸν / εὔκλειαν ἂν κτήσαιτο μᾶλλον ἢ ψόγον), and the song (κελαδη-

The First Isthmian Ode

ease (εὐμαρέως, line 195) in praise is used to bring the gnomic crescendo to bear on Hieron's glory (cf. κοῦφα in *I*. 1.45), and that the whole follows a victory catalogue.

Beside this passage we may place *P*. 9.96–99:

> οὕνεκεν, εἰ φίλος ἀστῶν, εἴ τις ἀντάεις, τό γ'
> ἐν ξυνῷ πεπονᾱμένον εὖ
> μὴ λόγον βλάπτων ἁλίοιο γέροντος κρυπτέτω·
> κεῖνος αἰνεῖν καὶ τὸν ἐχθρὸν
> παντὶ θυμῷ σύν τε δίκᾳ καλὰ ῥέζοντ' ἔννεπεν.

Here the transformations of the topic are due in the main to its use as foil for a single entry in a victory catalogue.[67] Once we observe that topical considerations force us to join παντὶ θυμῷ σύν τε δίκᾳ to αἰνεῖν rather than to ῥέζοντα, we see that this doublet, along with μὴ κρυπτέτω,[68] carries the leading idea of praise without stint and praise *to match* (σύν τε δίκᾳ) the worth of the laudandus;[69] that the condition, expressed in the participle ῥέζοντα resuming the generic phrase τό γ' ἐν ξυνῷ πεπονᾱμένον εὖ (note also εἴ τις), follows the injunction to praise; that the ancient authority for the vaunt is the old man of the sea, as in Bacch. 5.191–194 it was Hesiod; that the word ἀντάεις brings in the motive of the imaginary objection (see pp. 40 f.); and that ξυνῷ echoes ξυνόν in *I*. 1.46 as πεπονᾱμένον echoes ἀντὶ μόχθων in *I*. 1.46.

Passing from this pair we may look to passages which make the theme of ease in praise (which we marked in Bacch. 5.195) carry the burden of the whole. *I*. 2.33–46 is of this type. The passage is complicated and cannot be discussed here in its entirety, but lines 33–37 will give us the main elements:

> οὐ γὰρ πάγος, οὐδὲ προσάντης ἁ κέλευθος γίνεται,
> εἴ τις εὐδόξων ἐς ἀνδρῶν ἄγοι τιμὰς Ἑλικωνιάδων.
> 35 μακρὰ δισκήσαις ἀκοντίσσαιμι τοσοῦθ', ὅσον ὀργὰν
> Ξεινοκράτης ὑπὲρ ἀνθρώπων γλυκεῖαν
> ἔσχεν.

σαι, line 88) and its truth (ἀλαθέσιν λόγοις, lines 89 f.) are proof to the mind (γνῶναι, line 89) that the poet and his chorodidaskolos possess the good grace and understanding to praise where praise is due, *N*. 7.49 (οὐ ψεῦδις ὁ μάρτυς, on which cf. frag. 106.21, *N*. 1.18, *O*. 4.19 f., *O*. 6.21, *O*. 13.104, *I*. 5.54, *I*. 4.10, *O*. 4.3).

[67] See Stud. Pind. I 17 ff.
[68] For μὴ κρυπτέτω, cf. *O*. 2.107, *N*. 9.7, *I*. 2.44.
[69] καλά is all the qualification that ῥέζοντα requires. For δίκᾳ defining enkomiastic propriety, cf. *O*. 2.105 f. (mere length does not ensure a just enkomion), *N*. 7.48 (a just praise will require but few words; on τρία, cf. Dem. 19.209), *N*. 3.28 (the laudator must, in justice, turn from Herakles to Aigina and her heroes), Bacch. 13.202, *O*. 6.12. ἀλάθεια (cf. also ψεῦδος) is used in the same way. Cf. Bacch. 3.96, 5.187, 8.20 f., 9.85, *N*. 5.17, *O*. 10.4, *N*. 7.25. See n. 54.

The κούφα δόσις of *I*. 1.45 and the εὐμαρέως of Bacch. 5.195 head this passage in the words οὐ πάγος and οὐδὲ προσάντης. Note that ἁ κέλευθος matches κελεύθου in Bacch. 5.195, and that since the metaphor of line 33 anticipates the pulling out of all stops in lines 35 ff., the vaunt in effect both precedes and follows the conditional clause. Note ὀργάν here, ὀργάν in *I*. 1.41, and ὀργαῖς in *I*. 6.12. Note in ὅσον the idea of praise to match the deed. Observe, too, the metaphor in the vaunt of lines 35 ff. and the fact that it is a short step from this to passages of the type of *I*. 4.1 ff., *N*. 6.47–55 (the geographical topic of *N*. 6.50–55 occurs as a metaphor in *I*. 2.39–42: extent of ἀρετά is the unifying theme),[70] Bacch. 9.47–57, 5.9–36, and *I*. 6.20/1–26 (observe the geographical topic). I have already demonstrated the relation of these passages to such contexts as those of *O*. 11.7–21 (where Ὀλυμπιονίκαις does the work of the conditional clause in selecting the category), *O*. 9.107/8–120, and *N*. 1.25–30.[71] *O*. 2.91–105 also belong to this latter class, but to demonstrate this relationship is beyond the scope of this essay.

We may add one variation more—a very pretty one occurring at *N*. 5.50–54:

50   εἰ δὲ Θεμίστιον ἵκεις ὥστ' ἀείδειν, μηκέτι ῥίγει· δίδοι
     φωνάν, ἀνὰ δ' ἱστία τεῖνον πρὸς ζυγὸν καρχασίου,
     πύκταν τέ νιν καὶ παγκρατίῳ φθέγξαι ἑλεῖν Ἐπιδαύρῳ
          διπλόαν
     νικῶντ' ἀρετάν, προθύροισιν δ' Αἰακοῦ
     ἀνθέων ποιάεντα φέρειν στεφανώματα σὺν ξανθαῖς
          Χάρισσιν.

Note that a particular man rather than a category is selected by the conditional clause; note the sailing metaphor in the vaunt, which this time introduces a victory catalogue (as does *I*. 1.41–51). μηκέτι (not = μή) and the metaphor in ῥίγει are pointed: "Abandon (μηκέτι) all reserve (ῥίγει)."[72] Passages like this come alive only when one understands the principles involved in the tactical management of conventional themes.

Returning to our text, we find that light has been shed on a number of details by our excursion. We find that ὀργάν in line 41 recurs in other

---

[70] While more cautious souls strike sail before a too-favoring breeze (cf. Hor. *Carm*. 2.10), Xenokrates' liberality knew no bounds as he sailed to Phasis in the summer and to the Nile in the winter, so that the weather was always fair. For the literal use of this topic see the examples cited in n. 65.

[71] See Stud. Pind. I 14–17.

[72] Ordinarily these sailing metaphors introduce a warning against excess, and it is against this background of normal good sense that the laudator is forced, by Themistios' unusual qualities, to let out full sail. For the usual cautionary force of sailing metaphors, cf. Hor. *Carm*. 2.10, and see n. 70.

examples of the topic (for δαπάναις τε καὶ πόνοις, cf. I. 6.9 f.), that μὴ φθονεραῖσι . . . / γνώμαις is equivalent, not only in sense (see p. 58) but contextually too, to παντὶ θυμῷ in P. 9.99, and that certain details of lines 45 f. are conventional in such contexts. We may note further that the conventional character of lines 41-51 is overwhelmingly confirmed by the evidence of parallels, as is our observation that χρή is the pivot upon which all else turns. If we look now to certain aspects of lines 45 f., we shall be better able to state the full point of the injunction contained in χρὴ φέρειν.

Lines 45 f. further define the laudator's side of the χρέος (χρὴ αἰνεῖν), as lines 41 f. define the laudandus' side of the χρέος (χρὴ ἔρδειν). Deeds thirst for song as song thirsts for deeds. The introductory ἐπεί we have paralleled by γάρ in I. 5.28, ἀντὶ μόχθων by ἀντὶ πόνων in I. 5.27, and κούφα δόσις ἀνδρὶ σοφῷ by μελέταν δὲ σοφισταῖς in I. 5.31. It remains to relate these features to the total theme.

As we have already noted, the leading motive occurs in the words κούφα δόσις, and ἐπεί marks these words as explanatory of μὴ φθονεραῖσι . . . / γνώμαις, thus determining the specific reference of δόσις. The motive is so common in the rhetoric of enkomia that it is difficult to choose among the many parallels ready to hand. But particularly pleasing in its aptness is an elegiac couplet from a memorial inscription (IG II/III[2] 11169): οὐθεὶς μόχθος ἔπαινον ἐπ' ἀνδράσι τοῖς ἀγαθοῖσιν / ζητεῖν, εὕρηται δ' ἄφθονος εὐλογία. Comparisons are easy: οὐθεὶς μόχθος is parallel to κούφα δόσις; ἄφθονος εὐλογία, "praise without stint," repeats μὴ φθονεραῖσι . . . / γνώμαις; ζητεῖν, like ὀρθῶσαι in I. 1.46, is subject, and οὐθεὶς μόχθος, like κούφα δόσις, predicate; ἔπαινον ζητεῖν yields the same idea as do ἔπος εἰπόντ' ἀγαθόν and ὀρθῶσαι καλόν; ἐπ' ἀνδράσι τοῖς ἀγαθοῖσιν points, as does ἀντὶ μόχθων παντοδαπῶν, to the laudandus; in nearly every detail of form and thought this couplet is identical with I. 1.45 f. We see that what κούφα δόσις means is, "It is no expense (effort) at all," and that these words imply a merit so great that, in the words of Demosthenes (60.12), ἡ 'κείνων ἀρετὴ δείκνυσιν αὑτὴ ἃ καὶ πρόχειρα καὶ ῥᾴδι' ἐπελθεῖν ἐστιν. The deeds speak for themselves, thus lightening the laudator's task. In the words μὴ φθονεραῖσι . . . / γνώμαις he urges all within hearing to join him in putting aside the modest preliminaries of lines 1-40 and getting down to the real business of praise. He has been careful in building to this point, and now, fearful that his high spirits may betray to more cautious souls an uncritical mind, he acquits himself of hyperbole by pointing to the extravagant merit it is his privilege to praise. Thus the formally hyperbolic πᾶσαν (line 41) and παντοδαπῶν (line 46) are extremely important to the economy of the passage.⁷³ So too, the universalizing doublet of line 42 emphasized by ἀμφότερον (cf. O. 6.17).⁷⁴ The point of I. 5.26 f. is similar. μὴ φθόνει κόμπον τὸν ἐοικότ' ἀοιδᾷ / κιρνάμεν ἀντὶ πόνων means, "Don't hesitate to praise them as fully as they deserve." The laudator goes on to explain (I. 5.28 f.), "For the principle of rewarding valor (ἐκέρδαναν) by praise (λόγον) was fully established in the days of the heroes."⁷⁵ Similarly, he explains in I. 1.47–51 that the principle of rewarding (κέρδος, line 51) valor (note πολεμίζων in line 50 and πολεμισταί in I. 5.28) by praise (εὐαγορηθείς, line 51) is, so to speak, a law of nature.

κοῦφα has other parallels in Pindar and Bakkhulides, some of which we have already encountered. Besides εὐμαρέως in Bacch. 5.195, and οὐ πάγος and οὐδὲ προσάντης in I. 2.33, we find μυρία παντᾷ κέλευθος and εὐμαχανίαν in I. 4.1 f., μύριαι ... κέλευθοι in I. 6.20/1, πλατεῖαι πάντοθεν πρόσοδοι in N. 6.47, μυρία κέλευθος in Bacch. 19.1, μυρία πάντᾳ κέλευθος in Bacch. 5.31, δι' εὐρείας κελεύθου/μυρία πάντα φάτις in Bacch. 9.47 f., ἐλαφρόν in N. 7.77, αἶνος ἑτοῖμος in O. 6.12, ὄρθιον ὤρυσαι, contrasted with αἰπειναί, in O. 9.116 f. ("the ways of art are difficult, but in this case just sing out"), the whole of N. 5.19 ff. (note that ἐλαφράν implies ease), βουλαὶ ... / ἀκίνδυνον ... ἔπος ... / ἐπαινεῖν παρέχοντι in P. 2.65b f., λεγόμενον ἐρέω ("Others more artful than I praise him; I shall say only what everyone knows and no one can contradict: he has all the qualities") in P. 5.108, ἑτοῖμος ὕμνων / θησαυρός in P. 6.7 f., χαρίεντα ... πόνον in N. 3.12 (cf. οὐδεὶς μόχθος in IG II/III² 11169, cited above), ἴδια ναυστολέοντες ἐπικώμια, ... / δυνατοὶ παρέχειν πολὺν ὕμνον (cf. I. 4.1 ff.) in N. 6.33 f., and τὸν αἰνεῖν ἀγαθῷ παρέχει in I. 8.69 (cf. κοῦφα δόσις ἀνδρὶ σοφῷ ... ὀρθῶσαι καλόν). These parallels confirm the conventionality of κοῦφα δόσις in I. 1.45 along with their sense, "an easy *assignment*" (i.e., "expense," "task"), and indicate that the sentence means, in simple prose: εὖ λέγειν πάρεστιν, εἰ σὺν πόνῳ τις εὖ πράσσοι. With κοῦφα δόσις ὀρθῶσαι we may compare further E. Ba. 893, κοῦφα δαπάνα νομίζειν; frag. trag. adesp. 350 N., οὐδεὶς κάματος εὐσεβεῖν (cf. also E. Ba. 66 f., πόνον ἡδὺν / κάματόν τ' εὐκάματον).

The phrase ἀντὶ μόχθων παντοδαπῶν repeats in a more concrete form the condition of lines 41 f.; ἔπος εἰπόντ' ἀγαθόν is equivalent to the prose εὖ εἰπόντα; ἀνδρὶ σοφῷ ("an expert") is the laudator. As for the particular meaning of the phrase ξυνὸν ὀρθῶσαι καλόν (= "to glorify with true report a man and his state"), we must consult Pindar's use of (δι)ορθόω (ὀρθός)

---

⁷³ On the hyperbolic style in hymnal poetry (and the enkomion is a class of hymns), see K. Keyssner, op. cit. 28–48. (See n. 21 above.)

⁷⁴ For other universalizing doublets, see Stud. Pind. I 24, 24 n. 56.

⁷⁵ ἐκέρδαναν implies their preference of glory to gold (on this choice, see pp. 82–90); so Bury, ad loc., "The 'gold' which they gained was fame." Better is, "Their gold was glory": μισθὸς αὐτοῖς οὐ χρυσὸς ἀλλὰ λόγος. Cf. Isoc. 9.1–4.

and ξυνός (κοινός). The phrase ξυνὸν καλόν recalls ξυνὸν κόσμον in *I*. 6.65 signifying a glory common to the individual and the state. We encountered the same idea in *P*. 9.96, in the phrase τό γ' ἐν ξυνῷ πεποναμένον εὖ, where πεποναμένον and ξυνῷ suggested comparison with *I*. 1.46. Similar is κοινὰν χάριν in *P*. 5.102, "a glory common" to Arkesilas and his ancestors in the royal line. In *P*. 6.15 ff., κοινὰν νίκαν is a victory for both Xenokrates and his clan, as κοινὸν θάλος in *I*. 7.24 is a crowned glory common to Strepsiades and his uncle. So in *P*. 11.54 the laudator, on behalf of Thrasudaios, expresses a devotion to ξυναὶ ἀρεταί, "distinctions that bring credit to a man and his state." ξυνὸν . . . / χάρμα in Bacch. 10.12 f. extends the shared nature of the glorious report to all men. Often the laudator is concerned with both the private and the public aspects of his χρέος. In *O*. 13.47–50 he passes from the private to the public in the pronominal cap ἐγὼ δὲ ἴδιος ἐν κοινῷ σταλείς / . . . γαρύων . . . / . . . / οὐ ψεύσομαι ἀμφὶ Κορίνθῳ (note the participle and future indicative, on which see pp. 45, 48). But since the private may be taken for granted, it need not be emphasized. Hence in *O*. 10.11 f. occurs the promise, κοινὸν λόγον / φίλαν τείσομεν ἐς χάριν: the laudator will satisfy the demands of both the private and the public.

As for (δι)ορθόω and ὀρθός, these words, applied to the laudator or any of his representatives, emphasize the truth-telling (i.e., praise to match) aspect of the laudator's χρέος. Aineas, the chorodidaskalos, in *O*. 6.90, is an ἄγγελος ὀρθός whose true report (presentation of an ode equal to the occasion) will give evidence of the laudator's sense of truth and justice (λόγοις in line 90 is dativus commodi), and the words ἀγγελίας ὀρθᾶς in *P*. 4.279 speak of the true report which is a credit to the Muse. Similarly the verb ὀρθόω is used of true report. Homer's sense of justice (πᾶσαν ὀρθώσαις ἀρετάν) brought posthumous honor to Aias (*I*. 4.38); in *O*. 3.3b the laudator will keep the record straight in honoring Theron (ὕμνον ὀρθώσαις); in *O*. 7.21, as in *I*. 1.46, the two motives are combined (ξυνὸν ἀγγέλλων διορθῶσαι λόγον): the laudator will adhere to the facts in reporting a tale that is of interest not only to Diagoras and his father, but to all the Rhodian stock (note the participle and ἐθελήσω with the infinitive, on which see pp. 45, 48).

The only doubtful point that remains, now that we have assembled the evidence, is whether καλόν in *I*. 1.46 is the song (cf. ὕμνον ὀρθώσαις and διωρθῶσαι λόγον) or the deed of glory (cf. ὀρθώσαις ἀρετάν). I feel sure that it is the former. καλόν is inner accusative, and we may compare κόσμον κελαδήσω (*O*. 11.13 f.), γεγωνεῖν στεφάνωμα (*P*. 9.3 f.), μνᾶμα κελαδῆσαι (*I*. 8.63), ἐπιχώριον χάρμα κελαδέων (*N*. 3.63), and the like.[76]

---
[76] See Stud. Pind. I 20 f., 21 n. 47.

In summing up, we may note first that πᾶσαν (line 41) and παντοδαπῶν presume considerable agonistic effort and success. Together with ἀγάνορα κόμπον (line 43), these words set and maintain the fervent tone of the passage. χρή (line 43) and δόσις bespeak the laudator's obligation, while κοῦφα points to the eagerness with which he accepts it. φθονεραῖσι reflects a lack of warmth impossible on this occasion, and ἀγάνορα the laudator's straining to match the level of Herodotos' felicity. ξυνόν magnifies his agonistic glory by emphasizing its national significance. ὀρθῶσαι, insisting on the truth, will not permit the laudator to fall short of his theme. The whole, as we have seen, is highly conventional both in its details and in the ensemble. We may add that it praises a particular by putting the general case; for in this form it can serve as gnomic foil for the concrete victory catalogue of lines 52–63, a topic difficult to enliven without resort to foil in the form of prefixes, inserts, and suffixes of a rhetorical nature.[77] But to make the concrete climax (ἄμμι δ' ἔοικε, line 52) more effective the tone must first be lowered, as it was in the mythological matter (lines 12 f.) before the first crescendo, in χαίρετε before the pronominal name cap of line 32, and in the gnome of line 40 before the high vaunt of lines 41–46.

This rhetorical function (diminuendo) is fulfilled in lines 47–51 by explanatory (see p. 57) gnomic material cast in the form of a priamel. Priamel form and its myriad transformations I have treated in brief elsewhere and must refer the reader to that discussion for the distinctions employed here.[78] In *I.* 1.47–51 the climactic term appears in lines 50 f., and the foil term in lines 47 ff. The foil term employs three separate foil devices, any one of which, under appropriate circumstances, may suffice. Here each is allotted a single line as follows: summary foil of the ἄλλος ἄλλα type (line 47), list foil (line 48), summary foil of the πᾶς–πολύς type (line 49). The last two are amplifications of the first, which contains the leading idea. In the standard priamel the thought would be cast in the form: "The shepherd gains nurture from his sheep, the fowler from game birds, the fisherman from fish, but the athlete from praise." In *I.* 1.47–49 the unifying principle governing foil and climax is extracted and stated as a general proposition in line 47; then in line 48 it is applied to the list of occupations comprising the foil; line 49 discovers a unity among the foil terms that will not apply to the climax, and in this way sets up a contrast between the two terms that gives the climax a preferred value. The principle controlling the contrast is well expressed in Phoc. 9 D³:

---

[77] Prefix: *O.* 9.86–89; inserts: *P.* 9.92b f., 96–99 (on these passages, see Stud. Pind. I 17 f.); suffix: *I.* 1.60–63. So Homer, before catalogues, addresses the Muses.
[78] See Stud. Pind. I 4–10.

The First Isthmian Ode

δίζησθαι βιοτήν, ἀρετὴν δ', ὅταν ᾖ βίος ἤδη, and is employed again in the concluding priamel of P. 1.99–100b, and in that of N. 4.1–8.[79] In O. 11.1–6 appears a weaker contrast between foil and climax. μισθός (line 47), a frequent χρέος word,[80] controls the foil, and κέρδος (line 51: cf. λόγον ἐκέρδαναν, I. 5.29) applies its meaning to the climax; both are extensions of χρή and δόσις in the preceding antistrophe.

The form of the climax we recognize from our analysis of lines 41–46. We have in line 50 a relative condition repeating the condition of lines 41 f., followed by a vaunt repeating that of lines 43–46 in a form which retains little of the imperative force of χρή, although the explanatory γάρ extends some of the excitement of χρή and κοῦφα δόσις through μισθός to κέρδος. The form of the climax is very close to that of I. 3.1–3 (see above, pp. 55 f.):

Εἴ τις ἀνδρῶν εὐτυχήσαις ἢ σὺν εὐδόξοις ἀέθλοις
ἢ σθένει πλούτου κατέχει φρασὶν αἰανῆ κόρον,
ἄξιος εὐλογίαις ἀστῶν μεμεῖχθαι·

In the vaunt, ἄξιος and κέρδος are the χρέος words; εὐλογίαις μεμεῖχθαι = εὐαγορηθείς; ἀστῶν = πολιατᾶν. In the condition, the disjunctive phrases "athletic contests or wealth" and "athletic contests or warfare," present wealth and warfare as foil. The athletic contests gain luster from comparison with things so desirable as wealth and glory in war. This is a frequent device. With πολεμίζων in I. 1.50 we may compare πολεμισταί in I. 5.28, which sets the agonistic success of Lampon's sons against the valor of the warriors of old. With πλούτου in I. 3.2 we may compare the phrase κρέσσονα πλούτου μέριμναν in P. 8.96, used to enhance the importance of athletic success. In N. 5.19 the device takes precisely the form it has in I. 1.50 and in I. 3.1 f.: εἰ δ' ὄλβον ἢ χειρῶν βίαν ἢ υιδαρίταν ἐπαινῆσαι πόλεμον δεδόκηται, in which athletic prowess and warfare are foils for ὄλβος (either the first or last term of a series may be the focal point, the central terms never). So too the epithet ἁβρόν in I. 1.50 tacitly employs wealth as foil, and its conventional force in this sense is heightened by contrast with λιμόν in the preceding line.

The doublet πολιατᾶν καὶ ξένων presents a common universalizing motive (cf. O. 7.89 f.):[81] the fame of Herodotos and Asopodoros flowers on the lips both of their fellow citizens and of outlanders. For the superlative adjective with κέρδος, illustrating a common motive in priamels, we may compare the phrase στέφανον ὕψιστον δέδεκται in P. 1.100b (see p. 39).

---
[79] See Stud. Pind. I 2, 23.
[80] Cf. N. 7.63, P. 11.41, P. 1.77.
[81] See Stud. Pind. I 24, 24 n. 56.

Such is the structure of lines 47–51. They repeat the movement of lines 41–46 in a lower key, in order to make the thought a suitable foil for the pronominal name cap of line 52. The priamel is long enough and the images of lines 48 f. forceful enough to engage our interest for their own sake. Though we never lose sight of its relevance, the priamel begins to assume digressive proportions, and this is the desired effect. The focus becomes more exact (ἀέθλοις, line 50), but the scene now provokes more reflection than emotional fervor, and precisely in proportion as it does so, we shall respond more vividly to the concrete term of the crescendo. The extreme formality of these lines is another index to their quasi-independence. In the stately march of ideas each line represents a separate and discrete unit of form and thought. There is no enjambement, as there is in the excited lines 41–46, and this very formality in the deployment of motives is an aid to the process of decrescendo. Yet despite their quieter tone, these lines have greatly deepened and enriched the scene in which Herodotos stands as the principal figure. The tacit simile suggests that praise of valor is a law of nature, and it is an extraordinarily effective stroke to include in the background something of everyday life on a level far below the luxury of the games, and yet to unify it in principle with the pursuit of athletic success. From the fairy world of Kastor and Iolaos we have moved through the vicissitudes of political life to those of the occupational world. Against each of these as background we have viewed the athletic success of Herodotos, at which, for its own sake, we at last arrive in lines 52–63.

Against the triple foils of (1) the χρέος words in lines 41–51 (χρή, κούφα δόσις, μισθός, and κέρδος), (2) ἀέθλοις in line 50, which provides the appropriate category (the category posed in πολεμίζων is rejected), and (3) the decrescendo provided by lines 47–51, the laudator now focuses full attention on the athletic achievements of Herodotos. As ἔοικε, the new χρέος word, takes its cue from those of the preceding lines, so the list of games which it introduces takes its cue from ἀέθλοις in line 50. The pronominal name cap (ἄμμι δ' . . . Κρόνου σεισίχθον' υἱόν) and the imperative force of ἔοικε, which applies to the present the general obligation of lines 41–51, thrust the foil firmly aside to concentrate upon Herodotos' agonistic successes. We note that the new crescendo has the same structure as that of the two preceding ones. ἀμειβομένοις gives us the participle, and ἔοικε with κελαδῆσαι matches ἐθέλω with the infinitive in lines 14 ff.

It must be clear that this is the moment for which the ode, *as epinikion*, exists. The opening foil promised us Herodotos, but he yielded place in the first crescendo to Kastor and Iolaos; the second crescendo promised us Herodotos again, but he yielded place to his father Asopodoros; the foil of lines 41–51 promised us Herodotos, and whetted our enthusiasm to hear of his exploits; now at last we shall hear of them. It is true that the preliminaries have enhanced his glory, but it is equally true that the approach in these lines is tentative, that in them the laudator is still selecting his theme. The first and second crescendos are foil for the third, and ἔοικε corrects in particular, as χρή had chastened in general, the comparative irrelevance of Asopodoros and the pair Kastor and Iolaos as compared to the achievements of Herodotos himself. Propriety now demands strict attention to Herodotos' agonistic success.

The catalogue has two parts. In the first of these (lines 52–59) are recorded six triumphs; the second (lines 60–63) presents in summary fashion victories too numerous for itemized inclusion.[82] Since the second part constitutes a dismissal of the topic, it can be used as foil for the concluding crescendo, which takes the form of a wish for the future. The manner of the cataloguing is in both parts entirely conventional. We may take first the six victories recorded by name.

Heading the list is the current Isthmian success, hinted at in lines 9 and 32. The entry takes the form of a thank offering to Poseidon, lord of the Isthmos, and near neighbor at Onkhestos of Erkhomenos and Thebes. Two conventional motives appear here—the thank-offering and the neighbor motives.

A thank offering very like this one appears at *P.* 5.43 f., not in a victory catalogue but in the long tribute to Karrhotos, Arkesilas' charioteer:

ἑκόντι τοίνυν πρέπει
νόῳ τὸν εὐεργέταν ὑπαντιάσαι.
45   'Αλεξιβιάδα, σὲ δ' ἠΰκομοι φλέγοντι Χάριτες.

As the name cap shows, Arkesilas is expressing his gratitude not to Apollo, but to his charioteer.[83] πρέπει and εὐεργέταν are, in *I.* 1.52 f., ἔοικε and εὐεργέταν. *P.* 8.40–63, one of two interruptions that prolong the victory catalogue of lines 36–84, are a long tribute to Alkman, which is capped by a thank offering (lines 58–63) to this hero for predicting to Aristomenes (the chorus speak urbanely as if they were he) his victory

---

[82] For the manner, cf. *N.* 4.69–72, 33 ff., *N.* 10.19 f., *P.* 8.30–33. On priamels of the τᾶς–πολύς type, see Stud. Pind. I 8 ff.

[83] The need for gratitude to both Apollo and Karrhotos has been expressed in lines 25 f., but only the latter is developed (lines 27–42), the former remaining as foil. Apollo returns as the patron of Battos (archetype of Arkesilas) in lines 60–69. Χάριτες (line 45), representing Alexibiadas' place in the congratulatory ode, particularizes for him the principle of gratitude embodied in lines 43 f. For the untenable view that the gnome refers to Apollo, see Mezger (*ad loc.*), who actually believed that εὐεργέτης stands in opposition to 'Αλεξιβιάδα. But no one would argue that σοφοί (line 12) is similarly contrasted with σέ (line 14).

at Pytho.[84] The neighbor motive is employed here (P. 8.61), as it is in I. 1.53. In P. 9.90–92b, in a catalogue, thanks are offered to Herakles and Iphikles for a victory in the Herakleia.[85] There the language of the original prayer is quoted.[86] In N. 7.86–97 the neighbor motive is used to justify a prayer to Herakles for *future* benefactions, and a thank offering to Apollo for a Pythian victory is found at P. 5.103–107 (note πρέπει . . . Φοῖβον ἀπύειν).

The second entry records a victory in the Herakleia at Thebes. Although the games belong to Herakles alone, both he and Iphikles must be addressed (ἔοικε προσειπεῖν). This figure (see scholia: κατὰ σύλληψιν) appears also at P. 9.90–92b, where both (τοῖσι, line 92) are thanked for the victory, and where Amphitruon is also named (line 84b), as he is in I. 1.55.[87] Other than this (σέθεν, line 55, and τὸ τεόν, line 58), I find no more than two passages in which the god or hero honored by the games is addressed in a catalogue: P. 6.50 (τίν) and P. 8.62 (τύ), but this stylistic mannerism occurs also at P. 4.89 (Ὦτον καὶ σέ, τολμάεις Ἐπιάλτα ἄναξ), in a catalogue of divine and heroic names (cf. also O. 9.120, O. 9.19, frag. 27). προσειπεῖν here, like προσεννέπω in I. 6.15, is "call upon by name."[88]

The third item, a victory in the Minueia, is very briefly recorded in the words τὸν Μινύα τε μυχόν (ἔοικε προσειπεῖν). This kind of brevity is frequent in catalogues, as are forms of the word μυχός (cf. μυχῷ τ' ἐν Μαραθῶνος, P. 8.83). Note that the Boiotian victories are connected by τε as representing a unity.

The fourth and fifth entries, victories at Eleusis and Euboia, are given in the phrase καὶ τὸ Δάματρος κλυτὸν ἄλσος Ἐλευσῖνα καὶ Εὔβοιαν. For the

---

[84] So scholia: τῇ Ἀριστομένους οἰκίᾳ παρίδρυτο Ἀλκμάονος ἡρῷον, ἴσως δὲ καὶ τῇ αὐτοῦ μαντείᾳ χρησάμενος ἐπὶ τὸν ἀγῶνα ἐπορεύθη καὶ ἐνίκησεν. It is here, as in lines 103 ff., the chorus that is speaking. On the accepted view (that the subject is Pindar) the passage makes little if any sense. Alkman's role in aiding Aristomenes to victory sets up the pronominal name cap (τὸ δ', ἐκαταβόλε) in line 64 which rejects Alkman in favor of Apollo. Thanks must be rendered also to the god. The catalogue to which this passage belongs begins in line 36. First, family victories are listed, which then yield place to Aristomenes and his success (line 40). But before adding the particular list of his victories, the laudator will compare him generally to Alkman, who, as it happens, had predicted the young man's current success. By this means the laudator is enabled to acknowledge the favor of both Alkman and Apollo in introducing the first of Aristomenes' successes, his recent victory at Pytho (lines 66 ff.), and to proceed from these to local wins in the festival of Apollo and Artemis at Aigina. At this point the catalogue is again interrupted (lines 70–81) by a prayer for the future (for this type of interruption in catalogues, see pp. 78 f.). After the prayer, the remaining victories are recorded (lines 82 ff.) before the laudator turns again (lines 85–91) to the Pythian success which is the principal concern of the ode.

[85] See Stud. Pind. I 17 f., 18 n. 43.

[86] Cf. Thgn. 341 f.: ἀλλά, Ζεῦ, τέλεσόν μοι, Ὀλύμπιε, καίριον εὐχήν· / δὸς δέ μοι ἀντὶ κακῶν καί τι παθεῖν ἀγαθόν. P. 9.92 f. has τέλειον, εὐχᾷ, and τι παθών / ἐσλόν.

[87] See Stud. Pind. I 17 f.

[88] On προσεννέπω in I. 6.15, see E. Fraenkel, *Aeschylus, Agamemnon* (Oxford, 1950) vol. II, p. 172 n. 2.

bare name Εὔβοιαν, cf. Πέλλανά τ' (O. 7.86), Πέλλανά τε καὶ Σικυὼν καὶ Μέγαρα (O. 13.105), ἄτ' 'Ελευσίς (O. 13.106), ἄτ' Εὔβοια (O. 13.108). For ἄλσος in catalogues, cf. Αἰακιδᾶν τ' εὐερκὲς ἄλσος (O. 13.105). The phrase ἐν γναμπτοῖς δρόμοις at the end of line 57 ("when speaking of bending race-courses"), which goes closely with ἔοικε κελαδῆσαι καὶ προσειπεῖν, is emphatic, and unifies the first five items in the catalogue, thus giving the sixth and last an independent status, emphasized, as we shall see, by συμβάλλομαι in line 59.

The final entry in the first part of the catalogue records a victory in the games held at Phulaka in honor of Protesilaos. τέμενος shows the same manner of recording victories as does ἄλσος in line 57. With τέμενος here, cf. also N. 6.40 ff. and N. 6.63. συμβάλλομαι in line 59 emphasizes the independent status of this entry and converts it into foil for the second part of the catalogue. The force of the word, set against ἐν γναμπτοῖς δρόμοις in line 57, which seemed to bring the individual list to an end, is, "I can't resist adding one item more." πάντα δ' ἐξειπεῖν, breaking the pattern in the next line, adds, "but only one."

Lines 60–64 conclude the catalogue of victories and are transitional foil forming a bridge to the final topic. The pattern is conventional in these two functions, and its multiforms, some of which we have already discussed in connection with ἀσχολίας in line 2, occur in a variety of positions. It may be used to conclude legendary or historical matter in any of the positions in which these occur, or to abbreviate particular elements of a larger pattern, or to interrupt the presentation of material in order to heighten the audience's sense of the importance of a particular point still to come. Together with the matter for which it is foil, it forms a priamel of the πᾶς–πολύς type.[89] In N. 4.69–72 (note πάντα) it concludes a catalogue of Aiginetan heroes and introduces praise of the Theandridai. At lines 33 ff. (note τὰ μακρά) of this same ode the pattern merely interrupts the catalogue in order to heighten our sense of the latter's importance.[90] In O. 13.39 ff. (note μακρότεραι), N. 10.4 (note μακρά), and N. 10.5 (note πολλά) the pattern abbreviates single items in a catalogue.[91] In O. 13.45 f. (note ἑκάστῳ) it dismisses a victory catalogue and prepares

---
[89] See Stud. Pind. I 8 ff.
[90] See Stud. Pind. I 3–4 n. 11.
[91] See Stud. Pind. I 12 ff. Passages of this type are often construed as arrogant and dogmatic literary judgments. A frequent object of such misinterpretation is the *praeteritio* of O. 2.91–97, in which the laudator informs us that his quiver is full of arrows that speak only to the συνετοί. Far from doctrinaire is his subsequent refusal to employ them on the ground that a plain blunt vaunt (φυᾷ) is more truly sentient (σοφός) than are the ways of art. On the force of φυᾷ, see Stud. Pind. I 16–17. The σοφὸς φυᾷ (the plain blunt man) is in this passage *contrasted* with συνετοῖσιν (men of art). Here, as in O. 6.1–4 (see n. 49), the laudator prefers the virtues of clarity and force to those of allusiveness and insinuation.

for legendary material. In each of these passages the motive both abbreviates one topic and sets up the introduction of another. Further examples will be given below, but these will be sufficient to mark the pattern.

Observing now that in *I*. 1.60–63 the topic comes near the end of the ode and that it is preceded by a victory catalogue and followed by a prayer for the future, we may seek parallels exhibiting the same or similar dispositions. *O*. 13.94–110b come immediately to mind. After the itemized part of the catalogue comes the following:

καὶ πᾶσαν κάτα
Ἑλλάδ' εὑρήσεις ἐρευνῶν μάσσον' ἢ ὡς ἰδέμεν.
109b ἄνα, κούφοισιν ἐκνεῦσαι ποσίν·
110 Ζεῦ τέλει', αἰδῶ δίδοι
110b καὶ τύχαν τερπνῶν γλυκεῖαν.

"One may scour the whole of Greece and find more cities than the eye can encompass that have honored the Oligaithidai in victory." In this situation the laudator enjoins upon himself, in a metaphor from swimming, a speedy and graceful exit.[92] This injunction is followed by a prayer for the "double crown" of success and good repute.[93] The same pattern occurs at *N*. 2.19–25, save that the prayer is replaced by an exhortation to celebrate Timodemos both in the revel and in the song.[94] Virtually identical are *O*. 7.80–95, where the itemized catalogue (lines 80–87) is dismissed by the simple ἀλλά (see pp. 36, 38, 45, 48, and n. 3), which introduces a prayer (note αἰδοίαν χάριν in line 89 = αἰδῶ in *O*. 13.10). Thus the parallels show that the summary conclusion of the catalogue in *I*. 1.60–63 is conventional not only in matter, but in sequence too.

The summary part of the catalogue falls into two parts. The first contains the abbreviated section of the list and uses the pressure of time as its excuse; the second consists of an explanatory gnome further justifying the curtailment of the list. The two motives are conventional, both

---

[92] ἐκνεῦσαι codd.; ἐκνεύσω or ἔκνευσον Maas. For the metaphor, cf. E. *Hipp*. 469 f.: ἐς δὲ τὴν τύχην / πεσοῦσ' ὅσην σὺ πῶς ἂν ἐκνεῦσαι δοκεῖς;

[93] αἰδῶ (passive) is "honor," "glory," rather than (active) "modesty." For the formula, cf. *O*. 7.89 f.: δίδοι τέ οἱ αἰδοίαν χάριν / καὶ ποτ' ἀστῶν καὶ ποτὶ ξείνων. For the double crown (εὖ τε παθεῖν καὶ ἀκοῦσαι), cf. further *P*. 1.99–100b, *I*. 5.13–18, *N*. 9.46 f., *I*. 6.9–11b (ἀρετάς and δόξαν), *P*. 10.22 (εὐδαίμων δὲ καὶ ὑμνητός).

[94] The catalogue begins in line 19, and the summary motive bringing Timodemos' local wins into the ledger comes in line 23. An oddity, revealing for choral technique, is that the entry recording the Nemean successes is placed just before the summary of local wins, but is syntactically completed after this summary in order that the name of Nemean Zeus may give the current Nemean success a climactic position and provide the transition (Διός ... τόν) to the close. The conclusion can thus include the customary acknowledgment to the god or hero or human agency that has made the victory possible. For this type of acknowledgment in conclusion, cf. *I*. 4.72: σὺν Ὀρσέᾳ δέ νιν κωμάξομαι τερπνὰν ἀποστάζων χάριν.

singly and in combination. For πάντα δ' ἐξειπεῖν . . . / . . . / . . . ἀφαιρεῖται βραχὺ μέτρον ἔχων / ὕμνος we may compare N. 4.33 ff., τὰ μακρὰ δ' ἐξενέπειν ἐρύκει με τεθμός / ὧραί τ' ἐπειγόμεναι· / ἴυγγι δ' ἕλκομαι ἦτορ νεομηνίᾳ θιγέμεν. Here, ἐρύκει and ἕλκομαι represent the force of circumstances, as does ἀφαιρεῖται in I. 1.62; and τεθμός, ὧραι, and ἴυγγι represent the circumstances (obligation, time, and desire), as does βραχὺ μέτρον ἔχων / ὕμνος (time) in I. 1.62 f.[95] Note βραχύ (I. 1.62) opposing τὰ μακρά (N. 4.33); βραχύς and μακρός are key words in such passages. We may compare also P. 4.247 f., μακρά μοι νεῖσθαι κατ' ἀμαξιτόν· ὥρα γὰρ συνάπτει καί τινα / οἶμον ἴσαμι βραχύν. Cf. also βραχύ . . . πάντα (N. 10.19), πολλῶν . . . / ἐν βραχεῖ (P. 1.81 f.), πολύμυθοι· / . . . ἐν μακροῖσι . . . / . . . / παντός (P. 9.79–82),[96] μακρὸν πάσας (I. 6.53).

The gnome of line 63 has likewise many parallels. The key word is σεσωπαμένον, marking the entire passage as a decrescendo. For the order πάντα (line 60) . . . σεσωπαμένον (line 63) we may compare ἅπασα . . . σιγᾶν (N. 5.16 ff.), ἅπαντας . . . σιγᾶς (frag. 246), σεσιγαμένον / . . . ἕκαστον (O. 9.111 f.), and πολλὰ . . . σιγᾷ (I. 5.51–57). In three of these passages the force of the summary word is somewhat different from that of πάντα in I. 1.60, but in the other it is exactly the same.[97] In I. 5.51–57 the laudator cannot let fly all the arrows of his song, just as in I. 1.60–63 he cannot count the entire tale of Herodotos' successes. Elsewhere the σιγά motive occurs in isolation from the πᾶς–πολύς priamel motive; always it marks a decrescendo, a dismissal of one topic or another. We may compare ἀπό μοι λόγον / τοῦτον, στόμα, ῥῖψον (O. 9.38 f.) and διασωπάσομαι (O. 13.87b). Considerations of propriety dictate the use of this motive; it is therefore but another version of the countless appeals to propriety (cf. ἔοικε in I. 1.52) in introductions, transitions, and conclusions, where words and phrases like κόρος (N. 10.20, O. 2.105,[98] N. 7.52, P. 1.82, P. 8.33), πρέπει (O. 2.50/1, N. 3.64, P. 5.104), χρεών (P. 2.52), καιρός (P. 1.81, O. 9.41, N. 1.18, O. 13.46, P. 10.4), μέτρον (O. 13.46), τὸ πρὸ ποδός (I. 8.13), τὸ ἐν ποσί . . . τράχον (P. 8.33), τὸ παράμερον ἐσλόν (O. 1.99), τὸ πὰρ ποδί (N. 6.57), φροντίδα τὰν πὰρ ποδός (P. 10.62), χρή (O. 1.103, O. 6.4, O. 13.90, P. 4.1), πρόσφορος (O. 9.87, N. 3.30), and the like govern the scene. All such words and phrases attach to the laudator's χρέος and to the appropriate manner of discharging it. Thus when the occasion demands, the σιγά motive may be con-

---

[95] On this passage, see Stud. Pind. I 2 n. 11.
[96] On this passage, see Stud. Pind. I 17 ff.
[97] ἅπασα (N. 5.16), ἅπαντας (frag. 246), and ἕκαστον (O. 9.112) all reject themes for the song, but in a manner slightly different from that of πολλά in I. 5.51 and that of πάντα in I. 1.60. Discussion of the first three of these passages is beyond the scope of this essay.
[98] On the point of κόρος (= ἄκαιρον μῆκος) in this praeteritio, see Stud. Pind. I 29 n. 71, and see n. 123 of the present study.

verted into crescendo by the addition of a negative (*I.* 2.44, *N.* 9.7), and this is hardly different from the endless imperatives (*N.* 9.8, *N.* 9.50, *I.* 7.20, *N.* 10.21, *N.* 7.77, *N.* 3.10) to "wake the lyre" which can be converted into decrescendo by the addition of a negative (*O.* 9.43); it is hardly different from the verbals (*O.* 2.6/7), from ἐθέλω with the infinitive, from the numerous voluntative futures that direct the impulse of the song. All these motives work together to create the *appropriate* hymn of praise.

To return then to *I.* 1.63, σεσωπαμένον reflects, as does βραχὺ μέτρον in the previous line, the laudator's sense of propriety in determining the content and proportions of the song that will constitute the laudandus' claim to posthumous glory and incite him and others to even greater efforts. We may, then, ask what particular consideration urges silence in *I.* 1.63. The scholia offer two suggestions: (1) There is an allusion to a defeat suffered by Herodotos at Nemea. (2) The other victories were ἀνάξιοι and for this reason are better omitted.[99] The former is a foolish guess, and if the latter has a certain reasonableness, it is nevertheless unjustifiable, as will become evident from parallel contexts.

In *N.* 5.18 and *O.* 9.38 f. the σιγά motive becomes a highlighting device whereby unpropitious matter is converted into foil for a subsequent crescendo. This might seem to bear out the general purport of the conjectures recorded by the scholia, but we are bound to observe that in both of these examples the nature of the unpropitious material is clear from the context, and that this is not the case in *I.* 1.63. The same situation prevails in *O.* 13.87b, where the laudator avoids reporting Bellerophon's untimely end, but converts the dark circumstance into foil for the bliss achieved by Pegasos. In *I.* 5.57, σιγᾷ, set against πολλά, is simply a rhetorical abbreviation, but the laudator subtly balances it against φόνῳ in the previous line in order to gain dark foil for the following crescendo (lines 59 ff.) and to conceal the mechanical nature of the transition.[100]

---

[99] See Bury, *ad loc.*

[100] Note the affinity of lines 53–56 with the topic discussed on pp. 48–52. Technically the transition depends on πολλά ... ἀλλ' ὅμως ... τά τε καὶ τά, and the plain prose sense of the passage is therefore, "I have many things to say on the subject of Aigina's glory, not only in ancient times, but quite recently at the battle of Salamis. Nevertheless I pass this by, for variety (τά τε καὶ τά) is the spice of life, and even such high and serious subjects as these may admit of treatment side by side with athletic achievement." Despite this, the deliberately contrived φόνῳ is what prompts the recoil in line 57 (on death in battle as dark foil, see pp. 48 ff.), as the deliberately contrived impiety in *O.* 9.31–38 prompts the recoil of lines 38–44, and as the deliberately contrived μέγα ἐν δίκᾳ τε μὴ κεκινδυνευμένον of *N.* 5.14 prompts the recoil of lines 16 ff. Despite (or perhaps because of) the stylization (most notable in the sentence Ζεὺς τά τε καὶ τά νέμει = ἀνάπαυσις ἐν παντὶ γλυκεῖα ἔργῳ in *N.* 7.52) and the ceremoniousness of the language, there prevails throughout this passage a mood of heady gaiety in which the laudator pokes fun at his own seriousness.

In all of these passages the nature of the dark foil is not left to the imagination: we know precisely the reason for the silence. In *I*. 1.63, by contrast, the reason is not divulged and hence we must look further for the thought behind the silence. In *N*. 10.19 f. the σιγά motive (βραχύ μοι στόμα) follows a catalogue of Argive glories. Since the order of topics in these lines is the same as it is in *I*. 1.60–64, let us see whether we can determine what prompts in them the use of the σιγά motive and whether its form invites comparison with ours.

For an analysis of the catalogue (*N*. 10.1–18), I refer the reader to the first essay of this series.[101] We are concerned here with the summary that concludes the list of Argive glories set as foil for Theaios' Nemean victory:

βραχύ μοι στόμα πάντ' ἀναγήσασθ', ὅσων
 'Αργεῖον ἔχει τέμενος
20 μοῖραν ἐσλῶν· ἔστι δὲ καὶ κόρος ἀνθρώπων
 βαρὺς ἀντιάσαι·
ἀλλ' ὅμως εὔχορδον ἔγειρε λύραν,
καὶ παλαισμάτων λάβε φροντίδ'·

Note πάντα = πάντα in *I*. 1.60, βραχύ μοι στόμα = βραχὺ μέτρον ἔχων / ὕμνος in *I*. 1.62 f., and ὅσων 'Αργεῖον ἔχει τέμενος / μοῖραν ἐσλῶν = ὅσ' ἀγώνιος Ἑρμᾶς / 'Ηροδότοι' ἔπορεν ἵπποις. These equivalences suggest that the gnomic gloss ἔστι δὲ καὶ κόρος ἀνθρώπων βαρὺς ἀντιάσαι = the gnomic gloss ἦ μὰν πολλάκι καὶ τὸ σεσωπαμένον εὐθυμίαν μείζω φέρει in *I*. 1.63. The former implies that to overdo a subject brings the speaker little pleasure, and the latter that to know when to cease may actually increase it; and this gnomic topic (cf. Stob. περὶ σιγῆς and περὶ βραχυλογίας) invariably concerns itself with the advantage or disadvantage of the *speaker* in terms of audience reaction. εὐθυμία is thus the *laudator's* reward for producing a well-proportioned enkomion. Exactly the same sentiment in very nearly the same formulaic dress (the *overt* appeal to temporal considerations is lacking; cf., however, ταχείας, implying that the audience want the laudator to get on with his subject) appears at *P*. 1.81–84, where again the laudator's concern is to avoid the criticism (proceeding from a combination of boredom and ill will directed against the laudandus) that he may provoke among his audience if he dilates too long on one aspect of his theme. *P*. 8.30–33 (following a summary catalogue of Aiginetan glories) is identical with *N*. 10.19 f. and *I*. 1.60–63. The laudator has no time (ἄσχολος) to tell the whole long tale (πᾶσαν μακραγορίαν) for fear of irritating his audience with his prolixity (μὴ κόρος ἐλθὼν κνίσῃ). Thus the evidence of *N*. 10.19 f. and two of its congeners suggests that the laudator

---
[101] See Stud. Pind. I 13 f.

in *I.* 1.63 fears rather the criticism he may provoke among his general audience than the embarrassment he may cause the laudandus. Any displeasure that the latter might feel would proceed from the cause described by Euripides (*I. A.* 979 f.) : αἰνούμενοι γὰρ οἱ ἀγαθοὶ τρόπον τινὰ / μισοῦσι τοὺς αἰνοῦντας, ἢν αἰνῶσ' ἄγαν. Quality, not quantity, is the measure (cf. also Call. *h. Ap.* 105-113, *O.* 2.105-110) of εὐθυμία. We may pause to observe, before returning to *I.* 1.63, that *N.* 10.19 f. and its congeners have in common with other uses of the σιγά motive that they *all* resort to silence in fear of the disapproval of the general audience, rather than out of a direct solicitude for the laudandus himself. To be effective, the hymn of praise must be acceptable to those who will hear it and judge the actions it praises.

As we return to *I.* 1.60-63, we may recall that we have discovered parallels in form and function for each clause and each phrase of the ensemble. πάντα δ' ἐξειπεῖν = τὰ μακρὰ δ' ἐξενέπειν in *N.* 4.33, ἅπαντα διελθεῖν in *N.* 4.72, πάσας ἀναγήσασθαι in *I.* 6.53 or πάντ' ἀναγήσασθαι in *N.* 10.19; the ὅσα clause in *I.* 1.60 ff. is equivalent to that introduced by ὅσων in *N.* 10.19 f.; the temporal appeal in *I.* 1.62 f. is matched in numerous passages, as is the σιγά motive employed in *I.* 1.63. Smaller units are also conventional. For ἀγώνιος Ἑρμᾶς, cf. *O.* 6.79, Ἑρμᾶν . . . ὃς ἀγῶνας ἔχει; for ἔπορεν in recording victories, cf. πόρε (*I.* 2.18) and ἔπορεν (*P.* 4.66); for πολλάκι, cf. πολλάκις (*N.* 5.18), ἕκαστον (*O.* 9.112), ἔσθ' ὅτε (frag. 246.2); for μείζω, cf. κερδίων (*N.* 5.16), σκαιότερον (*O.* 9.112), πιστότεραι (frag. 246.2), σοφώτατον (*N.* 5.18); for the form of the phrase εὐθυμίαν φέρει, cf. προμάθειαν φέρει (*I.* 1.40), ἡσυχίαν φέρει (*Pa.* 2.26), κόσμον ἡ σιγὴ φέρει (S. *Aj.* 293), ὃ (τὸ σιγᾶν) . . . τιμὴν φέρει (Chares 2 N²).

THE CONCLUDING CRESCENDO, LINES 64-68: PRAYER FOR THE FUTURE

If the σιγά motive concludes the summary part of the catalogue, the silence it enjoins is a perfect foil for the spirited εἴη (in adversative asyndeton) of line 64 and the ringing words that follow (εὐφώνων, ἀερθέντα, Πιερίδων). In all its occurrences the σιγά motive is foil—usually for a rousing crescendo. Thus the gnome of line 63 has a transitional function like that of line 40, of χαίρετε in line 32, and of the briefly invoked legendary matter of lines 12 f. These, the major transitions of the ode, precede clean breaks in subject matter. ἀλλ' ἐγώ in line 14, ἐγὼ δέ in line 32, εἰ δέ in line 41, and now εἴη in line 64 each introduce a new aspect of the theme. After the prooimion, dedicated to the spirit of Thebes, Herodotos is linked first to Kastor and Iolaos (the legendary panel), and then to

Asopodoros (the familial panel), before he himself becomes the direct theme of the song. The order is climactic, and the foil with which the victorious charioteer is introduced (lines 41–51) lends emphasis to that order with its fervid and resolute acceptance of the debt that is owed to ἀρετά. In ἄμμι δ' ἔοικε (line 52), completing the transition to Herodotos begun in εἰ δέ, the laudator recognizes the currency of that debt. Now, having made due return to Herodotos for his successful efforts, the laudator looks forward to the future in the wish incorporated in εἴη, so that the temporal order, beginning with Kastor and Iolaos, is past, present, and future. This order is one mark of unity; another is the grouping of names: Thebes and the Isthmos in the opening foil; Herodotos and Thebes in the first crescendo; Herodotos, Asopodoros, Poseidon, and the Isthmos in the second crescendo; Herodotos and Poseidon in the third crescendo; and now, as we come to the final crescendo, Herodotos and Thebes. Still another is the system of emerging and receding foils that keeps the emphasis on Herodotos, but withholds the full view of his achievements for the climactic position which it occupies in lines 52–63. Now as we move to the final crescendo the focus again widens; for the moment to which the song as epinikion is dedicated has been realized. The unqualified present, whose overwhelming importance the hymn of praise exists to enhance and perpetuate, must now be surrendered; for the moment of happiness that must be enjoyed to the full when it is upon us does not abide (cf. *O.* 1.99 f., *P.* 10.61 f., *P.* 3.62), and the future looms ahead both to concede and to withhold the objects of our heart's desire (cf. *P.* 12.32). Herodotos' hope is that he will be proclaimed victorious at Pytho and Olympia, and this hope the laudator now expresses for him. Before considering the particular implications of the prayer, it may be well to gain some idea of the role played by the unknown future within the system of conventions that govern the composition of hymns of this class.

We shall confine our attention to appeals to the future in the form of prayers and wishes. These conclude a number of odes (*O.* 1, *O.* 6, *O.* 8, *O.* 13, *P.* 5, *P.* 8, *N.* 9, *I.* 7). The concluding prayer is sealed sometimes by a gnomic sentence (*O.* 5, *O.* 7, *N.* 7) and sometimes by other explanatory material (*O.* 4, *P.* 11). Yet prayers and wishes are by no means confined to the concluding position, and we shall gain a better idea of their formal function from a brief examination of the prayer motive in other settings.

Our analysis of *I.* 1.14–32 showed clearly how parts of a given ode may be treated as complete generic wholes. *I.* 1.14–32 is a complete hymn of praise to Kastor and Iolaos. χαίρετε in *I.* 1.32 is a concluding hymnal motive adapted to the purpose of transition. The situation is similar in respect to prayers and wishes. This type of appeal to the future is in essence a concluding motive belonging to the hymnal form. We may compare typical endings from the *Homeric Hymns*. In *h. Hom.* 2.494 Demeter and Persephone are asked to grant a pleasant life in return for the song: πρόφρονες ἀντ' ᾠδῆς βίοτον θυμήρε' ὀπάζειν. This type of prayer appears in Pindar at *O.* 2.13–17, where all elements of the vocabulary reflect hymnal conventions.[102] The prayer may be for the song (see *h. Hom.* 25.6, ἐμὴν τιμήσατ' ἀοιδήν, and 10.5, δὸς δ' ἱμερόεσσαν ἀοιδήν), and such prayers often court indirectly the deity's more general favor (see *h. Hom.* 9.7, 16.5). The prayer for the song may be contrasted with a prayer for other blessings, as in 24.4 ff.:

ἔρχεο τόνδ' ἀνὰ οἶκον, ἐπέρχεο θυμὸν ἔχουσα
4b ⟨   ⟩
σὺν Διῒ μητιόεντι· χάριν δ' ἄμ' ὄπασσον ἀοιδῇ.

The latter form occurs in Pindar at *O.* 1.115 ff. (prayer for Hieron, prayer for the singer), at *O.* 6.101–105 (prayer for the Stymphalians and Syracusans, prayer for the song), and, with modifications, at *I.* 2.43–46 and *N.* 7.98–104.[103]

Such prayers and wishes may be used by Pindar to conclude formally independent units within the song, as well as the song itself. The prayer μὴ θραύσοι χρόνος ὄλβον ἐφέρπων is combined with another hymnal prayer motive (δέξαιτο, line 98)[104] to conclude the brief "hymn to Hieron" in *O.* 6.92–100 and to set up a transition to Hagesias. We may compare also *P.* 1.56 f. (concluding praise of Hieron and preparing a transition to Deinomenes), *O.* 8.28 ff. (concluding praise of Aigina and preparing a transition to the past), and *O.* 13.23–28 (concluding praise of Korinth and introducing praise of Xenophon and the Oligaithidai). In this way the prayer motive comes to serve the same transitional function as is served by the χαῖρε motive in *I.* 1.32, with which it is often combined

---

[102] These conventions need not be fully illustrated; but for ἰανθεὶς ἀοιδαῖς ("in pleasure at our songs"), cf. Bacch. 17.130 ff., Δάλιε, χοροῖσι Κηΐων / φρένα ἰανθεὶς / ὄπαζε θεόπομπον ἐσθλῶν τύχαν; *h. Hom.* 9.7, καὶ σὺ μὲν οὕτω χαῖρε ... ἀοιδῇ; 16.5, λίτομαι δὲ σ' ἀοιδῇ; 19.48, ἵλαμαι δὲ σ' ἀοιδῇ; *h. Orph.* 31.6, ἔλθοιτ' εὐμενέοντες ἐπ' εὐφήμοισι λόγοισι; Aristonoos 1.45–48 (*Collectanea Alexandrina*, ed. Powell), χαρεὶς ὕμνοις ἡμετέροις, / ὄλβον ἐξ ὁσίων διδοὺς / ἀεὶ καὶ σῴζων ἐφέποις / ἡμᾶς, ὦ ἰὲ Παιάν.

[103] In *I.* 2.43–46 the hymnal address becomes an address to a mortal, who is asked to bestow his favor both on the greatness of Xenokrates and on the song that acclaims him. In *N.* 7.98–104 a prayer for the future of the Euxenidai is thrust aside by a pronominal cap (τὸ δ' ἐμὸν ... κέαρ, line 102) which intrudes the laudator's concern for the future (οὔ ποτε φάσει) reputation of his "hymn to Neoptolemos." Here the prayer motive yields to asseveration. "I shall never [etc.]" is a very strong "May I never [etc.]."

[104] For the δέξαι motive (ordinarily addressed to gods; here addressed to a godlike mortal), cf. *P.* 8.5, *P.* 12.5, *O.* 4.10, *O.* 8.10, and often.

in the *Homeric Hymns* (cf. 6.19 f., 10.4 f., 11.5, 13.3), and it is as a transitional motive that it assumes its position between items in a catalogue, although even here it retains its concluding function. *N.* 10.29-33, a prayer for an Olympian victory, completes the Panhellenic series Pytho (line 25), Isthmos (line 26), Nemea (line 26), and Olympia, and provides the transition from the Panhellenic to the local successes itemized in lines 33-36.[105] Similarly in *O.* 13.94-103 the Panhellenic series Isthmos, Nemea, Olympia, Pytho (repeating the principal items in the list of lines 28-44b) adds weight to the list of local successes that follows. In lines 39-44b the laudator had declared beyond count the family's wins at the Isthmos and at Nemea (at Delphoi too). Returning to that subject in lines 94-96 he puts the number at sixty. He then passes over the family's Pythian wins to recapitulate the Olympian, three in number, recorded in lines 28 ff. and 34 f. The reason for the anticlimactic position of the Pythian wins (lines 102 f.) is simply that Xenophon himself can boast no Pythian successes, and by convention his victories must stand first in the catalogue. This convention is indeed the reason for recapitulating in lines 94-98 the successes of the family at the Isthmian, Nemean, and Olympian festivals; for these are the festivals in which Xenophon has been crowned victor (lines 28-33). Thus the prayer for future Olympian triumphs in lines 99-102 separates the two groups of entries. Pytho heads the second group by virtue of the greater distinction attached to it and thus completes the tale of Panhellenic successes. Here again the prayer, used in transition, retains its concluding function. Indeed, the careful reader will find that there is no prayer in Pindar that does not follow these conventional rules.

We see that subjective appeals to the future (prayers and wishes) may conclude any topic used to praise a currently existing entity and acquire, so used, a transitional function. We have further observed that the prayer motive in the epinikion is hymnal in origin: a prayer puts a hymnal seal on the matter that precedes it, and often too this matter is introduced by a hymnal invocation or other subjective crescendo the force of which is ἀείδειν χρή (cf. *O.* 8.74-88, *P.* 1.42-57). Prayers and wishes, then, are regularly preceded by praise of blessings achieved, and call for continuation or amplification of a present happiness.

As we turn our attention now to the prayer of lines 64-68, we shall find that many of the details are already familiar. The lines express the hope that Herodotos will be victorious at Pytho and Olympia. The order of the listing is climactic, like that of Λακεδαίμονι and Θήβαις in line 17, and

---

[105] The victories itemized in lines 37-48 are those of other members of the clan and form, therefore, a discrete section of the catalogue.

the climax is emphasized by the word ἐξαιρέτοις, giving preference to the Olympic wreaths.[106] As we have seen, prayers for crowns more desirable than those already achieved are conventional following catalogues, subunits of catalogues, or, when a single victory has been granted, praise of the current agonistic success. Thus praise of Strepsiades' Isthmian victory in *I.* 7.20–39 is followed by the concluding prayer (lines 39–51), which is capped by a request for a Pythian success. In *N.* 10.29–33 and *O.* 13.99–102 prayers for Olympian successes conclude subsections of catalogues. In *P.* 5.103–124 praise of Arkesilas' Pythian victory in the form of a thank offering to Apollo introduces a catalogue of Arkesilas' native qualities; the summary statement that God currently fulfills these qualities in action smoothes the way to the concluding prayer, "May God's favor abide; may the house of Battos add to its splendors an Olympian success." *O.* 13.94–110b and *O.* 7.80–95 provide the closest contextual parallels to *I.* 1.52–68. Since both occur in odes for Olympian victors, the concluding prayers for continued success (*O.* 13.110b, *O.* 7.92 ff.) are general (there are no games to cap the Olympian), but the same topical sequence (catalogue followed by prayer) is observed; *O.* 13.108 ff. matches the abbreviation topic of *I.* 1.60–63, whereas *O.* 7.94 f. matches the gnomic gloss of *I.* 1.67 f. To parallel the form of the prayer itself in *I.* 1.64–68 we must turn to other passages. *P.* 1.1–28, formally a hymn to the phorminx, describes (in lines 2–28, beginning with the hymnal relative τᾶς)[107] the actual performance of a hymn to Zeus. Accordingly it is concluded by the hymnal prayer εἴη, Ζεῦ, τὶν εἴη ἀνδάνειν (i.e., ἄμμιν εὔφρων γένοιο, Ζεῦ).[108] This εἴη is frequent in prayers and wishes. We may compare *P.* 2.83, *P.* 2.96, *I.* 6.6, and *N.* 4.11—all prayers for the laudator; but the closest parallel is *O.* 1.115 ff.—a concluding prayer for both laudator and laudandus—where εἴη σέ . . . πατεῖν formally matches εἴη μιν . . . / . . . / . . . φράξαι in *I.* 1.64 ff. For ἔτι in such prayers, cf. *O.* 1.109, *N.* 2.6, *O.* 2.16.

To pursue our inquiry further, we must look to the structure of the prayer itself. We observe first that it is sealed by inverted gnomic foil in a form already familiar to us from our examination of lines 41–45

---

[106] That ἐξαιρέτοις modifies ἔρνεσι with respect only to Ὀλυμπιάδων seems clear from the fact that a second modifier, Ἀλφεοῦ, intervenes between ἐξαιρέτοις and ἔρνεσι. In any case, the epithet is not applicable to Πυθῶθεν in the presence of Ὀλυμπιάδων.

[107] For this hymnal relative, cf. *h. Hom.* 2.2, 3.2, 4.3, 5.2, 6.2, etc., *h. Orph.* 3.10 (any number of epithets may precede or follow), 12.11, 13.8, 14.2, 17.7, 18.4, 6, 8, 11, *N.* 8.2, *P.* 9.5, *P.* 12.2, *N.* 11.1, *O.* 14.1.

[108] ἀνδάνειν is another example of the motive appearing in λανθείς in *O.* 2.14/5 (see n. 102): the suppliant must please the god. For ἁδεῖν, cf. *O.* 3.1. Cf. *h. Orph.* 1.10, εὐμενέουσαν ἀεὶ κεχαρηότι θυμῷ; 6.10, βαῖνε γεγηθώς; 18.19, ἵλαον . . . μολεῖν κεχαρηότα μύσταις; 27.14, ἔρχεο γηθόσυνος; 29.2, κεχαρισμένα δ' ἱερὰ δέξαι. Cf. also ἀφθόνητος (*O.* 13.24), εὔφρων (*O.* 2.16), καρδίᾳ γελανεῖ . . . δέκεν (*O.* 5.2 f.), and the like.

and 50 f. As for the prayer itself, we see that it contains three provisions. The main point is carried by φράξαι, to which τεύχοντα adds a secondary provision. To this prayer for the well-being of individual and state (cf. O. 8.88, αὐτούς τ' ἀέξοι καὶ πόλιν, and O. 13.23–27) is subordinated (ἀερθέντα, line 64) the equally conventional prayer for the song. Thus the concluding crescendo has two parts: the prayer proper (lines 64–67) and its gnomic gloss (lines 67 f.). We must consider the relation between the two.

Gnomic foil, whether it precedes or follows its focal point, provides by analogy or contrast a category appropriate to the point of interest which it glosses (see pp. 53 f.). Here the principle of contrast is invoked in order to highlight Herodotos' devotion to generous pursuits against the background of miserly self-preoccupation. This simple fact directs suspicion against certain widely held views on the point of the prayer and the foil. We may take first the prayer.

We have already observed the bipartite (ἀερθέντα, φράξαι) structure of the prayer. What we must determine is the relation of the two provisions to each other. The point is passed over by all but a very few commentators and translators. Ludwig Wolde renders, "O würd' ihm dies: es trüge der singenden Musen Fittich, der / Glänzende, hoch ihn empor, *weil* pythische Zweige, erlesne, ihm den Arm, / Und die olympischen vom Alpheios füllen; Theben, der Stadt / Der sieben Tore, brächt' er die Ehre [italics mine]."[109] This seems to make of ἀερθέντ' . . . / . . . / . . . φράξαι a kind of hysteron proteron (= ἀερθείη φράξας); but the time of ἀερθέντα is either previous to or identical with that of φράξαι, about which we are not left in doubt, since from Πυθῶθεν and 'Ολυμπιάδων we see that these crowns will be received at the scene of victory. Thus, if the time of ἀερθέντα is not that of I. 1 or of victories succeeding the Isthmian but preceding the envisioned Pythian and Olympian successes, then the odes for these future victories will be sung at Pytho and Olympia. But the performance of the formal victory ode ordinarily took place in the victor's homeland, and the few exceptions to this rule (e.g., O. 8) will not justify Pindar's assuming the exception in I. 1. A spontaneous κῶμος (cf. O. 9.1 ff.) is one thing; an elaborate victory ode such as that alluded to in I. 1.64 f., another. Not a few translators cover up the difficulty with additions of their own. C. J. Billson translates: "May sweet-voiced Muses *in yet loftier flight* / Bear him on wings of light! / O may he thus accoutre his hands once more / At Pytho . . . [etc.] [italics mine]."[110] This still gives a hysteron proteron, but, by the insertion of the phrase

---

[109] Ludwig Wolde, *Pindar, Die Dichtungen und Fragmente, verdeutscht und erläutert* (Leipzig, 1942).

[110] C. J. Billson, Πινδάρου ἐπινίκια, *The Nemean and Isthmian Odes, with an introduction and a translation* (Oxford, 1930).

"in yet loftier flight" (note the transfer of ἔτι from φράξαι to ἀερθέντα) and the division of the sentence into two distinct prayers, the second glossing the first, Billson unfairly avoids the difficulty.

From these considerations, it seems evident that the songs alluded to in lines 64 f. do not belong to the prospective victories of lines 65 ff. The sense is therefore, "May he, borne aloft on *these* wings of song, yet gird his hand with wreaths from Pytho and Olympia." There may even be the suggestion that *I*. 1 and the victory it celebrates may inspire Herodotos to yet greater efforts and achievements (see my remarks on *P*. 8.92–96 below), and this thought is in accord with the implicit exhortation μὴ κάμνε λίαν δαπάναις (cf. *P*. 1.90) contained in lines 67 f. Herodotos may not rest on his laurels.

The flight motive is one of a number of conventional themes used to express the supernatural potency of victory and song. In *P*. 9.130 and *O*. 14.24 the victory crowns are winged; in *N*. 7.22 the poet's art is winged, as in *P*. 8.35 the debt owed to Aristomenes takes wing by the poet's art. Similarly, the song is winged in *I*. 5.70. In *P*. 8.92–96 a present victory lends wings to the aspirations of the victor, who will count no cost to win future glories (this passage, it will be seen, is very like our own), while in *N*. 6.50 the fame in song and story of the Aiakidai flies to every corner of the world; and the extent of Hieron's fame likewise determines the laudator's flight as eagle in Bacch. 5.16–36.

The second division of the prayer contains, as we have noted, two provisions, reflecting the laudator's concern first for the personal, then for the public aspects of agonistic success. The personal and public aspects of ἀρετά (often expressed in Attic by the adjectives ἴδιος and δημόσιος) are the two principal concerns of the epinikion, and many of its formal conventions serve to articulate the relation between the two. In *O*. 13.47 the phrase ἴδιος ἐν κοινῷ σταλείς expresses these two components of the laudator's χρέος: he must do justice both to the Oligaithidai and to Korinth.[111] Similarly in *N*. 6.59 he carries a δίδυμον ἄχθος, must serve both the ἴδιον and the κοινόν.[112] As applied to the laudandus this motive designates his agonistic labors and expenses as a public service, a χορηγία culminating in his outlay of substance in the production of the victory ode and the public festival that attended it. This act marked him as φιλόξενος and φιλόπολις and provided an occasion for general rejoicing and merrymaking. Thus the concluding prayer of *O*. 7 is grounded on the well-known (τοι) fact that Ἐρατιδᾶν ... σὺν χαρίτεσσιν ἔχει /

---

[111] So in lines 48 f., μῆτιν and πόλεμον are the singer's themes regarding Korinth, while ἐν ἡρωΐαις ἀρεταῖσιν represent the interests of the Oligaithidai. See n. 45.

[112] For other forms of the motive, cf. *N*. 11.3 ff. (Ἀρισταγόραν and Τένεδον), *O*. 9.15 (ἓ and υἱόν), *O*. 13.26 f. (τόνδε λαόν and Ξενοφῶντος).

The First Isthmian Ode

θαλίας καὶ πόλις, and the prayer of O. 4.13 f. is explained by the fact that Psaumis is φίλιππος, φιλόξενος, and φιλόπολις. The opening prayer of this ode has the similar ground that Psaumis κῦδος ὄρσαι / σπεύδει Καμαρίνᾳ (lines 12b f.). The prayer of N. 9.28–32 for peace, lasting political unity, and festive glory in which the people share (i.e., enkomia which are both ἴδια and κοινά) is grounded on the evident truth (τοι) that Aitna's lords are dedicated to the agonistic virtues πόνος and δαπάνα: they are φίλιπποι and κτεάνων κρέσσονες.

In our passage the laudator expresses his hopes for Herodotos and Thebes. Herodotos, in adding to the tale of his own glory successes at Pytho and Olympia, will magnify the glory of Thebes. With this thought the prayer is concluded and the laudator has exhausted his theme. The prayer is briefly this: "May Herodotos be inspired by the acclaim accorded these successes to achieve further crowns at Pytho and Olympia for himself and his city." The prayer puts a hymnal seal on the ode, and the word Θήβαισι in line 67 strikes briefly the note of civic pride enlarged on in the opening foil. The focus widens at the close from Herodotos to Thebes, as at the beginning it narrowed from Thebes to Herodotos.

That this widening of focus brings a relaxing of tension is clear. That it touches on the suprapersonal aspect of ἀρετά is equally plain. Yet the laudator will not leave it at this. He will further relax the tension of the prayer crescendo and overtly call attention to the unselfishness of agonistic success by adding at the close an inverted gnomic foil praising the dedication required of Olympian and Pythian victors. In form the concluding gnomic sentence is the same as that of lines 41–45 and lines 50 f.; in thought it is the inverse of these (see pp. 59–62, 67), in the sense that it condemns rather than praises the category selected by the conditional clause. Yet the difference is merely rhetorical. The earlier passages provided by *analogy* a category for praise of Herodotos' current agonistic successes. Lines 67 f. now provide by *contrast* a category to embrace the envisioned successes at Pytho and Olympia. Thus the inversion has a cautionary force. Pytho and Olympia lie in the unknown future. Their favors may be bestowed or withheld. Yet certain it is that they will not be achieved without labor and expense. The laudator encourages as well as praises the qualities required to win enduring fame. At the same time he tempers the celebratory mood with sober reflection. The resulting decrescendo is therefore both aesthetically and ethically proper.

The thought of the sentence is simple. Lines 41–46 declare that if a man work and spend to achieve ἀρετά, he must, when he achieves it, win glory. Lines 47 f. declare that if a man *refuse* to spend, he will *not* win glory. Aside from the precise force of νέμει in line 67,[113] only the clause ἄλλοισι δ' ἐμπίπτων γελᾷ gives trouble. ἄλλοισι are thought to be "those who spend" in the hope of winning glory, and commentators infer that in the words ἐμπίπτων γελᾷ Pindar is alluding to certain individuals who had mocked Herodotos' "foolish" outlay of substance on his agonistic hopes. But whatever the reference of ἄλλοισι, the word can hardly designate a category appropriate to Herodotos; for this type of foil sets up a category antithetical in its prime terms to the focal point—here Herodotos—so that these terms (here νέμει, γελᾷ, and οὐ φράζεται) refer by contrast to the laudandus. The laudator is not interested in the fact per se that some hoard their wealth; he mentions the type to point up by contrast the merits of Herodotos. It would then defeat the strategic purpose of the foil and confound its simple clarity to conceal another reference to Herodotos in ἄλλοισι, which is formally antithetical to the prime terms. The point is that the foil warns *Herodotos* not to laugh at others, as it warns *him* not to hoard. The principle may be illustrated by *O*. 10.95-100:

95   καὶ ὅταν καλὰ ἔρξαις ἀοιδᾶς ἄτερ,
     'Αγησίδαμ', εἰς 'Αΐδα σταθμόν
     ἀνὴρ ἵκηται, κενεὰ πνεύσαις ἔπορε μόχθῳ
97b βραχύ τι τερπνόν. τὶν δ' ἀδυεπής τε λύρα
     γλυκύς τ' αὐλὸς ἀναπάσσει χάριν·
     τρέφοντι δ' εὐρὺ κλέος
100 κόραι Πιερίδες Διός.

Here the terms referring by contrast to the laudandus are ἀοιδᾶς ἄτερ and κενεὰ πνεύσαις ἔπορε μόχθῳ / βραχύ τι τερπνόν. These inapplicable foil terms are rejected in the pronominal name cap that follows:[114] song *is* Hagesidamos' portion, and the Muses *are* taking care that his fame will be broad (even after death). Thus the name cap makes it clear that the foil terms apply, by contrast, to the laudandus, and are meant purely as foil, not as descriptions of real persons near to or far from the scene of the celebration. The principle holds in *I*. 1 also. νέμει, γελᾷ, and οὐ

---

[113] The scholia paraphrase ἀποταμιευσάμενος, "lock away." To Bury (*ad loc*.), νέμει = "dispense" and ἔνδον νέμει = οὐ νέμει, and Fennell explains, "lords it over." Farnell (*ad loc*.) finds in the word the idea of "shepherding." Rumpel's gloss is "fovet." I suspect that the scholia are right and that νέμει κρυφαῖον = κατακρύψαις ἔχει (*N*. 1.31). νέμει may have the further implication of "enjoy": he is the only one who benefits from his wealth.

[114] ἀλλά (line 90) breaks away from Zeus and turns to Hagesidamos. Lines 90-94 are then foil for the gnomic cap of lines 95-97b and the concrete pronominal caps of lines 97b-100 (objective) and lines 101-110 (subjective). The entire passage carries out the tacit injunction of ἀλλά (line 90) to do justice at long last to the laudandus of the ode.

φράζεται describe a type rather than a real person or personages. To assume a definite reference for these verbs (certain maligners of Herodotos) and for ἄλλοισι (Herodotos) is not only to invent history but to destroy the integrity of the conventions that give the lines their position and force in the ensemble.

It is to be doubted, moreover, that ἄλλοισι refers to people of a different *temper* from the miserly τις—for this too contravenes convention and obstructs communication. ἄλλοισι are rather, as Schmid suggested,[115] those in less favorable circumstances than the miser, who lose the benefit of his wealth when it brings them and their city no glory and deprives them of his munificence on celebratory occasions such as this. Thus the contrast in this sentence is between πλούσιός τις and ἄλλοισι, not between ἄλλοισι and the category of miserly self-preoccupation embraced by the conditional clause and emphasized in ἔνδον.

"Non ita divitibus" is Schmid's gloss, the correctness of which is borne out by all the relevant parallels. We may take first N. 1.31–33b:

οὐκ ἔραμαι πολὺν ἐν μεγάρῳ πλοῦτον κατακρύψαις ἔχειν,
ἀλλ' ἐόντων εὖ τε παθεῖν καὶ ἀκοῦσαι φίλοις ἐξαρκέων.
κοιναὶ γὰρ ἔρχοντ' ἐλπίδες

πολυπόνων ἀνδρῶν. ἐγὼ δ' Ἡρακλέος ἀντέχομαι
33b προφρόνως κτλ.

It will be observed that the gnomic material is foil for the pronominal name cap of lines 33 f., which introduces Herakles as laudandus. From this it is clear that Herakles is a type of εὐεργεσία and that his exploits are a paradigm of Khromios' own liberal pursuits.[116] The first person of ἔραμαι is not, of course, Pindar, but (by a figure called by the scholia, with only slight inaccuracy, "persuasive hortatory soliloquy" [πιθανῶς ὁ θέλει παραινέσαι τῷ Χρομίῳ, ἐφ' ἑαυτοῦ ἐξενήνοχεν]) brings forward the chorus's approval of a principle espoused by Khromios and Herakles. The foil theme that concludes *I.* 1 is here used to effect a transition from the present to the past, from the laudandus to his archetype, from Khromios to Herakles. Here the foil is analogous, whereas in *I.* 1 it is antithetical; yet in both odes it attributes to the laudandus the highest of the agonistic virtues, liberality. What we require is a thematic analysis of the foil in *N.* 1 to determine its relevance to the problem presented by ἄλλοισι in *I.* 1.68.

The point of this theme is always its praise (and encouragement) of

---

[115] His view is reported by Dissen, *ad loc.*
[116] Herakles' adventures are regularly a paradigm of εὐεργεσία. So Theseus at Athens was the type of the εὐεργέτης. Cf. Lys. 33.1 f.

εὐεργεσία. Within the conventions this means praise of wealth and its proper use. The motives regularly employed in the elaboration of this theme are three: (1) εὐεργεσία (good works, liberality, indifference to gain); (2) human expectations (shared humanity, human dependence on God or fate); and (3) enduring fame (occasionally literal immortality). One or more of these themes may be implicit or not fully developed, but the theme as a theme is unmistakable and its use is carefully regulated by convention. While the individual motives that make up the ensemble may appear in isolation anywhere, the composite theme is confined to transitions and conclusions. P. 5.1–22, though very like O. 2.56–105, a genuine version of the theme, are no exception to this rule, seeing that they employ only the first of the three characteristic motives.

Let us take first the motive of εὐεργεσία. In N. 1 this theme is treated first negatively (οὐκ, line 31) and then positively (ἀλλ', line 32): one must not hoard; one must spend. Such a use of polarity, though characteristic (cf. P. 1.90 ff.) in the handling of this motive, is by no means required. In Bacch. 1.159–184, where the theme is introduced by the word [εὐε]ργεσιᾶν in line 157, πλουτεῖν (πλοῦτος, lines 160 f.) is simply contrasted with εὖ ἔρδειν (εὖ ἔρδων, line 163, glossing ἀρετάν in line 160); in O. 2.56–105, πλοῦτος (lines 58/9) is simply contrasted with ἀρεταῖς (lines 58/9); in N. 7.14–20, the sentence σοφοί . . . / . . ., οὐδ' ὑπὸ κέρδει βλάβεν (cf. κέρδεσσ', P. 1.92) is all that is required to commend εὐεργεσία and censure φιλοκέρδεια. In P. 11.50b–58, however, the condemnation of πλοῦτος (μέμφομ' αἶσαν τυραννίδων, line 53 = οὐκ ἔραμαι πλουτεῖν [cf. ἐραίμαν, line 50b]) is followed by praise of ξυναὶ ἀρεταί (line 54 = εὐεργεσίαι).[117]

Certain uses of the motive outside the body of epinikian literature are informative. Thgn. 573 f. reads: εὖ ἔρδων εὖ πάσχε· τί κ' ἄγγελον ἄλλον ἰάλλοις; / τῆς εὐεργεσίης ῥῃδίη ἀγγελίη: "If you wish to be well served, serve others well; issue no other call: benefaction speaks for itself." To be observed here is the coupling of εὖ ἔρδων (= εὐεργετῶν) and its passive, εὖ πάσχε. This formulaic coupling is frequent in Pindar. We may compare P. 8.6 (τὸ μαλθακόν = εὖ), P. 2.24, P. 5.44, I. 1.53. The two members of the doublet appear in N. 1.32 as εὖ τε παθεῖν καὶ ἀκοῦσαι and φίλοις ἐξαρκέων. The former phrase exhausts the possibilities of the passive—being honorably treated in word as well as in deed—thus broaching the theme of (enduring) fame; the latter forbears to add εὖ εἰπεῖν to εὖ ἔρδειν,

---

[117] For the form of such disclaimers preceded or followed by the expression of the speaker's προαίρεσις, cf. Thgn. 885 f., εἰρήνη καὶ πλοῦτος ἔχοι πόλιν, ὄφρα μετ' ἄλλων / κωμάζοιμι· κακοῦ δ' οὐκ ἔραμαι πολέμου; 1155 f., οὐκ ἔραμαι πλουτεῖν οὐδ' εὔχομαι, ἀλλά μοι εἴη / ζῆν ἀπὸ τῶν ὀλίγων μηδὲν ἔχοντι κακόν; 1191 f., οὐκ ἔραμαι κλισμῷ βασιληΐῳ ἐγκατακεῖσθαι / τεθνεώς, ἀλλά τί μοι ζῶντι γένοιτ' ἀγαθόν; N. 8.35–39, frag. 134. Cf. also Anacr. 8 D², Arch. 60 D³, 22 D³ (incomplete). This form is implicit in numerous Pindaric contexts. Cf., e.g., N. 8.4 f., N. 3.29 f.

and employs the formulaic φίλοις ἐξαρκέων (cf. ἀρκέων φίλοις, Pa. 2.24) to encompass the idea of εὐεργεσία. Germane to the passage, then, is its insistence on harmony between self-interest and altruism. One serves one's own best interests by serving those of others. This balanced altruism is the point of ἀρεταῖς in O. 2.58/9 (cf. ἀρετᾷ . . . καθαρᾷ in P. 5.2), of εὖ ἔρδων θεούς in Bacch. 1.163, of μὴ κάμνε λίαν δαπάναις in P. 1.90 (where εὖ ἀκοῦσαι is the stake), of οὐδ' ὑπὸ κέρδει βλάβεν in N. 7.18, and of ξυναῖσι... ἀρεταῖς (see pp. 64 f.) in P. 11.54 (where εὐώνυμον χάριν, line 58 [= εὖ ἀκοῦσαι] is the stake).[118] The implication is that balanced altruism is the point also (by the principle of contrast) of ἄλλοισι δ' ἐμπίπτων γελᾷ in I. 1.68.

This implication is strengthened by the fact that all of these passages (O. 2.56–110,[119] Bacch. 1.159–184, P. 1.86–100b, N. 7.11–20, P. 11.50b–64) share the remaining two motives that constitute the theme we are examining. The second of the three motives is concerned with human expectations. In its most incisive form the motive insists that with respect to ἐλπίδες all men are equal. The point of this traditional gnome may be either that death is no respecter of persons or that the hopes of rich and poor, if quantitatively different, are qualitatively the same. Thus Bacch. 1.172 ff. declares: ἴσον ὅ τ' ἀφνεὸς ἱ- / μείρει μεγάλων ὅ τε μείων / παυροτέρων, while in N. 7.19 f. the thought takes the other form: ἀφνεὸς πενιχρός τε θανάτου πέρας / ἅμα νέονται. The formal difference between the passages is unimportant, since in both, the shared humanity of rich and poor becomes the ground for the preferment of liberality to close-fistedness. In N. 1.32 f. the thought is stated in a general form that accommodates both ideas: κοιναὶ γὰρ ἔρχοντ' ἐλπίδες // πολυπόνων ἀνδρῶν: because bad times may come upon all men, the wise man will turn his own good fortune to the service of other men; because all men must equally entertain the expectation of death, the wise man will turn his own good fortune to the service of others with an eye to achieving enduring fame. Here it is the paradigm (lines 33–72) that makes clear, at its close (lines 69–72), that in ἐλπίδες the poet is thinking of that life after death achieved in good works. In the remaining passages the motive of shared humanity is implicit in their common use of "death" to broach the third motive—that of enduring fame. As fame (or life) after death is the concern of N. 7.11–20, of Bacch. 1.178–184, and (implicitly) of N. 1.32–72, so is it

---

[118] Topical considerations suggest that the proper reading in line 55 is ἄτᾳ· τίς κτλ. and that in the corrupt line 57 the first person singular of the future indicative is required, e.g., μέλανα δ' ἂν' ἐσχατιάν / καλλίονα θάνατον ⟨σχήσω⟩, γλυκυτάτᾳ γενεᾷ κτλ. This brings the passage into line with its congeners in both sense and form.

[119] On this passage, see n. 63.

of O. 2.62–91 (note particularly οἶδεν τὸ μέλλον / ὅτι θανόντων κτλ. in lines 62 f., with which cf. μέλλοντα . . . / ἔμαθον in N. 7.17 f.), of P. 11.56–64, and of P. 1.92–100b. In all of these passages, moreover, the theme of expectation, hope, ambition, longing underlies the whole. We may observe μέριμναν in O. 2.60; ἐλπίδι and μέριμναι in Bacch. 1.164, 179; ἐραίμαν, μαιόμενος, τέταμαι in P. 11.50b, 51, 54; φιλεῖς in P. 1.90.[120] In passages that exhibit this theme we find the three motives interlocked: a man soon finds that the human condition limits his hopes, and seeks the most he can have in a nice balance between εὖ ἔρδειν and εὖ πάσχειν that brings him the admiration of his fellows both in life and in death.

The thematic and motivational grammar of passages cast in the same conventional mold as I. 1.67 f. makes it extremely difficult to interpret ἄλλοισι in I. 1.68 in the accepted manner. ἄλλοισι ought to be οἱ πενιχροί— the poverty or indifferent circumstances traditionally subject to the mockery of the rich, but not of those lordly rich who understand the vanity of human pretensions in the face of death and the fickleness of fortune. Fame is the end and wealth the mere means.

Mockery of those in evil circumstances is, as I have suggested, a frequent motive in the tradition from which choral lyric borrows its gnomic foils. We may compare the warning attributed to Khilon: ἀτυχοῦντι μὴ ἐπιγέλα· κοινὴ γὰρ ἡ τύχη (Stob. 4.48.11 [cf. Democr. frag. 107a D-K⁶]). N. 1.31 ff. is but a poetic form of this gnome—a fact which strongly suggests that ἄλλοισι δ' ἐμπίπτων γελᾷ in I. 1.68 refers to mockery of those in evil circumstances rather than to the niggard's mockery of Herodotos. At E. Cyc. 687 we find οἴμοι γελῶμαι· κερτομεῖτέ μ' ἐν κακοῖς, and at Arch. frag. 65 D³, οὐ γὰρ ἐσθλὰ κατθανοῦσι κερτομεῖν ἐπ' ἀνδράσιν (cf. χ 412). In the same vein Thgn. 1217 f. (cf. also 1041 f.) enjoins, μήποτε πὰρ κλαίοντα καθεζόμενοι γελάσωμεν / τοῖς αὐτῶν ἀγαθοῖς, Κύρν', ἐπιτερπόμενοι. Here the second line provides, in the joys of self-interest, a thematic equivalent for ἔνδον νέμει πλοῦτον in I. 1.67 and ἐν μεγάρῳ πλοῦτον κατακρύψαις ἔχειν in N. 1.31. Indeed, here is the motive in the full form exhibited in I. 1.67: "Do not enjoy yourself at the expense *of others*." In further examples of the use of this motive, the poor are often the objects of mockery, and the rich the mockers. In Aes. Prov. 140 (Perry), ὁ καεὶς ἔζησεν καὶ ὁ γελῶν ἀπέθανεν, ὁ καεὶς is glossed as ὁ πένης, and ὁ γελῶν as ὁ πλούσιος. Krantor *apud* Stob. 4.32.33 (Wachs.-Hense) complains, καὶ γὰρ ἂν φύσει σπουδαῖος ᾖς, πένης δέ,

---

[120] These words (see n. 117) belong to a very large group of words and expressions used to introduce general or specific human προαιρέσεις. Usually comparison is explicitly involved. Cf. θηρεύων (P. 3.23), μαστεύεμεν (P. 3.59), σπεῦδε (P. 3.62), ἀσκήσω (P. 3.109), μάτευε (I. 5.16), διώκων (I. 7.40), παπταίνει (I. 7.44, P. 3.22), ἐρευνασάτω (frag. 120.2), and many others.

καταγελως ἔσῃ. Theognis (155-158) grounds the warning μήποτέ τοι πενίην θυμοφθόρον ἀνδρὶ χολωθεὶς / μηδ' ἀχρημοσύνην οὐλομένην πρόφερε on the vanity of human expectations, and Hes. Op. 717 f. exhibits the same use of the motive: μηδέποτ' οὐλομένην πενίην θυμοφθόρον ἀνδρὶ / τέτλαθ' ὀνειδίζειν, μακάρων δόσιν αἰὲν ἐόντων (cf. χ 411 ff.). God gives and God takes away (the theme of human expectations). This, we remember, is the point of N. 1.42 f., κοιναὶ γὰρ ἔρχοντ' ἐλπίδες / πολυπόνων ἀνδρῶν, and of Khilon's κοινὴ γὰρ ἡ τύχη.[121] The rich man who possesses also understanding sympathizes with others in the knowledge that what he has is the gift of powers who can take it away, and lays out his wealth in good works. Thus Hieron is praised for his εὐεργεσίαι in a straightforward use of the liberality motive in Bacch. 3.10-21:

> 10 ἁ τρισευδαίμ[ων ἀνήρ,
> ὃς παρὰ Ζηνὸς λαχὼν
> πλείσταρχον Ἑλλάνων γέρας
> οἶδε πυργωθέντα πλοῦτον μὴ μελαμ-
> φαρέϊ κρύπτειν σκότωι.
>
> 15 βρύει μὲν ἱερὰ βουθύτοις ἑορταῖς,
> βρύουσι φιλοξενίας ἀγυιαί·
> λάμπει δ' ὑπὸ μαρμαρυγαῖς ὁ χρυσός,
> ὑψιδαιδάλτων τριπόδων σταθέντων
>
> πάροιθε ναοῦ, τόθι μέγιστον ἄλσος
> 20 Φοίβου παρὰ Κασταλίας ῥεέθροις
> Δελφοὶ διέπουσι.

Hieron (like Herodotos) *does not hoard his wealth in dark coffers*, but brings it (and his fame) to light *in benefactions*, such as ἑορταί and φιλοξενίαι, which bring gladness to *others*, and in dedications to Apollo. These φιλοξενίαι point, among other things, to victory celebrations as a form of public benefaction,[122] and this form of service is in part what Pindar has in mind in N. 1.31 ff. (cf. 19-24) and I. 1.67 f. Finally, returning at length to ἄλλοισι in I. 1.68, we may recall the language in which

---
[121] For the pattern "Be generous (Don't mock); we are all human and subject to the whims of fate," cf. Men. frag. 673K, E. frag. 130 N², 406 N², Andr. 462 f., Alexis frag. 150K, S. *Aj.* 265 ff., Isoc. 1.29, Democr. frag. 107a, 293D.-K.⁶, Demosth. 18.252, *P.* 2.49-53.

[122] Cf. frag. 106.23 (προξενίαισι), N. 9.2, O. 4.4/5, O. 9.89, N. 7.61, 65. In all these passages ξενία points to the liberality of the laudandus in appointing the present celebration with its throng of guests. The notion that προξενίᾳ in O. 9.89 and N. 7.65 proclaims Pindar a political πρόξενος of Opous and Aigina (or Epeiros) is false.

Theron εὐεργέτης is praised in O. 2.101–110 (I omit the first part of the *praeteritio* of lines 105–110) :[123]

αὐδάσομαι ἐνόρκιον λόγον ἀλαθεῖ νόῳ,
102/3   τεκεῖν μή τιν' ἑκατόν γε ἐτέων πόλιν φίλοις
        ἄνδρα μᾶλλον
        εὐεργέταν πραπίσιν ἀφθονέστερόν τε χέρα

105   Θήρωνος. . . .
        . . . .
        . . . .
        . . . ἐπεὶ ψάμμος ἀριθμὸν περιπέφευγεν,
        καὶ κεῖνος ὅσα χάρματ' ἄλλοις ἔθηκεν,
110   τίς ἂν φράσαι δύναιτο;

ὅσα χάρματ' ἄλλοις ἔθηκεν: that is the measure of εὐεργεσία and the point of the warning in the words ἄλλοισι δ' ἐμπίπτων γελᾷ. Herodotos may not and will not keep his wealth to himself, taking pleasure in the lot of others less fortunate than himself, but will labor and spend to achieve a fame on men's lips that will live after him.[124]

Thus the effect of the concluding foil, in which all the terms are generic, describing a type antithetical to the laudandus, is to set off the central figure of Herodotos against the dark foil of a spiritless ease loathsome to the heroic temper. It is against such foil that Pelops makes his choice in O. 1.81–85:

        ὁ μέγας δὲ κίνδυνος ἄναλκιν οὐ φῶτα λαμβάνει.
        θανεῖν δ' οἷσιν ἀνάγκα,
82b   τά κέ τις ἀνώνυμον
        γῆρας ἐν σκότῳ καθήμενος ἕψοι μάταν,
        ἁπάντων καλῶν ἄμμορος; ἀλλ' ἐμοὶ μὲν οὗτος ἄεθλος
85   ὑποκείσεται· τὺ δὲ πρᾶξιν φίλαν δίδοι.

---

[123] The prose sense of the *praeteritio* is: "Having declared Theron the greatest benefactor of mankind produced in the last hundred years, I must stop short of listing his benefactions. For in praising there comes a point when continued eulogies, far from enhancing the reputation of the laudandus, actually detract from it. To attempt to enumerate Theron's benefactions here would imply that the number of them is finite, whereas in actual fact they outnumber the sands of the sea." Cf. O. 13.43–44b, where the laudator's quarrel with other laudatores is that they attempt to number the numberless.

[124] For an excellent parallel, free from the allusive stylization of the Pindaric examples, see Theocr. 16.22–33. Note also the "mockery" quoted in lines 16–21. Finally, on the purpose behind the theme employed in I. 1.67 f., cf. Aristotle's discussion of topics for praise at *Rhet.* 1367a: (καλὰ) καὶ ὅσα τεθνεῶτι ἐνδέχεται ὑπάρχειν μᾶλλον ἢ ζῶντι· τὸ γὰρ αὑτοῦ ἕνεκα μᾶλλον ἔχει τὰ ζῶντι. καὶ ὅσα ἔργα τῶν ἄλλων ἕνεκα· ἧττον γὰρ αὑτοῦ. καὶ ὅσαι εὐπραγίαι περὶ ἄλλους ἀλλὰ μὴ περὶ αὑτόν, καὶ περὶ τοὺς εὖ ποιήσαντας· δίκαιον γάρ. καὶ τὰ εὐεργετήματα· οὐ γὰρ εἰς αὑτόν. The motive of kindness to *others* is so basic to the topic that we cannot spare it in I. 1.68.

Here again humanity's common end in death becomes the ground for preferring ἀρετά (εὖ ἔρδειν) to the easy enjoyment of life.[125] In the pronominal cap (ἐμοί, with ἀλλά to dismiss the foil) Pelops commits himself to the kind of heroic undertaking (ὑποκείσεται) to which the laudator commits Herodotos at the close of I. 1. Such too was Akhilleus' choice.

Thus the τις of I. 1.67 joins the other foil figures of the ode, all of which, as they emerge into the foreground and recede again into the background, add in their turn to the impression of Herodotos' greatness. The closing reminder of humanity's common end in death greatly enlarges the dimensions of the whole. Other odes, too (cf. P. 1, N. 10, N. 1, I. 7), turn in conclusion to the inevitability of death in order to define and illumine the essence of ἀρετά. The least stylized and allusive of such conclusions is perhaps Bacch. 1.178–184:

>   ὄντινα κουφόταται
>   θυμὸν δονέουσι μέριμναι,
> 180 ὅσσον ἂν ζώηι λάχε τόνδε χρόνον τι-
>   μάν. ἀρετὰ δ' ἐπίμοχθος
>   μέν, τ]ελευταθεῖσα δ' ὀρθῶς
>   ἀνδρὶ κ]αὶ εὖτε θάνηι λεί-
>   π[ει πολυ]ζήλωτον εὐκλείας ἄ[γαλ]μα.

The preeminently praiseworthy actions are those which, as Aristotle says (Rhet. 1367a), "it is possible for a man to possess after death rather than during his lifetime, for the latter involve more selfishness."

In conclusion, I should like to stress two points: first, that the ode is a perfect unity, that its linear development from start to finish is perfectly lucid, and that the transitions from topic to topic are handled with superb tact; and second, that to follow the movement of the ode is not to follow the development of a thought that has a beginning, a middle, and an end, but to pursue the fulfillment of a single purpose through a complex orchestration of motives and themes that conduce to one end: the glorification, within the considerations of ethical, religious, social, and literary propriety, of Herodotos of Thebes, victor in the chariot race at the Isthmos. If unity means "oneness," the ode is a unity. There is never loss of control, and apparent irrelevancy (e.g., lines 12 f.) is only comparative and is deliberately contrived in the interest of variety and as foil for a point of commanding interest. In the determination of sense and effect as they subserve the harmony of the whole,

---

[125] Pelops is here a paradigm of Hieron εὐεργέτης. The method of such comparisons is included by rhetorical theorists under the means of "amplification" (αὔξησις). Cf. Arist. Rhet. 1368a. On the choice, cf. Plu. 2.32F f., where Akhilleus' choice is contrasted with that of the man who διερρύηκεν ὑπὸ πλούτου καὶ μαλακίας.

convention rules. Language which admits, on the assumption of its uniqueness, a wide variety of interpretations, becomes, when the conventional elements have been isolated and identified, unambiguous, or ambiguous only in a controlled sense.

If my analysis is correct, it seems apparent that in this genre the choice involved in composition is mainly a choice of formulae, motives, themes, topics, and set sequences of these that have, by convention, meanings not always easily perceived from the surface denotations of the words themselves. And if I am right to any appreciable degree, then the methods employed in studying the odes have been wrong and we must start anew, seeking through careful analysis of individual odes the thematic and motivational grammar of choral composition. The study of Pindar must become a study of genre. No longer can we view the odes as the production of an errant genius whose personal interests cause him to violate the ordinary canons of sense and relevance.

It is true that the ode examined here is not one of the "problem" odes. Yet I believe that those too will yield to the same techniques of interpretation, and in subsequent essays to be published in this series I shall apply the principles established in this and the previous essay to the examination of odes celebrated for their obscurity or willful irrelevance, in the hope of arriving at a more satisfying conception of the technique of choral song.

SELECTED WORKS
CITED IN STUDIA PINDARICA

Billson, C. J. Πινδάρου ἐπινίκια, *Pindar's Odes of Victory: The Nemean and Isthmian Odes*. Oxford: Oxford University Press, 1930.
Bury, J. B. *The Isthmian Odes of Pindar*. London and New York: Macmillan, 1892.
Dissen, L. *Pindari carmina quae supersunt*. Gotha: Henning, 1830.
Dornseiff, F. *Pindars Stil*. Berlin: Weidmann, 1921.
Drachmann, A. B. *Moderne Pindarfortolkning*. Copenhagen: Forlagt af Universitets Boghandler, 1891.
Farnell, L. R. *The Works of Pindar*. London: Macmillan, 1930.
Fennell, C. A. M. *Pindar, The Olympian and Pythian Odes*. Cambridge: Cambridge University Press, 1879.
Fraenkel, E. *Aeschylus, Agamemnon*. Oxford: Oxford University Press, 1950.
Fraenkel, H. *Dichtung und Philosophie des frühen Griechentums*. Philological Monographs of the American Philological Association, 13. New York: American Philological Association, 1951.
Gasper, C. *Essai de chronologie pindarique*. Brussels: H. Lamertin, 1900.
Gildersleeve, B. *Pindar, The Olympian and Pythian Odes*. New York: Harper & Brothers, 1890.
Kazantzakis, N. *The Odyssey: A Modern Sequel*. Translated into English by Kimon Friar. New York: Simon and Schuster, 1958.
Keyssner, K. *Gottesvorstellung und Lebensauffassung im griechischen Hymnus*. Würzburger Studien zur Altertumswissenschaft, 2. Stuttgart: Kohlhammer, 1932.
Kröhling, W. *Die Priamel (Beispielreihung) als Stilmittel in der griechisch-römischen Dichtung*. Greifswalder Beiträge für Literatur- und Stilforschung, 10. Greifswald: Julius Abel, 1935.
Lattimore, R. *The Odes of Pindar*. Chicago: University of Chicago Press, 1947.
Mezger, F. *Pindars Siegeslieder*. Leipzig: Teubner, 1880.
Norwood, G., *Pindar*. Sather Classical Lectures, 19. Berkeley and Los Angeles: University of California Press, 1945.
Perrotta, G. *Safo e Pindaro*. Bari: G. Laterza, 1935.
Puech, A. *Pindare, Olympiques*. Coll. G. Budé. Paris: Les Belles Lettres, 1949.
Riemschneider-Horner, M. "Die Raumanschauung bei Pindar." *Zeitschrift für Aesthetik und allgemeine Kunstwissenschaft* (Stuttgart) 36 (1942) 104–109.

Rose, H. J. "Iolaos and the Ninth Pythian Ode." *Classical Quarterly* 25 (1931) 156–161.

Rumpel, I. *Lexicon Pindaricum*. Leipzig: Teubner, 1883.

Sandys, J. *The Odes of Pindar*. Cambridge, Mass.: Harvard; London: Heinemann, 1946.

Schadewaldt, W. "Der Aufbau des pindarischen Epinikion." *Schriften der Königsberger gelehrten Gesellschaft, Geisteswissenschaftliche Klasse*, 5 (1928) 2: 259–343.

Schroeder, O. *Pindari carmina*. Leipzig: Teubner, 1900.

———. *Pindars Pythien*. Berlin and Leipzig: Teubner, 1922.

Snell, B. *Pindarus*. Leipzig: Teubner, 1949.

Turyn, A. *Pindari carmina*. Krakow: Academia Polona Litterarum et Scientiarum, 1948.

Wolde, L. *Pindar: Die Dichtungen und Fragmente*. Leipzig: Dieterich, 1942.

INDEX LOCORUM

Prepared by Thomas R. Walsh,
with the assistance of Andrew Miller and Donald Mastronarde

AELIUS ARISTIDES	περὶ τοῦ παραφθέγματος	56	30, 30n73
AESOP	*Proverbia*	140	88
ANACREON		8 D²	86n117
ANTAGORAS		1 (Powell)	45n32
ARCHILOCHUS		22 D³	86n117
		60 D²	86n117
		60 D³	86n117
		65 D³	88
ALEXIS		150 K	89n121
ARIPHRON		1 D².3–14	45n32
		1 D².7	56n50
		1 D².9	56n50
ARISTONOUS		1.45–48 (Powell)	78n102
ARISTOTLE	*Rhetoric*	1365a	50n40
		1367a	90n124, 91
		1368a	91n125
		1414b	43n26

[95]

BACCHYLIDES *Epinikoi*

1.157	86
1.159 f.	17
1.159–184	86, 87
1.160	86
1.160 f.	86
1.163	86, 87
1.164	88
1.172 ff.	24n56, 87
1.178–184	87, 91
3.5	46
3.10–21	89
3.57 f.	3
3.63 ff.	17
3.63–66	25, 25n60
3.63–71	25, 59n60
3.67–71	59n56
3.69	25
3.70	25n61
3.92 f.	17
3.94–98	58n54
3.96	61n69
4.4	46
5.1–6	26
5.9–36	62
5.16–30	32n78
5.16–35	15
5.16–36	82
5.31	64
5.31 f.	15
5.40	17
5.42	40n18
5.42 f.	17
5.43	59n60
5.51	26
5.187	61n69
5.187–190	58n54, 59n55, 59n59
5.187–197	60
5.191–194	60, 61
5.195	60n66, 60–61, 62, 64
8.19 f.	17
8.19 ff.	58n54
8.20 f.	61n69
8.22	17, 59n60
8.22 ff.	17

Index Locorum

BACCHYLIDES	*Epinikoi*	(*Continued*)		
			9.47	15, 62
			9.47 f.	64
			9.47–57	62
			9.85	61n69
			10.12 f.	65
			10.35–56	11n34
			10.36	15
			10.38	15
			11.12 f.	2
			11.22	18n42
			11.22–30	17
			13.193	18n42
			13.202	61n69
			14.1–11	15
			14.1–18	37
			14.6 f.	37
			14.8	37n7, 15
			14.8 f.	17, 37
			14.8 ff.	16
			14.12–20	16
			14.19 f.	5n18
			14.20	37
	Dithyramboi		17.130 ff.	78n102
			19.1	15, 64
	fragments			
		Paianes	4.39 f.	2
		Hyporchemata	14	60n66
		Enkomia	20C.19 f.	15, 16
			20C.19–24	15–17
			20C.20	16, 30
			20C.21	17, 59n60
CALLIMACHUS	*Hymns*		2.105–113	76
CHARES			2 N^2	76

CHILON. *See* STOBAEUS 4.48.11

CRANTOR. *See* STOBAEUS 4.32.33

Index Locorum

DEMOCRITUS		68 B 107a D.–K.⁶	88, 89n121
		68 B 293 D.–K.⁶	89n121
DEMOSTHENES	*Orations*	18.252	89n121
		19.209	61n69
		60.1	58n54
		60.6	19n45, 40n14
		60.12	63
		60.13 f.	40n14
		61.7	58n54
		61.27	18–19
		61.33	40n14
	Epistles	2.13–16	45n32
DIOGENES APOLLONIATES		64 B 1 D.–K.⁶	55n49
EURIPIDES	*Andromache*	462 f.	89n121
	Bacchae	66 f.	64
		893	64
	Cyclops	687	88
	Hippolytus	469 f.	72n92
	Iphigenia in Aulis	979 f.	9, 76
	fragments	130 N²	89n121
		237 N².3	52n44
		406 N²	89n121
		745 N².2 f.	52n44
HERODOTUS		9.69	48
HESIOD	*Works and Days*	717 f.	89
HIMERIUS	*Orations*	38.9	40n15
HOMER	*Odyssey*	14.228	7

Index Locorum

HOMER *Odyssey*	*(Continued)*	19.303	17n41
		22.411 ff.	89
		22.412	88
HOMERIC HYMNS		2.2	80n107
		2.494	78
		3.2	80n107
		3.19	45
		3.207	45
		4.3	80n107
		5.2	80n107
		6.1 f.	46
		6.2	80n107
		6.19	46
		6.19 f.	79
		7.1 f.	46
		7.58	46
		9.7	78
		9.7	78n102
		10.1	46
		10.4	46
		10.4 f.	79
		10.5	78
		11.5	79
		13.3	79
		16.5	78, 78n102
		19.48	78n102
		24.4 ff.	78
		25.6	78
HORACE	*Carmina*	1.1	11n11
		2.10	62n70, 62n72
		4.3	11n11
HYPERIDES	*Orations*	6.4	19n45
ISOCRATES	*Orations*	1.29	89n121
		2.9	19n45
		9.1–4	64
		9.34	18–19
		9.69 f.	45n32
INSCRIPTIONES GRAECAE		II/III^2 11169	63, 64
		V.i.213	45n31

Index Locorum

LYRICA ADESPOTA	34.8–11 (Powell)	45n32
	84 Bgk.⁴	45n32
LYSIAS	2.1 f.	58n54
	2.2	14, 60n65
MENANDER	673 K	89n121
ORPHIC HYMNS	1.10	80n108
	3.10	80n107
	6.10	80n108
	12.11	80n107
	13.8	80n107
	14.2	80n107
	17.7	80n107
	18.4	80n107
	18.6	80n107
	18.8	80n107
	18.11	80n107
	18.19	80n108
	27.14	80n108
	29.2	80n108
	31.6	78n102
PHOCYLIDES	9 D³	2n9, 66–67
PINDAR *Isthmian Odes*	1.1–3	36
	1.1–4	32n78
	1.1–13	36–44
	1.5	11n33
	1.8	36n6
	1.13	36n6
	1.14	7n25, 36, 39
	1.14–32	44–47
	1.16	36n6
	1.19 ff.	36n6, 44n28
	1.21 f.	56n51
	1.23 f.	56n51
	1.24	57n52
	1.24–27	56
	1.26	57, 57n52
	1.26 f.	64
	1.28	57
	1.31	57

PINDAR *Isthmian Odes* (*Continued*)

1.32–40	47–53
1.33–50	56n51
1.41–63	53–76
1.47–51	7, 10, 11n34
1.50	32n78
1.50 f.	7
1.53–56	74n100
1.56	74
1.57	74n100
1.59 ff.	74
1.64–68	76–92
1.67 f.	28
2.18	76
2.20	18n42
2.30 f.	26n62
2.30 ff.	26
2.33	7n23, 15, 17, 62, 64
2.33–37	61–62
2.33–42	15n39, 60n65
2.33–46	58, 59, 61
2.35 ff.	58n54, 62
2.39	25n60
2.39–42	62
2.41 f.	15n39, 24n56
2.43–46	78, 78n103
2.44	61n68, 74
3.1	58
3.1 f.	67
3.1 ff.	45n32, 55–56, 59n59
3.1–3	67
3.2	67
3.3	57n52
3.5	56n50
3.7 f.	11
3.9 f.	26n62
3.10	2n8
3.15	17n41
3.18	28
conclusion	28
4.1	7n23, 15
4.1 f.	64
4.1 ff.	55–56, 60n64, 62, 64
4.1–6	25

PINDAR *Isthmian Odes* (*Continued*)

4.1–19	14–15
4.2	7n23, 43n25
4.2 f.	14–15
4.4–15	14, 25
4.7 ff.	25
4.9	14
4.9–13	25, 44
4.10	61n66
4.13	14, 59n55
4.14	25
4.15	14
4.16–19	49, 51, 52
4.17b	51
4.18	14, 51
4.24 f.	58
4.25 ff.	14n38
4.28 ff.	14n38
4.30	26n62
4.31	59n55
4.37–42	14n38
4.38	65
4.41 f.	15n39, 24n56
4.43	14n38
4.45–48	29
4.48	53
4.72	21, 23, 72n94
5.1–11	11n34, 36
5.5	36n6
5.5 f.	24n56
5.12	53
5.13–18	44n28, 56, 72n93
5.15	24, 58
5.16	88n120
5.17	26n62
5.23	27n65
5.23 f.	23n53
5.24	59
5.24–32	56–58
5.26	57n52, 59
5.27	57n52, 58, 63
5.28	57n52, 63, 64, 67
5.29	67
5.31	57n52, 63
5.51	73n97
5.51 ff.	3n11
5.51–57	73
5.51–61	6n21, 13n36

PINDAR *Isthmian Odes* (*Continued*)

5.51–65	9
5.54	61n66
5.57	13n37, 74
5.58	7n23
5.70	82
6.6	80
6.9	57
6.9 f.	57n52, 63
6.9–11b	24n56, 44n28, 56, 59n59, 72n93
6.10	57n52, 58
6.12	57n52, 62
6.12 ff.	44n28
6.15	70, 70n88
6.18	11
6.19	23n53
6.20/1	15, 64
6.20/1 ff.	60n64, 60n65
6.20/1–26	15n39, 62
6.22–26	60n65
6.53	73, 76
6.53–56	6n21, 9
6.57	43n25
6.58	26n62
6.59	82
6.65	65
7.1	36–37
7.1 ff.	6, 8, 13
7.1–22b	6, 36, 45, 45n22
7.2	11n33
7.16 ff.	8, 13
7.16–19	38n11
7.16–21	10n29
7.20	5n18, 74
7.20–39	80
7.21	43n25
7.23–38	48–49, 51, 52
7.24	65
7.27	17n41
7.27–30	59n60
7.37	36n3, 49
7.38 f.	51
7.39–51	80
7.40	88n120
7.44	88n120
conclusion	77, 91

PINDAR *Isthmian Odes* (*Continued*)

	8.13	5n18, 73
	8.13b	11n33
	8.63	65
	8.69	64
	8.70	26n62
Nemean Odes	1.13–18	60n63
	1.18	4n12, 58n54, 61n66, 73
	1.19	27n67
	1.19–24	89
	1.25	15, 16, 37n7
	1.25–30	15, 59, 62
	1.29 f.	59n56
	1.31	84n113, 86, 88
	1.31 ff.	88, 89
	1.31–33b	85
	1.32	7n23, 86
	1.32 f.	87
	1.32–72	87
	1.33	36n2
	1.33 f.	85
	1.33 ff.	56n51
	1.34	52n45
	1.42 f.	89
	1.53 f.	28, 53
	1.61–72	87
	conclusion	91
	2.6	80
	2.19–25	72
	3.1–5	27
	3.6	42
	3.6 f.	10
	3.6 ff.	11
	3.10	74
	3.12	64
	3.18–25	44, 59n55, 59n58, 59n61
	3.19	59n55, 72n94
	3.19 f.	44
	3.20	59n55
	3.21–24	43n26
	3.21–25	44
	3.23	72n92
	3.25 f.	44n27
	3.28	61n69
	3.29 f.	86n117

Index Locorum

PINDAR *Nemean Odes* (*Continued*)

3.30	73
3.38–40	15
3.40	15
3.48	27
3.63	65
3.64	73
3.67	26n62
3.74	21, 27n66
3.77 f.	32n78
3.77–80	32
4.1	2, 2n9
4.1–6	10n30
4.1–8	2, 11n35, 22, 67
4.3	2
4.11	80
4.11 ff.	25n58
4.20–79	27n64
4.25 ff.	3n11
4.33	7n23, 11, 76
4.33 f.	42
4.33 ff.	3n11, 69n82, 71, 73
4.33–43	13n36
4.33–44	32, 42
4.33–46	8, 10
4.34	42
4.35	42
4.36	13n37, 42
4.36–43	3n11
4.37	42
4.39	4n11
4.41 f.	16
4.41 ff.	3n11
4.43 ff.	4n11
4.68	3n11
4.69–72	69n82, 71
4.69–75	8, 54, 58
4.72	76
4.74	27n65
4.82–85	60n66
4.82–90	10n30
4.91–96	7
4.93	7
4.93–96	13n36, 59n56, 59n58
5.2 f.	27
5.14	74n100

PINDAR *Nemean Odes* (*Continued*)

5.14–21	10
5.16	11n33, 21, 73n97, 76
5.16 ff.	73
5.17	61n69
5.18	11n33, 74, 76
5.19	11n33, 67
5.19 ff.	64
5.40 f.	15
5.48	17n41
5.50	59n55
5.50 f.	58n54, 59n58
5.50–54	62
6.1	32n78, 39
6.1 f.	38
6.1–7	37–39
6.2 ff.	38
6.4–7	38
6.6 f.	36n5
6.8	5n18, 38
6.9	7n23
6.22	18n42
6.26	17, 59n60
6.27 ff.	58n54
6.33 f.	64
6.40 ff.	71
6.47	15, 19, 64
6.47 ff.	56n51
6.47–55	10, 15n39, 19, 59, 60n65, 62
6.47–65	10
6.48	43n25
6.50	82
6.50–55	62
6.55 ff.	19
6.55–59a	19
6.57	73
6.57–69	19
6.58	11n33, 26
6.59	56n51
6.59–63	7n25
6.63	71
7.1	37
7.1–8	36
7.7–10	26
7.11–20	87
7.14–20	86

Index Locorum

PINDAR *Nemean Odes* (Continued)

7.17 f.	88
7.17–30	31n75
7.17–34	10
7.18	87
7.19	7n23, 10, 24n56
7.19 f.	87
7.20	10
7.20 f.	7n25
7.22	82
7.24–30	10
7.25	61n69
7.30	7n23, 10
7.30 ff.	10
7.30–34	10
7.32	10n29
7.33 f.	10
7.34	10n29
7.48	61n69
7.49	58n54, 61n66
7.49 f.	17
7.50–53	10
7.52	73, 74n100
7.54–63	10
7.55	7n23
7.60	52n44
7.61	89n122
7.63	10, 11, 58n54, 59, 67n80
7.64	40
7.64 f.	40n15
7.64–69	4n13
7.65	60n66, 89n122
7.65 ff.	58n54
7.77	64, 74
7.82 ff.	27n68
7.83	23n53
7.86–97	70
7.98–104	78, 78n103
7.102	4n14, 22n49, 78n103
7.102 ff.	17, 58n54
7.102–105	4n13
7.104 f.	28
7.107 ff.	17
conclusion	28, 77
8.1–5	36
8.2	80n107

PINDAR *Nemean Odes* *(Continued)*

8.3	36n6
8.4 f.	36n6, 86n117
8.6–12	36n6
8.8	24n55
8.13–16	36n6
8.18 f.	43n26
8.19–22	10, 40
8.19–34	31n75
8.19–39	10, 32
8.20	40n16
8.20 ff.	10, 40n16
8.23–24	40, 40n16
8.23–34	10
8.30–34	31n75
8.35–37	40n16
8.35–39	10, 31n75, 86n117
8.37–40	40n16
8.40–44	40n16
8.42 ff.	60n66
8.44	40n16
8.44–48	10
8.48 f.	59
9.1	22
9.1 f.	23–24
9.1 ff.	27–28
9.1–3	22
9.2	89n122
9.3	6n3, 22
9.7	61n68, 74
9.8	32n77, 36n3, 74
9.28–32	83
9.33	24n54, 40
9.45	17n41
9.45 ff.	56, 59n60, 59n61
9.46	58
9.46 f.	44, 57n52, 72n93
9.47	59n55
9.48	23
9.48 f.	2
9.48 ff.	11n35
9.48–55	10, 22–23
9.49	23, 23n51
9.49–53	23

Index Locorum 109

PINDAR Nemean Odes	(Continued)		
		9.50	23, 74
		9.53 ff.	23
		conclusion	77
		10.1 ff.	13–14
		10.1–18	75
		10.1–24	7
		10.2 f.	13
		10.4	13, 71
		10.5	13, 71
		10.19	73, 76
		10.19 f.	58n54, 69n82, 75, 76
		10.19–22	75
		10.20	26n62, 40, 73
		10.21	13n37, 74
		10.25	79
		10.26	79
		10.29–33	18n43, 79, 80
		10.33–36	79
		10.37–48	79n105
		10.39 ff.	60n66
		10.41	46n35
		10.45–47	13
		10.45–48	41
		10.46	42
		10.49–54	3n10, 14
		10.72	28, 53
		conclusion	91
		11.1	80n107
		11.3 ff.	82n112
		11.7	32n77
		11.7 ff.	25
		11.8 f.	25n58
		11.13 f.	58
		11.13–18	59
		11.17	57n52
		11.24	11n33, 17
		11.29–32	32n78
		11.37–48	28
		11.38	7n23
		11.42	7n23
	Olympian Odes	1.1	11n33
		1.1 ff.	6
		1.1–11	59n55
		1.3 f.	11n33
		1.5	59n55

PINDAR *Olympian Odes* *(Continued)*

1.10	27n65
1.17 f.	59n55
1.25	8
1.28	8–9
1.28b f.	9
1.28–51	8
1.30	9
1.31	60n66
1.36	9, 21
1.36–45	9
1.81–85	90–91
1.84	36n3
1.97–105	6n21
1.99	5n18, 73
1.99 f.	77
1.100	11n33
1.103	60n66, 73
1.104	26n62
1.104 f.	26
1.105	5n18
1.109	80
1.114	59n55
1.115 ff.	3n11, 78, 80
conclusion	77
2.1 ff.	6n20
2.1–8	23n52
2.2	6n20, 21, 45
2.6/7	74
2.13–17	78
2.14/5	80n108
2.16	80, 80n108
2.17–52	50n40
2.39 f.	50n41
2.50/1	9n27, 11, 73
2.50/1–57	50n41
2.56–105	86
2.56–110	87
2.57	26n62
2.58/9	59n60, 86, 87
2.60	88
2.62	60n63
2.62 f.	88
2.62–91	88
2.63–91	60n63
2.91–97	3n11, 71n91
2.91–99	60n63
2.91–105	6n21, 13n36, 15, 32, 62

Index Locorum

PINDAR *Olympian Odes* (Continued)

2.94/5	16
2.94/5 ff.	32n78
2.96	29n71
2.99 ff.	17
2.99–105	60n63
2.101	21
2.101 ff.	40n18, 60n66
2.101–110	90
2.102/3 f.	17
2.105	73
2.105 f.	61n69
2.105–110	29, 29n71, 32, 76, 90
2.106	29n71
2.107	61n68
2.108 ff.	10n30, 58n54
3.1	80n108
3.3b	65
3.6	43n25
3.13	9n27
3.36b	5n18
3.40 f.	7n25
3.40b	30
3.44	11n33
3.44–48	59n55, 60n62
3.46/7	59n55
3.46/7 f.	28, 32n78
conclusion	44
4.2b	27n66
4.3	61n66
4.4/5	89n122
4.7	36n3
4.10	78n104
4.12b f.	83
4.13 f.	83
4.19	21
4.19 f.	4n12, 58n54, 61n66
4.20	26n62
4.24–29/30	28
4.28 f.	28
conclusion	77
5.2	80n108
5.23 ff.	24, 56, 58, 59n59, 59n61
6.1–4	10n30, 71n91

112   Index Locorum

PINDAR *Olympian Odes*   (Continued)

6.1–7	55
6.1–8	59n60
6.1–9	17
6.3 f.	33
6.4	55, 58, 73
6.4 ff.	11n33
6.4–7	55
6.4–21	55
6.6	7n23, 57n52
6.7	55, 57n52
6.8	55
6.8–21	55
6.10	24n56
6.12	61n69, 64
6.17	64
6.20	11n33
6.20 f.	40n18, 45n30
6.21	21, 61n66
6.22–28	24, 27n65
6.23 ff.	56
6.27 f.	58n54
6.71	9n27
6.77–81	59n60
6.79	76
6.82–91	60n66
6.84 ff.	60n66
6.84–89	60n66
6.87–91	58n54
6.88	61n66
6.89	61n66
6.89 f.	4n12, 61n66
6.90	65
6.92–100	78
6.101–105	78
conclusion	77
7.1–10	10n30
7.8 f.	45n30
7.11	7
7.13	5n18, 9n27, 20, 27n65
7.13–19	21
7.14–19	20
7.16	21
7.20 f.	45n30
7.21	65
7.26	24n56
7.77	9n27

Index Locorum

PINDAR *Olympian Odes* (*Continued*)

7.80–87	72
7.80–95	72, 80
7.83	17n42
7.86	71
7.87–95	28, 72, 80
7.89	58, 58n53, 72
7.89 f.	67, 72, 93
7.92 ff.	80
7.94 f.	80
7.94 ff.	28
conclusion	77, 82–83
8.6	58
8.10	17, 78n104
8.12	7
8.15	7
8.21–30	25n58
8.28 ff.	78
8.31	9n27
8.52	7
8.53 ff.	16
8.54 f.	40n15
8.74	36n3
8.74–88	79
8.86	26n62
8.88	81
conclusion	77
9.1 ff.	81
9.5	5n18, 36n3
9.15	82n112
9.16 f.	25n58
9.19	70
9.23/4–27	45n30
9.27	21, 27n66
9.30	9
9.30–50	9
9.31–38	74n100
9.31–50	7n24
9.38 f.	73, 74
9.38–44	74n100
9.41	73
9.43	74
9.86–89	30, 66n77
9.87	73
9.89	89n122
9.90	43n25
9.95	46n35

PINDAR *Olympian Odes* (*Continued*)

9.105 f.	18n42
9.107/8	30
9.107/8–116	16, 37–38
9.107/8–120	6n21, 15, 30, 32, 59, 62
9.111	30
9.111 f.	73
9.112	73n97, 76
9.112 f.	15
9.112 ff.	17
9.113/4	7n23
9.116	16–17
9.116 f.	64
9.120	70
10	1, 4
10.1–8	1n4
10.1–12	40
10.3	11
10.4	61n69
10.9	13n37
10.9b	1, 33, 41n20
10.11 f.	65
10.12	21
10.13 f.	25
10.13–15	25
10.81	5n18
10.90	84n114
10.90–94	84n114
10.90–97b	10
10.95–97b	84n114
10.95–100	84
10.97b–100	84n114
10.100–110	7n25
10.101–110	84n114
11	1–33
11.1	11–12
11.1–6	10–12, 31, 60n62, 67
11.1–10	20
11.1–15	4–22
11.2	23, 42
11.4 ff.	6
11.4–15	14
11.6	60n66
11.7	15
11.7 f.	59n57
11.7–10	14–15, 19

PINDAR *Olympian Odes* (*Continued*)

11.7–15	12
11.7–21	59, 62
11.8 f.	19
11.10	19, 30
11.11–15	6, 20–21
11.13 f.	65
11.14	33
11.16	23
11.16 f.	26
11.16 ff.	40n18
11.16–19	22, 27
11.16–21	22–32
11.17	27, 28
11.18	5, 5n18, 14, 27
11.19	26
11.19 ff.	22, 31
11.20	30
12.1–6	21
12.1–21	11n34, 36, 52
12.3	46
12.3 ff.	24n56
12.5	36n6
12.5–12	36n6
12.6	7n23
12.7–12	51–52
12.12	7n23
12.13	36n6
12.13–21	52
12.19	52
13.1–10	31
13.1–22b	31
13.2 f.	24
13.6	46
13.10	72
13.11	31
13.11 f.	31, 32
13.11 ff.	24, 31
13.11–16	31
13.12	32
13.13	29, 31, 32
13.14 f.	24
13.16–21b	24–25, 26
13.21b	25
13.22 f.	25
13.23–27	81
13.23–28	78
13.24	80n108

PINDAR *Olympian Odes* *(Continued)*

13.26	23n53
13.26 f.	82n112
13.28 ff.	79
13.28–33	79
13.28–44b	79
13.34 f.	79
13.39 ff.	71
13.39–44b	79
13.42	46n35
13.42–44b	10n30
13.43–44b	46n35, 58n54, 90n123
13.45	7n23
13.45 f.	71
13.45–52	6n21
13.46	11n33, 73
13.47	56n51, 82
13.47–50	65
13.47–52	7n25
13.48 f.	82n111
13.49	52n45
13.50	17, 21
13.80	3
13.87b	21, 73, 74
13.89–93	9, 58n54
13.89–96	6n21
13.90	73
13.93	27n65
13.94	46n35
13.94 f.	17, 60n66
13.94 ff.	40
13.94–96	79
13.94–98	79
13.94–103	79
13.94–110b	72, 80
13.99–102	18n43, 79, 80
13.102 f.	79
13.103	46n35
13.104	21, 61n66
13.105	71
13.106	71
13.108	71
13.108 ff.	80
13.109b	72n92
13.110b	26n62, 80
conclusion	77

Index Locorum

PINDAR *Olympian Odes* (*Continued*)

	14.1	80n107
	14.5–17	11n34
	14.7	11n34, 56n50
	14.24	82
Paeans	2.24	87
	2.26	76
	6	4, 14, 29
	9.1–21	45n32
Pythian Odes	1.1–28	80
	1.2–28	80
	1.3	8n27
	1.14	24n56
	1.26–28	3
	1.29	80
	1.33	5n18
	1.33 ff.	5n18
	1.34 f.	24
	1.36	5n18
	1.41	9
	1.41–45	58n54
	1.42	7n25
	1.42–57	79
	1.47–50	5n18
	1.50	5n18
	1.56 f.	78
	1.75	21
	1.77	67n80
	1.81	73
	1.81 f.	73
	1.81–84	75
	1.81–86	6n21, 9, 15
	1.82	73
	1.85	13n37
	1.86–100b	87
	1.90	82, 87, 88
	1.90 ff.	86
	1.92	86
	1.92–100b	88
	1.99–100b	2n9, 24n56, 28, 67, 72n93
	1.100b	67
	conclusion	91
	2	4
	2.4	27n65
	2.10	46n35
	2.13–20	7

PINDAR *Pythian Odes* (*Continued*)

2.18	7
2.24	86
2.34	53
2.34 ff.	28
2.42–52	3
2.46 ff.	13n36
2.49	9
2.49–53	89n121
2.49–61	6n21
2.52	73
2.58–61	17
2.59	25n60
2.60	17, 59n60
2.62	21
2.63–67	24n55, 24n56
2.65b f.	64
2.68	27n66
2.77	29
2.83	80
2.83 f.	32n78
2.83 ff.	29–30
2.96	80
3.20–23	28
3.22	88n120
3.23	88n120
3.59	88n120
3.62	77, 88n120
3.76	27n65
3.84	26, 62
3.109	88n120
3.114 f.	28
4.1	73
4.1 f.	27n69
4.66	76
4.89	70
4.247 f.	3n10, 42, 73
4.256	36n5
4.259	9n27
4.277 ff.	27n69
4.279	65
4.281 f.	24n55, 24n56
4.291 ff.	51
5.1–11	8, 38n9
5.1–22	86
5.2	87
5.5–11	51, 52

PINDAR *Pythian Odes* (Continued)

5.10	51
5.10 f.	52
5.12	69n83
5.12 f.	59n57
5.12 ff.	8
5.12–23	38n9
5.14	69n83
5.27–42	69n83
5.43 f.	69, 69n83
5.43 ff.	8
5.44	86
5.44 f.	59n57
5.45	36n2, 69n83
5.55	13n37
5.57	9n27
5.60–69	69n83
5.102	65
5.103–107	70
5.103–124	80
5.104	73
5.107 f.	24
5.107 ff.	24
5.108	64
5.109–112	24
5.113	24
5.114	24
5.115	24
5.116 f.	24
conclusion	77
6.7 f.	7n23, 64
6.15 ff.	65
6.43	5n18
6.44	5n18
6.45	11n33
6.48 f.	25
6.50	70
7.7	11n23
7.19b–22	28
conclusion	28
8.1–4	27
8.3 f.	26
8.5	78n104
8.6	46, 86
8.6 f.	25n58
8.22 ff.	56n51
8.22–35	7, 27n64

PINDAR *Pythian Odes* (*Continued*)

8.30	42
8.30–33	69n82, 75
8.30–35	41
8.33	5n18, 73
8.34	11, 42
8.35	82
8.36	70n84
8.36–84	69
8.40	70n84
8.40–63	69
8.50–57	50n40
8.58–63	69
8.61	70
8.62	70
8.64	70n84
8.66 ff.	70n84
8.70–81	70n84
8.82 ff.	70n84
8.83	70
8.85–91	70n84
8.92–96	82
8.96	67
8.96 f.	7n23
8.103 ff.	70n84
conclusion	77
9.1 f.	21
9.1 ff.	45n30
9.1–3	21
9.1–4	20–21
9.3 f.	65
9.5	9n27, 21, 80n107
9.69 f.	2, 3n10, 14
9.73	5n18, 9n27, 17
9.75/6	21
9.75/6 ff.	17
9.79–82	17, 31n75, 73
9.80	18
9.81	17, 18, 19
9.81 f.	17n42, 18n44
9.82	18n42
9.82 f.	17
9.83–89	17–18
9.84b	70
9.90–92b	18, 70
9.90–92b ff.	18
9.92	22n49, 70

PINDAR *Pythian Odes* (*Continued*)

9.92 f.	18n43, 70n86
9.92b f.	66n77
9.93 ff.	18
9.94	21n48, 23n53
9.96	24n56, 65
9.96–99	18, 58n54, 61, 66n77
9.99	63
9.100	18, 46n35
9.100–107	18
9.106	18
9.108	10
9.130	82
10.1 f.	32n78
10.1–3	38–39, 4n13
10.1–6	6, 38, 39
10.2	39
10.4	4n13, 11, 36n3, 73
10.4 ff.	38
10.10	24n56
10.22	72n93
10.22–26	59n55
10.22–30	56
10.23	57n52
10.24	57n52, 58
10.34 f.	2
10.38–40	2
10.48 ff.	3
10.48–50	14
10.51–63	6n21
10.61 f.	77
10.62	73
10.64–68	60n66
10.67–72	10n30
10.69–72	28
10.71 f.	28
11.38–40	4n13, 44n27
11.38–45	6n21
11.41	67n80
11.41–50	4n13
11.45	2
11.50b	86, 88
11.50b–58	86
11.50b–64	87
11.51	88
11.53	86

Index Locorum

PINDAR *Pythian Odes* (*Continued*)

		11.54	65, 86, 87, 88
		11.55	87n118
		11.56–64	88
		11.57	11n33, 87n118
		11.58	87
		conclusion	77
		12.2	80n107
		12.5	78n104
		12.28–32	28
		12.32	77
	fragments		
	Isthmian Odes	1.5	25n58
	Hymnoi	19.1–6	45
		27	70
	Partheneia	105.6	37n7
		106.21	61n66
		106.23	43n25, 89n122
	Hyporchemata	117.1–4	24n56
		120.2	88n120
	Enkomia	130.13	60n66
		134	86n117
	dubia	238.1 f.	26
		246.1	73n97
		246.1–2	73
		246.2	76
		254	45n32
		260	11n34
		283	30
PLUTARCH	*Moralia*	32F f.	91n125
SAPPHO	A.16 L.–P.	1–4	5
		3	6
		3 f.	5
		5–14	5
		15	5, 6
SCOLIA ANONYMA		33D^2	60n66
SOPHOCLES	*Ajax*	265 ff.	89n121
		293	76
	Electra	730	51
		1444	51

SOPHOCLES	*(Continued)*		
	fragments	101 N²	60n66
STOBAEUS		3.33 (περὶ βρα-χυλογίας)	75
		3.36 (περὶ σιγῆς)	75
		4.32.33	88
		4.48.11	88–89
THEMISTIUS	*Orations*	1.4b	1n4
		7.84b f.	33
THEOCRITUS		16.16–21	90n124
		16.22–23	90n124
THEOGNIS		155–158	89
		341 f.	18n43, 70n86
		573 f.	86
		885 f.	86n117
		1041 f.	88
		1155 f.	86n117
		1191 f.	86n117
		1217 f.	88
		1237	52n44
THUCYDIDES		2.35.2	40n14
VIRGIL	*Georgics*	2.503–515	11n11
	Aeneid	6.847–853	11n11
XENOPHON	*Agesilaus*	2.12	40n14
		2.25	40n14
		5.6	40n14
		8.7	40n14
ZENOBIUS		I.93	30n74

SUBJECT INDEX

Prepared by Thomas R. Walsh,
with the assistance of Donald Mastronarde

Abandonment, 33; of device, 13, 16, 20; of theme, 13, 41. See also Dismissal; Rejection
Abbreviation, 24, 25, 59n55, 73; catalogue and, 71; language of, 3n10, 33; of list, 5n18, 8, 72; of pattern, 71; of priamel, 10; rejection and, 37; rhetorical, 74; σιγά motive and, 74; time and, 42, 72; of topic, 13, 51, 72; vaunt and, 32, 44
Abruptness, 32, 35
Abstract, for concrete, 2
Abundance, in foil, 12–15
Achievement, 7, 10, 20, 77, 82, 83; athletic, 35, 38; vs. disposition, 58; limits of, 43–44; praise for, 55; reward for, 11, 22; song and, 2, 11, 12. See also Athletic success; Fame; Glory; Laudandus; Praise; Success; Victor
Address, in catalogue, 70, 78n103. See also Hymnal address; Names
Adjective, 59
Adverb, 59
Adversative, 48, 54, 76
Akhilleus, 91, 91n125
Alexandrians, 1; moderns and, 35. See also Modern scholarship; Scholia
Allusion, 35, 48, 90n124
Allusiveness. See Allusion
Altruism, selfishness and, 81, 85, 87–88. See also Liberality; Unselfishness
Ambiguity, 15, 46, 92
Amplification, 42, 58, 91n125; foil as, 40

Analogy, 12; contrast and, 7–8, 36, 52–55, 81, 83; gnome and, 7–8, 53, 81
Anaphora, 56
Antithesis. See Contrast
Apodosis, as cap, 54–55. See also Condition; Conditional clause; Conditional sentence
Apology, 4; for abruptness, 32; contrived, 33, 41; objections and, 40; prooimial, 33; tactfulness and, 41
Apostrophe, 70. See also Address
Appeal, to the future, 78. See also Future
Archetype, 85. See also Type
Arrangement, in catalogue, 24
Arrival motive, 22, 23–28; defined, 23, 27; future tense and, 27, 28; laudator and, 27; Muse and, 27; song and, 27
Arrows, of song, 71n91, 73; inspiration and, 9
Art, 4n11, 9, 16, 32, 37–38, 64, 71n91
Asseveration, 20, 43, 59, 59n60, 60n66, 78n103; cap and, 54, 55; in enkomia, 11n33; name cap and, 17, 52; objections and, 17, 17n41, 24, 24n54, 40, 40n18, 52n43; praise and, 24; vaunt and, 22
Athletic success: background and, 68; catalogue of, 16; as climax, 10, 11, 13, 30, 52; as foil, 67; Panhellenic, 79; praise of, 54. See also Achievement; Catalogue; Success; Victory catalogue
Attention: direction of, 9, 21, 43, 55–56; foil and, 53

Audience, 44, 60n66, 71; convention and, 16, 27, 46; disapproval of, 75–76; experience of enkomia, 26; poetry and, 27; powers of, 12, 13, 26, 35, 40; σιγά and, 75–76

Background: foil and, 52; foreground and, 12, 15, 20, 38, 44, 47, 52, 68, 81, 91; theme and, 39, 44
Bakkhulides, 12, 15, 26, 28, 30, 37, 50, 50n40, 59, 64
Bitter experience, as foil, 48–52, 53, 74n100. See also Bright foil; Dark foil
Brevity, in catalogues, 18, 70
Bridge, 71
Bright climax, 14, 48, 50n40
Bright foil, 47n37. See also Bitter experience; Dark foil; Foil
Business, pleasure and, 41

Cap, 7, 23, 36, 36n2; apodosis and, 54–55; concrete, 5, 54; defined, 5n18; generic, 36n6, 54; gnomic, 51–52, 54, 55. See also Capping; Climax; Concrete name cap; Concrete pronominal cap; Foil; Name cap; Priamel; Pronominal cap; Pronominal name cap
Capping: terms, 15, 16, 17n41, 60n62; vaunt, 56
Catalogue, 13–14, 43, 43n24, 70n84; address in, 70; arrangement in, 27; beginning of, 72; conclusion of, 16, 71, 72, 72n94; crescendo and, 53; elements of, 24; foil and, 14, 17–19, 37, 41, 53, 56n51, 61n67, 66, 69, 71, 74; gnomic foil and, 53, 66; Homeric, 18, 66n77; hymn and, 46; length of, 3n11, 8, 16, 28, 42; position of, 27; prayer and, 19, 72, 80; second entry in, 17; σιγά motive and, 75; summary and, 18, 46, 46n35, 69, 72, 72n94, 80; thank offering and, 18n43, 69, 70, 80; transition in, 71; of victories, 7, 13, 16, 17n42, 18, 28, 30, 41, 46, 47n37, 54, 61, 62, 62n69, 66, 72, 79. See also Victory catalogue
Categorical vaunt, 24, 31–32, 44; conditional clauses and, 55–59, 60n63; defined, 55; laudandus and, 37; praeteritio and, 31; subjective or objective, 44, 59, 59n59. See also Vaunt
Category, 27, 36, 37, 39, 44, 53, 62, 68, 83
Charioteer, praise of, 8, 45, 46, 69, 77
Choral style, 5, 32, 40, 40n15, 92
Chorodidaskalos, 60n66, 65
Chorus, 23, 41, 69, 70n84, 85
City, 9, 22; heroes and, 46; victor and, 56n51, 83. See also Home; Polis
Clan, 13, 14, 69. See also Family
Class, 56n51. See also Indefinite; Type
Climactic term, 14, 20; gnomic and concrete, 5–6; metaphor and, 5n18, 19; selection and, 37; subjective foil and, 14n38
Climactic vaunt, 60n63
Climax, 6, 10, 13, 36, 43, 77, 80; crescendo and, 8, 17; current success and, 52; dark foil and, 50; foil and, 14, 37–39, 47n37, 48, 53, 66–67; gnome and, 5, 53; νῦν and, 37, 48; of priamel, 13n36, 57; θαῦμα motive and, 3. See also Concrete climax; Crescendo; Descrescendo; Diminuendo; Gnomic climax
Combination. See Ensemble
Command. See Injunction
Community. See City
Comparative degree: in priamels, 11n33, 39. See also Superlative degree
Composition, 41, 77, 92
Conclusion, 14, 71, 72, 86, 90; acknowledgment in, 72n94; foil and, 28, 53, 67; future tense in, 77; gnome and, 28, 52, 53, 77; of hymns, 46, 77; prayer and, 77–79; propriety and, 73
Concrete, 2, 10, 23, 43, 45, 66
Concrete climax, 5, 6, 40n16, 66; name cap in, 10; victory list as, 7. See also Cap; Climax; Foil; Priamel
Concrete name cap, 20, 40n16. See also Cap
Concrete priamel, gnomic priamel and, 23

Subject Index

Concrete pronominal cap, 84n114
Concrete simile, 55
Concrete term, in crescendo, 68
Concrete vaunt, 28
Condition: alternatives for, 59; generic expression and, 59; suppressed, 59, 60, 60n63; vaunt and, 60, 67
Conditional clause, 56, 60n62, 60n63, 62, 85; crescendo and, 57; in gnomic sentence, 83; vaunt and, 54–59, 61–62, 60n63
Conditional sentence: conventional use of, 54–59, 61; as priamel, 59n55
Confidence, 10, 41–42; hesitation and, 30–31, 32, 40
Consolation, 53
Content, 49, 74
Context, importance of, 22, 29, 35, 48, 51, 74, 80
Contrast, 9, 12, 30, 36, 38n10, 38–39, 53–54, 66–67, 83–85, 87, 90; gnomic foil and, 7–8, 81
Control, 14, 47, 91
Convention, 2, 4, 14, 22, 24, 35, 44n29, 48, 50, 52, 55, 67, 69, 71, 73, 79; ambiguity and, 92; audience and, 16, 27; composition and, 77, 92; in ensemble, 85; form and, 3; hymnal, 45, 78, 78n102; knowledge of, 27, 32; meaning and, 3, 10, 21, 82, 88; metaphor and, 58; originality and, 42; of participles and future, 43; theme and, 62, 86; unity and, 1, 35–36
Conventional: particular and, 12; sequence, 26n62, 27, 66, 71, 72, 80, 85; topic, 49
Craft, 59
Crescendo, 3n11, 8, 9, 48, 66, 74; climax of, 47n37; concrete term of, 68; condition and, 54–59; final, 53, 77; full, 44–47; generic, 56, 57; gnomic, 12, 56, 61; movements of, 57; oath and, 17; objective, 52; opening, 1n4, 46, 49; preliminary, 41; σιγά motive and, 76; structure of, 44–45, 57–58; subjective, 52. *See also* Climax; Decrescendo; Diminuendo
Criticism, 40, 75–76

Dark foil, 14, 47–53, 74, 74n100, 74–75, 90; exile and, 51; in narrative, 50n40; present joy and, 50. *See also* Bright foil; Dark past; Foil
Dark past: as foil, 48, 53; present and, 57. *See also* Dark foil; Past
Day and night, as motive, 36, 36n5
Death, 14, 48–50, 51, 52, 74n100, 84, 87, 88, 91. *See also* Immortality
Debt, 41, 41n20, 57–58, 77
Decrescendo: defined, 73; formality and, 68; propriety and, 83; σιγά motive and, 73–76. *See also* Climax; Crescendo; Diminuendo
Deed, word and, 56n51, 58, 58n54, 62, 63. *See also* Word
Definite, 54–56
Denotation, 92
Desire, 3n11, 12, 20, 42, 73
Details, ensemble and, 66
Development, 36, 91
Device, 4, 16, 20, 32, 37, 38, 39, 45, 56, 56n50, 66, 67, 74
Digression, 44n27, 68; foil and, 8, 44
Diminuendo, 8, 9; defined, 66. *See also* Climax; Crescendo; Decrescendo
Disapproval, of audience, 76
Disclaimer, προαίρεσις and, 86n117
Disjunctives, 6, 45–46, 62, 67; effect of, 56n50; in hymn, 56; in selection, 45
Dismissal, 3n11, 5n18, 19, 73; of catalogue, 69–72; and hymnal χαίρετε, 47; of ὄκνος motive, 31n75; summary, 8; theme and, 8, 9. *See also* Abandonment; Rejection
Disunity. *See* Unity
Diversity, foil as, 7, 37–39
Double crown, 72, 72n93
Double priamel, 23, 23n51, 23n52, 38n9
Doublet, universalizing, 10, 24–25, 24n56, 25n59, 26, 36n5, 61, 64, 64n74, 67, 86
Duty. *See* Obligation

Eagerness, 66
Eagle, 82
Ease, 61–62, 64

Embarrassment, 1n4, 2, 4, 16, 32, 35, 40n15, 41, 68, 76
Embellishment, 60. *See also* Amplification
Emphasis, 13, 15, 21, 22, 45, 54, 56, 59, 71, 74, 77
Enjambement, 68
Enkomia, 3, 4, 35, 36, 40, 58, 60, 61n69, 63, 64n73, 75, 83
Ensemble: conventional, 66; conventions and, 85; of motives, 16, 24, 32, 42, 73, 76, 86. *See also* Order
Enthusiasm, of laudator, 32, 69
Envy, 56n51
Epinikion, 3, 43n26, 79; ἀρετά and, 82; song as, 68, 77, 82
Epiphany, of Apollo, 41
Epithet, 80n106, 80n107
Eulogy, 24, 35, 43, 48
Event, 20, 35
Evidence, 37n7, 48, 51
Exempla, 5, 5n18, 8n27, 10, 14n38, 31n75, 40n16; list and, 9; in prooimia, 36n6; purpose of, 43n26
Exhortation, 58n54; prayer and, 72
Exile, 52
Expectations, as motive, 86–89
Explanatory clause, 10, 39, 43, 45, 46, 57, 63
Explanatory gnome, 22, 32, 60, 66, 72
Explanatory matter, 77
Explanatory particle, 43, 46, 67

Fair weather: present joy and, 48; victory and, 51. *See also* Foul weather; Weather
Fame, 19, 52, 60, 60n63, 64n74, 67, 82, 84, 86, 87–88. *See also* Achievement; Glory
Family, 52, 70n84, 76. *See also* Clan
Father, of victor, 20, 47n37, 48, 50, 51–53, 56n51. *See also* Son
First person, 3, 6, 6n19, 21, 41, 45, 85, 87n118
Focus, 5, 11, 12, 20–21, 28, 39, 40, 46, 53, 54, 55, 67, 68, 77, 83, 84; ensemble and, 42
Focusing foil, 5, 9, 20, 21, 25, 36

Foil, 4n11, 32, 33, 42, 66–67, 84–85; broad types of, 28; catalogue and, 14, 17–19, 37, 41, 53, 56n51, 61, 61n67, 66, 69, 71, 74; climax and, 36, 37, 39, 47n37, 48, 53, 66; concluding, 28, 90; concrete pronominal cap and, 84n114; diminuendo and, 8; dismissal of, 6, 44, 50; diversity as, 37–39; embarrassment as, 1n4, 4; emphasis and, 74, 77; focus and, 9, 15, 53, 84; gnome and, 5n18, 7–8, 9, 12, 22n50, 28–31, 53, 54, 80–81, 84n114, 85; inverted, 53, 80–81; irrelevance and, 6n21, 43, 44, 91; χρέος and, 54; laudandus and, 28, 31, 84, 90; list as, 37, 66; name cap and, 39, 53, 44n28; names and, 38, 39, 46–47; objection as, 24, 24n54, 40, 41; objective, 12, 25n57, 28; occasion as, 5n18; occupational, 7, 10; opening, 44; φθόνος in, 57n51; priamel and, 28; pronominal name cap and, 44n28, 47, 68; protasis and, 54–55; recapitulation and, 6–7, 6n21, 13, 38, 38n11; selection and, 6–7, 11; σιγά motive and, 74; subjective, 12, 16n40, 28–29; summary, 5n18, 7, 12, 16, 20, 36, 37, 40n16; term, 66; thrust aside, 68; tradition and, 88–89; transition and, 13, 43, 71; unity of ode and, 6n21, 54, 77; vicissitude, 14n38, 51–52. *See also* Bright foil; Contrast; Dark foil
Foreground, background and, 20, 47, 52. *See also* Background
Form, 3, 49, 52, 56, 57, 59, 60, 68, 83
Formal invocation, 46
Formality, decrescendo and, 68
Formula, 3, 20, 21n48, 37, 38–39, 42, 46, 75, 86, 87, 92
Fortune, 52, 53, 57
Foul weather: past and, 49; politics and, 51. *See also* Fair weather; Dark foil; Weather
Fulfillment. *See* Desire
Function, 49
Future, 1, 12, 18n43, 20, 27, 28, 33, 48, 77–83, 80, 81, 87n118; conclu-

sions and, 77; participle and, 45, 45n 30, 65, 68; present and, 21–22, 77; voluntative, 43, 74; wishes or prayers and, 77. *See also* Past; Present

Genealogy, 60n66
General, 5, 10, 53, 66. *See also* Particular
Generic: cap, 36n6; climax, 40n16; crescendo, 56; expression, 59, 83; foil, 56–57, 56n51; phrase, 61
Genre: importance of, 92; requirements of, 35, 58
Geographical topic, 60, 60n65, 62
Gestures, conventional, 35
Glory, 3, 3n11, 8, 22, 23, 35, 36, 39, 40, 41, 47, 49, 50, 51, 61, 64n75, 65, 66, 67, 69, 72, 72n93, 74, 82, 83. *See also* Achievement; Fame
Gloss, 12, 15, 31, 38, 51–52, 75, 80, 81, 82
Gnome, 56, 73, 87; analogy and, 7–8; between topics, 53–54; cap and, 55; climax and, 5, 53; conclusion and, 28, 52, 77; contrast and, 7–8, 81; experience and, 52; explanatory, 22, 32, 60, 66, 72; focus and, 28; foil and, 5, 7–8, 12, 22n50, 30, 51–52, 54; following praise, 28; form of, 28; gloss as, 12; narrative and, 28; particulars and, 28, 29; preceding praise, 31; prooimia and, 28; subject and, 54; subjective or objective, 29; theme and, 7–8, 28; transition and, 28, 53; vaunt and, 28, 66
Gnomic cap, 84n114; invocation and, 51–52; summary foil and, 12–15, 20
Gnomic climax, 5, 6, 10, 37–38; list and, 7, 7n24, 37
Gnomic crescendo, 12, 56, 61
Gnomic foil, 9, 22, 28–29, 31; catalogue and, 53, 66; function of, 81; inverted, 28, 53, 80–81, 83; name cap and, 11–15, 53; priamels and, 23, 28; tradition and, 88–89
Gnomic generalization, 55
Gnomic gloss, 12, 31, 75, 80, 81, 82
Gnomic sentence, 77, 83

Gods, 3, 8, 8n27, 9, 25n60, 29, 38, 45, 56n50, 69–70, 69n83, 70, 70n84, 72n94, 78n102, 80, 80n108, 86
Good repute. *See* Glory
Grammar, 32, 33, 54, 56n51, 58, 88, 92
Gratitude, 8, 69, 69n83

Harmony, 91
Hendiadys, 2
Herakles, 9, 59n55, 61n69, 70, 85; epinikion and, 43n26; εὐεργεσία and, 43n26, 85, 85n116; limits of achievement and, 43–44, 43n26
Heroes, 44–47, 70, 72n94
Hesiod, 61
Hesitation, 3n11, 8, 17, 31, 31n75, 38
Hesukhia, 26
Highlighting. *See* Emphasis
Historical matter, conclusion of, 71
Historical persons, types and, 29n71
Historical references, 35
Home, of laudandus, 23n53, 38, 41, 81
Homer, 30, 65; Muses and, 18, 30, 66n77
Hope, 18n43
Hospitality, 18n43, 24, 25, 26
Hymnal address, 78n103; conventions of, 78, 78n102; form of, 56n50; invocation in, 36, 79; χαῖρε and, 47, 77, 79. *See also* Address
Hymnal seal, prayer and, 79, 83
Hymnal selection, 45–46, 56. *See also* Priamel
Hymnal structure, rhapsodic, 46
Hymns, 6, 45–47, 78–79; cult, 8n27; endings of, 78, 79; kletic, 27; praise and, 45, 64n73, 74, 76, 77; rhapsodic, 8n27
Hyperbole, 13, 63–64
Hypostatization, of success, 36, 36n6
Hysteron proteron, 81

Images, 68
Immortality, as motive, 11, 60n63, 86
Impatience, 28
Imperatives, 17n41, 55, 56, 57, 57n52, 58, 67, 68, 74
Indefinite, 56, 58, 85

Individual, state and, 46, 65
Individual topics, conclusions of, 53
Inevitability, of praise, 54
Injunction: to conclude prayer, 72; to praise, 54, 55, 56, 61, 63
Inspiration, 9, 14, 16, 18
Intent, 3, 20, 52
Interest, debt and, 41
Interpretation, 15, 48, 71n91, 92
Interrogative, in hymnal form, 56n50
Interruption, 69, 70n84, 71
Introductions, 46, 56, 63, 71, 73
Inverted gnome, 28, 31, 53, 80, 83
Invocation, 79; explanatory clause and, 46; formal, 46; hymnal, 36, 46; priamel as, 51. *See also* Hymnal address; Muse
Irrelevance, 3, 4n13, 6, 14, 21n48, 35; as foil, 2, 4, 43, 44, 69, 91, 92; variety and, 91

Justice, in treating a theme, 28–29, 29n71, 58n54, 61n69, 65

Key words, 17n41, 46n35, 73
Kharites, inspiration and, 18, 69, 69n83

Laudandus, 30, 76, 84n114; in cap, 5n18, 7, 36, 36n2; criticism of, 75; foil and, 4, 12, 28, 37, 38, 84, 90; glory of, 41; hypothetical, 54; χρέος of, 63; laudator and, 36, 56; limits of achievement and, 43–44; merits of, 31, 61; place names and, 21, 39; priamel as foil for, 38; public and private concerns of, 82–83, 89n122. *See also* Achievement; Victor
Laudator, 6n20, 18, 23, 27, 56n51, 72, 90n123; ἀσχολία and, 41–42; attitude of, 29, 55; audience and, 13, 60n66, 75–76; in cap, 5n18, 36, 36n2; confidence of, 10, 32; control of, 47; criticism of, 75–76; difficulty of, 41–42, 58n54; eagerness of, 66; enthusiasm of, 32; future and, 78; hypothetical, 54; intent of, 20, 52; χρέος of, 54; laudandus and, 7,

56; limits of achievement and, 43–44; obligation of, 42, 53–54, 66; προαίρεσις of, 40n16; reckless abandon of, 41–42; relation to foil, 28; reward of, 75; theme and, 6n21, 12, 13, 31, 31n75, 60n66, 66, 69. *See also* Pindar; Singer
Legendary matter, 6n21, 44–47; conclusion of, 71; connected with present, 8n27; introduction of, 71–72; in transitions, 76
Leisure, 41–42
Length, 61n69, 68
Liberality, as virtue, 85–87, 89
List, 5n18, 6, 8, 72, 75; of ἀρεταί, 43; choice and, 46; in exemplum, 9, 32; as foil, 37, 66; following gnome, 7n24; of merits, 32; on occupations, 7; of powers, 56n50; selection and, 46; summary, 18; of victories, 7
Literal, metaphorical and, 48–50

Manner. *See* Theme, treatment of
Mannerism, 45, 70
Marvels, 2–3, 8–9
Matter, sequence and, 72
Meaning, convention and, 1n5, 2, 3, 12, 26n62, 35, 39, 92
Mechanical, and natural, 3, 3n11, 16, 29, 74
Merit, 7, 10–11, 12, 15, 15n39, 24, 30, 31–32, 42, 54, 57, 63
Metaphor: convention and, 1n4, 5n18, 19, 48–50, 58, 59, 59n61, 60n65, 62; geographical, 60n65, 62; κέλευθος as, 15, 62, 64; χρέος motive and, 57–58; πανταχῇ motive and, 15n39; ποιμαίνειν in, 19; sailing as, 51, 62, 62n70, 62n72; shipwreck as, 48, 50–51; swimming as, 72, 72n92
Minor conventions, 11
Minor foil, climax and, 39
Misinterpretation. *See* Interpretation
Mockery, 88–89, 89n121, 90n124
Modern scholarship, 1, 2n7, 33, 35
Motives, 32, 46, 46n34, 55, 63, 67; abbreviated, 24; arrival, 22, 23, 27, 28; combination of, 22, 42, 72–73, 76, 86;

compressed or expanded, 25; context and, 29; day and night, 36, 36n 5; δέξαι, 78, 78n104; enduring fame, 86, 87–88; flight, 81–82; human expectations, 86, 87, 89; hymnal, 56n 50; immortality, 11, 60n63, 86; introducing new topic, 71–72; καιρός, 11n32; χαῖρε, 78–79; χρέος, 55, 56, 57–58; kindness, 90n124; lateness, 33; liberality, 89; limits of achievement, 44; many roads, 17; mockery, 88; neighbor, 69–70; objection, 40; obligation, 42; occupational, 7, 10, 11n34, 68; ὄκνος, 31n75; ὁμοίως, 17–19; πανταχῇ, 15n39; parental, 37–39, 41; as part of theme, 42, 86–87; πᾶς–πολύς, 66, 71, 73; praise of ξενία, 24; praising mind and body, 24–28; prayer, 77–83; of priamel, 45; purpose and, 91; rhetorical position of, 45; shared humanity, 86, 87; σιγά, 73–76; θαῦμα, 3n10, 13n86, 14; τόλμα, 31; transformation of, 59. See also Theme; Topic

Movement, 68

Multiforms, 59–60, 71

Munificence. See Altruism

Muse, 22, 23, 27, 42, 65, 84; in Homer, 18, 30, 66n77; sensibility and, 24–26

Myth, 1, 6n21, 8, 8n27, 66. See also Legendary matter

Name cap, 5n18, 6n19, 7, 17, 20, 31, 36, 36n2, 38, 43, 69; concrete climax and, 10, 40n16; foil and, 39, 44n28; gnomic foil and, 11–15, 53; vicissitude foil and, 52; vocative in, 9

Name patterns, 46, 77

Name priamel, 39

Names: foil and, 46–47; of heroes, 47; order of, 48, 79–80; of places, 39, 47; unity and, 39, 77; of victors, 20

Narrative, 2–3, 6n21, 8n27, 14, 14n38, 17, 20–21, 28, 41, 53

Nature, 4n11, 7, 10, 11, 16, 29, 31, 64, 68

Need to praise, 7, 9, 10–11, 54

Oaths: asseveration and, 11n33, 17, 27, 40, 60n66; force of, 27; key words in, 17n41

Objections, 40–41, 52n43, 61; asseveration and, 40n18; as foil, 24, 24n54, 40; types of, 40

Objective, subjective and, 12, 15–16, 28, 29, 44, 52, 59

Obligation, 56, 56n51, 68, 73; of laudator, 42, 54, 66

Occasions, 5n18, 22, 41

Occupational motive, 7, 10, 11n34, 68

Ode, 1, 21, 72, 80, 81; beginning of, 56; design of, 13, 36; as epideixis, 35; linear development of, 36, 92; orality of, 35; publicity of, 35, 89, 89n122; tact in, 35, 91. See also Unity

Opening: crescendo, 46; foil, 31, 36–44, 68, 83; hymnal, 46; prayer, 83; priamel, 2, 11–12, 22; vaunt, 21

Order, 22, 57; of foil and concrete, 23, 29, 31; of names, 48, 79–80; unity and, 77. See also Ensemble; Position; Sequence

Originality, 12, 42

Paian, 41

Paradigm, 27n64, 43, 60n63, 85, 85n 116, 87, 91n125

Parallel passages, as evidence of sense, 26n62, 48, 51, 57, 59, 63, 64, 72, 73, 74, 76, 80

Parental motive, 37–39, 41

Parenthesis, explanatory, 10

Participle, 48, 59, 61; future and, 43, 45, 45n30, 65, 68

Particular: gnome and, 28–29, 53, 57; τόλμα motive and, 31. See also General

Parts of song, as units, 77, 78–79

Past, 12, 48, 49, 52, 53, 57, 77. See also Dark past; Future; Present

Patron, 3, 14, 35, 46, 51, 60n66; as witness, 17n42

Pattern, 25, 40, 46, 71, 72

Pause. See Rhetorical pause

Peaks, in narrative, 53

Performance, 81
Personal apology: as foil, 4; in 7th *Nemean Ode*, 4
Personal embarrassments, 16, 40n15
Personal interests, of Pindar, 2, 3–4, 3n11, 4n15, 13, 35, 41, 92
Personification, 2
Perspective, 28, 47
Philosophical references, 35
Piety, appeals to, 9
Pindar, 38, 50, 50n40, 59, 64, 70n84, 78, 86, 89n122; aesthetic sensibility of, 26; control of, 14; humor of, 74n100; inspiration and, 14; originality of, 12; personal, 41, 92; personal outbursts of, 13; style of, 4, 12, 47, 90n124; tact of, 35; use of verb in first person by, 3, 85. *See also* Hymns; Style
Pindaric problem, 35
Place: in catalogue, 17n42; as foil, 38; name of, 38, 39, 47; as witness, 17n42
Pleasure, 41, 75
Poet, 2, 3, 4, 60n66
Poetry, 25, 26, 27, 64n73
Polarity, 86. *See also* Doublet
Polis, 27n64; victor and, 20–22, 36. *See also* City
Politics, 35, 48, 51, 52, 68. *See also* Dark foil
Poor. *See* Rich
Position, 27, 45, 49. *See also* Ensemble; Order
Praeteritio, 19, 31, 71n91, 73n98, 90, 90n123
Praise, 4n12, 5, 37; achievement and, 55; of athletic success, 54; blame and, 83; categorical, 24; of city, 22; command for, 54, 56, 61; debt and, 57–58; ease of, 61–62; following gnome, 31; ground for, 8, 43; hymns and, 45–46, 74; inevitability of, 54; inspirational vs. mechanical, 16; manner of, 45; matching deed, 61, 62, 66; narrative, 20–21; need for, 7, 54; φθόνος and, 61; of place, 20; in simple statement, 20; unqualified, 32; unstinting, 60; valor and, 64, 68; variation in, 24–25
Prayer: asseveration and, 72, 78n103; in conclusions, 78–80; conventional rules of, 79; future and, 76–83; for future victory, 18n43, 70, 70n84; hymnal, 78–79; hymnal seal and, 83; hymns, 46; for individual state, 81; χαῖρε and, 78–79; language of, 70; of laudator, 23; neighbor motive and, 70; praise and, 77–83; pronominal cap and, 78; recapitulating foil and, 25n57; for the singer, 78; for the song, 78, 81; transitional, 78–79; victory catalogue and, 18n43, 70n84, 72, 78–80; wishes and, 76–83
Present, 8n27, 21, 22, 48–50, 54, 57, 77. *See also* Future; Past
Priamel, 4–10, 5n17, 5n18, 40n16, 59n55; abbreviated, 10; climax of, 13, 57; comparative and superlative in, 11–12, 11n33, 39, 67; concluding, 67; concrete, 23; defined, 5; digression and, 68; in diminuendo, 66; double, 23, 23n51, 23n52, 38n9; in enkomia, 5; focusing foil and, 36; as foil, 38; gnomic cap and, 10, 51; gnomic foil and, 28; gnomic material and, 66; hesitatory, 8, 9–10; hymnal, 6; importance of, 4–5; invocation and, 36, 51; names in, 39; narrative and, 6n21; occupational, 11n34; opening, 11, 13, 22; πᾶς–πολύς type, 7–10, 7n23, 69n82, 71, 73; prooimia and, 6, 36–37, 36n6; rejected, 38; rhapsodic, 45; selection and, 5, 6, 45; structure and, 5, 10n30; summary, 6–10; transitional, 6n21, 9–10; two-term, 10, 10n30; variants of, 59–60
Principle, unifying, 36, 37, 38, 42, 66, 68. *See also* Unity
Private. *See* Public
Promise, by laudator, 1n4, 20, 21, 45, 52
Pronominal cap, 5n18, 6, 6n19, 9, 10, 56n51, 65, 78n103; combined with name cap, 7, 8, 36n2, 91; concrete,

Subject Index 133

84n114; concrete climax and, 40n16. See also Cap
Pronominal name cap, 36, 47, 85; defined, 5, 44, 56n51, 66, 70n84; foil and, 44n28, 68, 84; in prooimia, 36n6. See also Cap
Pronominal reference, 5n10, 6, 6n19, 8, 8n27, 21, 23n53, 36n2
Proof, 37n7. See also Evidence
Prooimia, 14, 33, 36–44, 76; cap and, 36n6; gnome and, 28, 36n6; priamel and, 6, 36n6, 37
Propriety, 37, 68–69, 83; δίκα and, 61n69; key words for, 73; in χρέος motive, 56, 73–74; σιγά motive and, 73–74; unity and, 16, 73, 79, 91
Prose, poetic topics and, 14, 15, 15n39, 18, 19, 40, 45, 45n32, 58n54, 63, 64
Protasis, as foil, 54–55, 59, 59n55
Public, private and, 64–65, 82–83, 82n111, 82n112, 89n122
Purpose, 18n44, 35, 41, 43n26, 90n124, 91

Quantity, quality and, 31, 76
Question, 6, 45

Recapitulation, foil and, 6–7, 6n21, 13, 25n57, 38, 38n11, 79
References, external, 9, 35
Reflection, emotion and, 68
Rejection, of themes, 6–7, 37, 38, 73n97. See also Dismissal
Relative pronoun, 21n48, 59, 67; exempla and, 43n26; in hymns, 8n27, 46, 80, 80n107; introducing mythic foil, 8, 39; in major transitions, 8, 8n27, 21
Relevance, 14, 38, 39, 45, 68; of exempla, 43n26. See also Irrelevance
Revel, song and, 2, 22–24, 26, 72
Reward, 64. See also Achievement; Praise; Song
Rhetoric, 12, 19, 24, 55n49, 60, 83, 91n125; choral, 40, 63; of list, 13; of pleading, 31; prose, 40
Rhetorical abbreviation, 74

Rhetorical conventions, meaning and, 1, 9, 10
Rhetorical elaboration, 13, 24, 28, 32
Rhetorical foil, 3n11, 4, 33, 66, 66n77
Rhetorical pause, 8, 9, 13, 17, 56n51
Rhetorical pose, 4
Rhetorical priamel, 8
Rhetorical purpose, understanding of, 18n44
Rhetorical situation, importance of, 17
Rich, poor and, 85–89
Ring form, 47
Rules, 3, 3n11, 36, 38

Sailing, as metaphor, 51, 62, 62n72
Scholia, 1n1, 4, 4n14, 24, 33, 48, 48n38, 51n42, 70n84, 74, 84n113, 85
Seal, 11; gnomic foil as, 80–81; hymnal, 83
Selection, 44, 56; in catalogue, 17–18, 21; of category, 83; comparative and superlative in, 11–12, 11n33, 39; conditional clause in, 62; focus and, 12; manner of treatment, 8; motive in prose, 45, 45n32; of parts of catalogue, 24; process of, 46; rhapsodic priamel motive in, 45; of subject, 8; of theme, 39, 69
Self-interest, 87. See also Altruism; Liberality
Sense, 14, 91, 92
Sequence, 15, 20, 26n62, 27, 32, 72, 80, 92. See also Ensemble
Shared humanity, as motive, 86, 87
Shift, of focus, 20–21
Shipwreck, as metaphor, 48, 50–51
Silence, as motive, 73–76
Simile, 6n20, 10, 55, 68
Singer, theme and, 20, 43, 45. See also Laudator
Son, as victor, 48, 50, 51–53, 54, 56n51. See also Father
Song: achievement and, 2, 11, 12, 42; arrows of, 73; as cap, 23; celebration and, 11; content of 74; as crown, 21; merit and, 10–11, 42, 54, 57; Muses and, 84; proportions of, 74; revel and, 2, 22–23, 26, 72; victory

Subject Index

and, 82. *See also* Achievement; Laudandus; Praise; Unity

Spirit, letter and, 17

Spring. *See* Fair weather; Weather

State, 65

Storm. *See* Foul weather; Weather

Story. *See* Narrative

Structure, 5, 45, 46, 47, 57, 58, 68, 70, 80

Style: choral, 32; conventional elements and, 4; enkomiastic, 21; hymnal, 64n73; of Pindar, 4, 35, 47, 64n73, 90n124, 91; ποικιλία and, 47. *See also* Hymns; Pindar

Subject, 4, 14–17, 38, 54–55

Subjective foil, 12, 14–16, 14n38, 16n40, 28, 29, 52, 59, 79, 84n114. *See also* Objective

Subject matter, transitions and, 76

Substance, form and, 57

Success, 13, 47n37, 52, 77; good repute and, 11, 72; personal and public, 82–83; praise and, 42, 54, 69; prayer for, 72; vicissitude and, 15

Summary: ἄλλος ἄλλα type, 66; ambiguity of, 15; in conclusion, 9, 72, 75; gnomic cap and, 20; list and, 7, 8, 9, 18, 43; πᾶς–πολύς type, 66; in prooimia, 36n6; subjective or objective, 15, 16

Summary catalogue, of victories, 14, 46, 46n35, 69, 72, 75

Summary dismissal, 5n18

Summary foil, 5n18, 7, 36, 37, 40n16

Summary gnome, 12–16, 14n38, 36n6

Summary praise, of clan, 14

Summary priamel, 6–7, 10, 12–14

Summary statement, prayer and, 80

Summary vaunt, 20

Summary word, 10

Superlative degree, 5n18, 11; in priamel, 11n33, 12, 39, 67. *See also* Comparative degree

Suppliant, god and, 78n102, 80n108

Suspense, 55, 56

Swimming, as metaphor, 72

Symbolism, 29, 30, 30n74, 44

Symbols, unity and, 32

Tact: apology and, 41; of laudator, 41; in ode, 35, 91

Tale. *See* Narrative

Technique, 59, 72n94

Tedium, catalogue and, 18

Temper, of Pindar, 35

Tension, 28, 36, 43, 43n26, 52, 54, 55, 67, 83. *See also* Focus

Terms, 36, 52, 54, 67

Tests, 60n66

Thank offering, 18n43, 69–70, 70n84, 80

Theme, 7–8, 28, 32; abandonment of, 6, 6n21, 9, 13, 73n97; comparative importance of, 6, 8, 27, 41, 45, 76; composition of, 62, 86, 91; ease of praise as, 61; of enduring fame, 86; of expectation, 88; foil and, 85; implicit, 86, 87; liberality, 85; of life after death, 60n63; management of, 16, 17n42, 62; modification of, 39; motives and, 88; singer and, 39, 45, 60n66; treatment of, 37, 44, 45, 73. *See also* Motives

Thirst, for song, 10–11, 10n31, 42

Thought, purpose and, 83, 91

Time, 42, 73, 75–76, 77

Tone, 66, 68, 74n100

Topic, 54–57, 66, 71, 73, 90n124; abbreviation of, 13, 72, 82; conventional, 33, 49; development of ode and, 36; digression and, 44; geographical, 60, 60n65, 62, 72; gnome and, 53–54, 57, 75; introduction of, 72; limits of achievement as, 43–44; marvels as, 2–3, 3n10; φυά, 62; pillars of Herakles as, 59n55; witness as, 60, 60n66

Touchstones, 60, 60n66

Tradition, 1, 9, 59, 88

Trainer, in catalogue, 17n42, 19, 21

Transformations, 59, 61, 66

Transition, 2–3, 6–7, 8, 8n27, 9–10, 13, 14, 17–18, 23, 28, 35, 43, 53, 60n63, 71, 72n94, 73, 76, 77, 78–79, 85, 86, 91

Translation, 18n44, 21, 50, 81–82

Truth, 17, 29, 60n66, 65, 83

Subject Index

Type, 3n11, 29n71, 85, 85n116, 90

Unity, 1, 2, 4, 32, 36, 37–39, 62, 66, 71, 72–79, 91. *See also* Principle
Universalizing doublet. *See* Doublet
Unselfishness, 83. *See also* Altruism; Liberality; Self-interest

Variation, 24–25, 39, 47, 59, 60
Variety, 18; irrelevance and, 91
Vaunt, 31, 37, 71n91; abbreviated, 19, 32; capping, 56; categorical, 22, 44, 55, 56, 59; climactic, 60n63; community and, 21; concluding, 16; concrete, 28; condition and, 54–58, 59–60, 61–62, 67; declarative categorical, 56; formal, 22; gnome and, 28, 66; high, 66; metaphor in, 62; opening, 21; summary, 20; victor and, 38; victory catalogue and, 62. *See also* Categorical vaunt
Verbals, 74
Vicissitude, 53, 68; success and, 15
Vicissitude foil: catalogue and, 28; in conclusions, 28; gnomic cap and, 51–52; in gnomic form, 7, 14n38; nature in, 7; need to praise and, 7
Victor, 12, 23; clan of, 13; dedication of, 83; father of, 20, 48; foil and, 4n13; legendary heroes and, 44–47; polis of, 20, 22, 38, 83; in sequence, 20; as subject, 38–44; as theme of song, 44; as witness, 17n42. *See also* Laudandus
Victory, 82; celebration of, 22, 89; as central theme, 42; hope for, 18n43, 81; place of in catalogue, 17; song and, 82; summary presentation of, 69
Victory catalogue, 14, 14n38, 17n42, 30, 54, 61, 69–72, 79; as foil, 69; gnomic foil and, 66; key words in, 46n35; preceding prayer, 72; summary and, 46, 46n35; thank offering and, 69
Vocative name cap, 7, 8, 9
Voluntative enkomiastic future, 43, 74

Warfare, as foil, 67
Wealth, 48, 67–68, 84n113, 86. *See also* Rich
Weather, 48–51, 62, 62n70, 62n72. *See also* Fair weather; Foul weather
Wish: in conclusion, 69, 78; for future, 77–78
Witness, 17, 17n42, 21, 40, 44, 60, 60n66, 61
Witnessing word, in catalogue, 17n42
Word, and deed, 58, 58n54, 86. *See also* Deed

INDEX OF GREEK WORDS

ἀλάθεια, 4n12, 9, 60n66, 61n69
ἀλλά, 13, 22, 22n50, 36, 36n3, 38, 45, 48, 84n114, 91
ἄλλος, 7, 7n23, 11, 15, 37n7, 38–39, 44, 45, 48, 66
ἀμφότερος, 38–39, 64
ἀπορία, 8, 20
ἀρετά, 16, 20, 23, 24, 26, 30, 43, 57, 57n52
ἀσχολία, 13, 41–42, 71, 75

βάσανοι, 60
βραχύς, 73, 74, 75

γάρ, 45, 46

δέξαι, 78n104
δημόσιος, 82
δίκα, 58n54
δίψα, 10, 10n31, 11, 42
δόσις, 54, 58, 66, 67, 68

ἐθέλω, 21, 45, 48, 65, 68, 74
εἰ, 54, 55, 56
εἷς, 38–39
ἔοικε, 54, 56, 68
ἐπεί, 43, 46, 63
ἕτερος, 7, 7n23, 15, 37n7
εὐδία, 51
εὐεργεσία, 85–89, 85n116
εὐθυμία, 75–76
εὑρίσκω, 58, 58n53
εὐφροσύνα, 2

ἤ, 6, 45

θάρσος, 30
θαῦμα, 3, 3n10, 8, 9, 10, 13, 13n36, 14
θεός, 2–3, 12, 15, 16, 21, 24, 30, 31

θυμός, 29, 63

ἴδιος, 65, 82–83

καιρός, 11n32, 18, 18n44, 29n71, 73, 73n98
κέλευθος, 14, 15, 60n65, 62
κέρδος, 54, 58, 67, 68n69
κοινός (ξυνός), 10, 61, 64–65, 66, 82–83, 86
κόρος, 13, 29n71, 40, 73, 73n98, 75
κορυφά, 18–19
κῶμος, 22–23, 27

μακρός, 13, 15, 71, 73
μαρτυρίαι, 60, 60n66
μῆτις, 29, 82n111
μισθός, 10, 54, 58, 64n75, 67, 68
μυρίος, 13, 14, 15, 16, 37, 37n7, 64, 73
μυχός, 70

νῦν, 5, 5n18, 8n27, 9, 14, 16–17, 20, 24, 37, 38, 48–50, 52, 53

ξενία, 24, 26, 89, 89n122

οἶδα, 17, 17n41, 20, 24, 31, 59n60
ὄκνος, 31n75, 38n11
ὁμοίως, 17–19, 33
ὅμως, 1n4, 13, 13n37, 74n100
ὀρθός, 64–65, 66

πᾶς, 13, 14, 15, 15n39, 18n44, 64, 66, 73, 73n97
πίστεις, 60
ποικιλία, 17n42, 18, 47
ποιμαίνειν, 19
πολύς, 13, 31, 71, 73, 73n97

[137]

Index of Greek Words

πρᾶγμα, 39, 41–42
πρέπει, 73
προαίρεσις, 40n16, 86n117, 88n120

σιγά, 73–76
σοφός, 69n83, 71n91

τεθμός, 10–11, 42
τέμενος, 71
τέχνα, 3n11, 29, 30, 32
τόκος, 1, 1n4, 33, 41n20
τόλμα, 29–31, 32, 38n11

φθόνος, 3n11, 12, 15, 17, 40, 40n16, 56–57, 56n51, 57n52, 58, 59, 60, 61, 63, 66, 80
φιλέω, 10–11, 23, 39
φυά, 3n11, 12–17, 30, 71n91

χάρις, 65
χαίρω, 46, 47, 66, 76, 77
χρέος, 10–11, 27, 54, 55, 56, 57–58, 63, 66, 67, 68, 73, 79
χρή, 5n18, 11, 16, 54, 55, 56, 57, 63, 66, 67, 68, 73, 79
χρῆσις, 10–11, 23, 42

ψεῦδος, 9, 60n66, 61n69

www.ingramcontent.com/pod-product-compliance
Lightning Source LLC
Chambersburg PA
CBHW021712230426
43668CB00008B/813